THE
GOOD NURSE

A True Story of Medicine,
Madness, and Murder

CHARLES GRAEBER

TWELVE

NEW YORK BOSTON

Grand Central Publishing
Hachette Book Group
1290 Avenue of the Americas, New York, NY 10104
grandcentralpublishing.com
twitter.com/grandcentralpub

Originally published in hardcover and ebook by Twelve in 2013
First Mass Market Edition: January 2018

Grand Central Publishing is a division of Hachette Book Group, Inc. The Grand Central Publishing name and logo is a trademark of Hachette Book Group, Inc.

The publisher is not responsible for websites (or their content) that are not owned by the publisher.

The Hachette Speakers Bureau provides a wide range of authors for speaking events. To find out more, go to www.hachettespeakersbureau.com or call (866) 376-6591.

ISBN: 978-1-5387-6097-0 (mass market), 978-1-4555-0612-5 (ebook)

Printed in the United States of America

OPM

10 9 8 7 6 5 4 3 2 1

AUTHOR'S NOTE

This is a true story built upon over six years of research and interviews with dozens of sources, including Charles Cullen.

Charlie is a proud and complicated man who, aside from our conversations, never issued a public statement or granted a single media interview. Our communication spanned several years, beginning with his attempt to donate a kidney from prison. He sees no reason to talk further.

His perspective appears throughout the book, but he is not the final arbiter of the facts herein.

Many other previously silent sources came forward to make this book possible. All risked their privacy, several risked careers or reputations. Some risked their freedom as well. Names and personal details have been altered when requested in order to protect their privacy and to shield those lives already altered by the events told here.

Every effort has been made to present this story accurately, through a relaying of the facts collected through police investigation reports, witness statements, transcripts, recorded wiretaps, surveillance tapes, court documents and legal depositions, and personal interviews. Some transcripts have been edited slightly for space and clarity, and some dialogue has been by necessity reconstructed based on cor-roborating documentation as above.

But as is true in any story of murder, the ultimate wit-nesses are voiceless. This book is dedicated to them, and to the good nurses everywhere who spend their lives caring for ours.

THE
GOOD NURSE

PART

I

1

October 3, 2003

Charlie considered himself lucky. The career had found him, by accident or fate he couldn't say. After sixteen years on the job, Charles Cullen was an accomplished veteran, a registered nurse with a GED and bachelor of science in nursing. His Advanced Cardiac Life Support (ACLS), Intra-Aortic Balloon Pump, and Critical Care Unit certifications earned him a healthy $27.50 an hour in hospitals across New Jersey and Pennsylvania. There was always work. Even within the rotted cores of Allentown or Newark, medical centers were still expanding profit centers, each proliferating with new specialties and services, and each locked in desperate competition to attract experienced RNs.

By 4:40 p.m., Charles Cullen was in his car, shaved, gelled, and dressed in his whites—white top and bottom with a soft yellow cardigan and a stethoscope draped across his neck, such that anybody might guess the handsome young man was a hospital professional, possibly even a doctor, despite his baby-blue Ford Escort station wagon, ten years old and freckled with rust. After a decade living in a basement apartment in New Jersey, Charlie's commute now started from across the border, in Bethlehem, Pennsylvania. His new girlfriend, Catherine, had a cozy little Cape there, which she'd dress up with little card-shop knickknacks—red paper hearts or singing jack-o'-lanterns or accordion turkeys, depending on the season—and though Charlie was growing bored with Catherine and her two teenage sons, he still liked being at her place okay, especially the little plot out back where he could putter on warm days, pinching deadheads or staking tomato plants. He also appreciated the five easy minutes it took to cross the Lehigh River to the familiar slipstream of I-78 East, an artery pumping thousands of workers to shifts at labor-starved hospitals across the Garden State, only five or six of which were, unofficially, closed off to hiring him.

Over the course of his sixteen years, Charles Cullen had been the subject of dozens of complaints and disciplinary citations, and had endured four police investigations, two lie detector tests, perhaps twenty suicide attempts, and a lock-up, but none had blemished his professional record. He'd jumped from job to job at nine different hospitals and a nursing home, and been "let go," "terminated," or "asked to resign" at many of them. But both his Pennsylvania and New Jersey nursing licenses remained intact, and each time he filled out a new application, Nurse Cullen appeared to be an ideal hire. His attendance was perfect, his uniform pristine. He had experience in intensive care, critical care, cardiac care, ventilation, and burns. He medicated the living, was the first code responder when machines screamed over the dying, and exhibited origamilike artistry when plastic-wrapping the dead. He had no scheduling conflicts, didn't seem to attend movies or watch sports, and was willing, even eager, to work nights, weekends, and holidays. He no longer had the responsibilities of a wife nor custody of his two children, and his downtime was spent primarily on Cathy's couch flicking through channels; a last-second sick call or an unexpected patient transfer could have him dressed and on the highway before the commercial break. His fellow nurses considered him a gift from the scheduling gods, a hire almost too good to be true.

His new job at Somerset Medical Center took forty-five minutes each way, but Charlie didn't mind the drive. In fact, he required it. Charlie considered himself a talker, and he was quick to share cringingly intimate details of his showdowns with Cathy or his comically crumbling home life, but there were some privacies he could never talk about— secret scenes that looped through his head, replayed for him alone. Between shifts, only the commute allowed Charlie to ruminate.

His little Ford hiccupped as it crossed from the cheap Pennsylvania asphalt to the smooth New Jersey tar. Charlie stayed in the left lane until the signs for exit 18, a fierce little one-way toward US 22 Somerville and Rehill Avenue. This was the nice New Jersey, wealthiest state of the union, the Jersey nobody ever joked about—suburban streets, lined with grand trees, well-tended yards uncramped by abandoned bass boats or broken trampolines, pristine driveways featuring leased Saturns rather than old Escorts. He killed the engine in the parking garage, early as usual, and hurried toward the hospital's back entrance.

Beyond the double doors lay a thrumming twenty-four-hour city lit by humming overhead fluorescents, the only place Charlie ever truly knew he belonged. He felt a thrill of excitement as he stepped onto the shining linoleum, a wave of familiarity as he breathed in the scents of home: sweat and gauze and Betadine, the zing of astringent and antibacterial detergent and, behind it all, the florid note of human decay. He took the back stairs two at a time. There was work to do.

The nursing profession had welcomed Charlie as few other aspects of life ever had, starting with childhood. Charlie described it as "miserable." He'd been a late-life mistake[1] that his working-class Irish-Catholic parents could hardly afford,[2] arriving soon before his father died and long after most of his seven siblings had grown up and moved out. Their narrow wooden house in West Orange[3] was a dark, unhappy place haunted by drug-addicted brothers, adult sisters who drifted in and out on tides of pregnancy or need, and strange, rough men who came at all hours to visit them both. Only Charlie's mother shielded him from the chaos of those upstairs rooms. He fed desperately on her affections, but there were never enough to go around. When she was killed in a car crash during his senior year in high school, Charlie was truly alone. He was furious with the hospital that had taken her body, and beyond consolation. He tried suicide, then the Navy, failing at both. Finally, he returned to the very same hospital at which his mother had died, and discovered his life's true mission.

In March 1984,[4] Charles Cullen was the only male student[5] at the Mountainside Hospital School of Nursing in Montclair, New Jersey. He was bright and did well. The coursework suited him, as did the uniform, and the sisterly dynamic was familiar and comfortable. When the honorary class president dropped out two weeks into the first semester, one of Charlie's classmates insisted he run in her place.[6] He was a natural choice for leadership, she told him: Charlie was bright, handsome, and, most important, male. Charlie was flattered, but running for president didn't sound much like him. The more he demurred, the more adamant she became. He wouldn't have to risk anything, she told him—she'd do it all. Charlie found himself happy in the passive role of grudging candidate, and even happier when he won. Class president was only a symbolic position, but it seemed to signal the arrival of a new Charlie. Six years after losing his mother to the Mountainside hospital morgue, Charlie was Mountainside's chosen son, crowned and confirmed by a white-uniformed navy of professional nurturers. For the first time in his life, he was special. It was as close to love as Charlie could imagine.

Charlie paid for his schooling with anonymous franchise shift work, racking up hours pushing powdered donuts or shoveling piles of shaved meat. He restocked boxes or filled condiment bars and mopped floors in between—there was always mopping to be done. He found it ironic that, just as the recruiter had promised, his military experience so neatly translated into civilian skills. And like the Navy, each of his civilian jobs required a uniform. For Dunkin' Donuts, it was the orange-and-brown shirt and a visor. For Caldor, the uniform was also orange and brown but the stripes were different. Charlie had to be careful to grab the right one from the pile from the floor. Roy Rogers required a rust-colored shirt seemingly designed to hide barbeque sauce the way casino carpets hide gum. It was a hideous garment, except when Charlie's manager, Adrianne, wore it. He especially liked the way her name tag hung.

Adrianne Baum[7] was a different class of girl from the ones Charlie had known in West Orange, an ambitious, newly minted college grad with a business degree and student loans to pay. Charlie watched her, mooning over his mop handle as he worked cleanup by the fixin's bar in her West Orange Roy's location. But Adrianne had a boyfriend and was scheduled to be transferred. Charlie quit, and doubled his hours at the Caldor next door, but he still took his lunch breaks at Roy's, just in case. When Adrianne was transferred back a month later without the boyfriend, Charlie was there, waiting.

The relationship moved as quickly as Charlie could accelerate it. Adrianne was surprised to discover that hidden inside the shy, wide-eyed boy she'd watched wiping the sauce station was a surprisingly confident man. He needed her attentions and pushed for them every way he could, showering her with gifts and playing the model boyfriend for her family. Charlie obsessed on gaining her affection, and he kindled its flame with constant flowers or candy, little things from the mall. Any little thing Adrianne mentioned liking, Charlie needed to get her. Adrianne finally had to tell him to stop. She pretended to be annoyed, but really, how could she be? She was aware how many girls would have killed to take her place. The boy was a catch. That Charlie seemed to be constantly quitting or getting fired could be chalked up to his high standards and busy schedule. Adrianne told her girlfriends, wow, here was a guy working three jobs, president of his nursing school class, as serious about his career as she was about hers. Yes, so, he was a goy—he wasn't perfect. But he was close enough.

Soon, whatever spare time the young couple could winnow between their respective shifts and Charlie's schooling was spent together. They were a unit, complete but closed. They called it love, and six months after their first date[8] they were engaged. They married the week after Charlie graduated nursing school. The rented hall in Livingston, the tuxedos, the honeymoon trip to Niagara Falls—it was like a fairy tale to Adrianne. They returned a day early so her prince[9] could start on his new job in the Burn Unit at Saint Barnabas Medical Center in Livingston, New Jersey. The hospital was willing to allow him extra time, but Charlie was adamant. It had to be that day; he didn't want to be late. Adrianne waved good-bye, and she felt the future rolling out before her like a strange red carpet.

2

June 1987[1]

Saint Barnabas Medical Center had the only certified burn unit in the State of New Jersey, so it took everyone—the horrible husks of humans, people burned in car accidents, house fires, industrial spills; men and women and, most often, children, some burned to stubs, without hair or eyelids, their body surfaces cooked beyond repair. Charlie's job was to clean these burn victims on a metal gurney—to scrape and wash away the charred, necrotic skin with antibacterial soap and a brush. Even within the field of critical care medicine, this is an almost unimaginably gruesome procedure; as a first job straight out of nursing school, it's something close to hell.

All burns start with a story. A mother in a nightgown reaching for the teakettle,[2] a paraplegic with a dropped cigarette, a drunk feeding a flagging campfire, the punctured gas tank of the crumpled car. Fire is the punch line. The body reacts predictably to the trauma. Third-degree burns are more deadly—complex layers of the skin, nerves, veins, arteries, and muscle cooked and dead—but second-degree burns are more painful because the nerves are still alive.

Even in the 1980s, burn wards were scream wards. The drug of consolation was morphine. Some patients will recover; others are kept on the ward only to suffer and die. The nurses know which is which. Fate in the burn unit is a statistic written on skin. Sooner or later, all nurses can read it.

It's always the same drawing on the burn sheet, a human figure, bald and naked. It's ageless, sexless, hairless. Its toes point toward an unseen ground. Its arms stretch palms up in the universal expression of supplication and surrender. The figure's eyes are open and lidless, its lips full but without expression. You can tally damage in the figure precisely, marking the drawing for pieces of thigh, a half a leg, a piece of the head. The damage corresponds to a point system: One point for the genitals, 1.25 for each palm, etc. But there is an easier way.

The nurses call it the rule of 9s. Each big piece—a leg, the back, the head—counts as 9. Add up the total, then add that to the patient's age; the sum is the mortality rate. By this rule, a fifty-year-old patient burned over half his body is 100 percent dead. If not now, soon. The rule helps soften the blow of the inevitable, indicate where on the burn ward the meager rations of hope are best invested. Every burn nurse knows the rule, there's no point talking about it; you use the formula, then try to forget it. The impending death is like a black car you see in the rearview mirror, always there if you look. So why look?

Meanwhile the pain on the burn ward is unbearable, and the nurses have no options for treatment except to hit their patients with more and more morphine. When these patients die, it isn't always clear whether they've overdosed or simply died of unsustainable wounds. All anyone knows is they aren't in pain anymore.

The burn victims arrive at all hours. They may arrive in

surprising ways, on stretchers or walking, alone or in packs. Sometimes they are lucid, talking, worried about their watch or a missed hair appointment. That's shock. Reality follows soon enough.

Burn victims are connected to machines, lines snaked into wrists and femoral arteries, plastic tubes shoehorned into holes top and bottom. Saline, electrolytes, pain meds, anxiety meds, liquefied food; the body swells with the fluids, sometimes doubling in size. The scrotum inflates like a beach ball, the eyes puff to slits, lips balloon and break like overcooked sausages. The body swells against the skin until the patient is as hard as carved marble. The blood vessels are squeezed shut. The core begins to die. And so they cut. It is simple surgeon's work. A blade runs the length of the arms and legs, front and back. Even the hands, puffed fat as udders, get cut. The knife runs tendon deep, five whisker-flicks beneath the knuckles like vents on a leather glove. The cuts[3] allow space for the insides to expand, like pleats on pants, pressure sighing open along a sudden fault line, exposing canyon walls of yellow fat, a valley welling blood. The smell can be terrible, but the bleeding is a good thing. If it bleeds it is alive. But bleeding makes more work.

The pleated skin is loose, a greased shirtsleeve of leather, shocking to the touch. It takes time for nurses to acclimate to the point where they can effortlessly handle these tactile details of damage. When these details become too much, they leave. Some nurses leave the burn Intensive Care Unit right away, switch to something —anything—less brutal. Others stay only until they encounter the burn patient who reminds them, too much, of a loved one—or of themselves.

Nearly a third of the patients on the unit were children. Sometimes their burns were delivered as punishments, for peeing on a mattress or forgetting a chore. Nurses recognize

the signs of abuse. There are burns from radiators and cig-
arettes, lighters and stove tops, red-hot water scalds and
blackened electrical scorches. Each has its unique signature
of pain. Charlie saw them all.

Some pain blossomed across skin in crenulated carna-
tions of tissue, some blistered or knifed in thin white stalks.
The nurses did their best to hide the pain beneath neat rows
of gauze and tape, behind the mask of drugs. But Charlie knew that pain could be held in secret. Pain could be a
banked ember, burning from the inside, endured without
expression. Especially by children. Unlike adults, children
didn't scream when he cleaned them, they didn't whimper in
their beds. Children tolerated the pain and held their secrets
to avoid being punished again. Charlie's mother had never
used a stove top or a hot pan to punish him, but he'd been
punished, pushed around, hit by his sister's boyfriends, big
guys with rings and Camaros and bulging jeans. He'd felt
their adult power, and he had never forgotten what it was to
be a child abnegated in its shadow. One of his sisters had a
live-in boyfriend, who had beaten her ruthlessly through her
pregnancy. She had run away, but the boyfriend would not
leave. And Charlie had known that man's relentless attentions, too.

He'd known pain in the military. Burns and punishment,
too, for "damaging Navy property," as they put it, after he
had woken up from a drunken shore leave with his bare feet
sunburned red and as swollen as kickballs. They'd forced
him into his dress shoes and gave him only aspirin. As he
worked, he reminded himself that, yes, he knew a hurt far
beyond what anyone could understand. Charlie dwelled
on these kids in the ward in tremendous pain that no one
could understand or properly address. At the time, nurses
weren't allowed to give children any pain medications more

powerful than Tylenol 3.[4] It wasn't nearly enough. Many nurses wanted to give more. Some did.

The kids came in hot and rising, hurting and reminding Charlie of his own hurt, too. He would pick them up, these screaming, melted little people, knowing that later the surgeons would open each like a baked potato, a Y-cut to keep them from exploding, only the first of many operations to come. In time, their melted skin would heal into scars, vinelike ropes that the surgeons would cut again and again to prevent the neck from locking into an unbendable trunk, to keep the arms flexible. Without these operations, the children would remain stunted within their baked bodies. Their hard scar casings were too inflexible to accommodate growth spurts and normal movements. Their only hope was the knife and the pressure suit, a wetsuitlike garment that squeezes a child in a painful hug. The pressure suit presses against the scars, thinning them, like a constant rolling pin against the hard rising tissue. Maybe, with enough work, after time and pain and pressure, the scarred cocoon might thin enough. The child might one day move and grow. One day, maybe, they might even forget their pain. Charlie knew that the children might live, they might age in years, but not in body; without a nurse's intervention, they would be forever trapped within the groaning cocoon of their childhood. Charlie considered it one of the neater equations in life: the world pushed, and the pressure suit pushed back.

Charlie liked the Saint Barnabas job. He knew he was helpful there, needed. He enjoyed caring for the infirm, bathing and feeding and dressing the dependent. He appreciated the one-on-one of the night shift and the professionalism of his veteran coworkers. He even liked the name of the hospital; raised Catholic, Charlie was familiar with Saint Barnabas, an apostle. He had a personal connection with this particular saint. The church celebrates Barnabas's feast day every year on June 11. It was the day Charlie Cullen started working at Saint Barnabas Medical Center.[5]

In church on Sunday, Saint Barnabas was suspended in the archway of the stained glass window—bearded Barnabas, the handsome young companion to Luke and Paul, the Aramis[6] of the early Christian Three Musketeers. As a Jew he had been Joseph, a landowner who sold his fields and gave cash to the apostles;[7] as a convert, Saint Barnabas was an inspiration: *Grant, O God, that we may follow the example of your faithful servant Barnabas, who, seeking not his own renown but the well-being of your church, gave generously of his life and substance...*

But Charlie had no use for those sorts of prayers. In preparing to marry Adrianne he had formally renounced the religion of his upbringing and converted to Judaism. Charlie felt like he was living the life of the saint in reverse.

It never ends well for saints, no matter how good they are. Castration, defenestration, hot pincers, prison—the saint is a scapegoat, a martyr, a patsy. Barnabas was stoned to death,[8] but his story lived beyond him. Every Catholic knew his name. It was the paradox of the saints, one thing Charlie held on to from his childhood: remembered well, remembered forever, but only after being hated to death.

3

Adrianne and Charlie Cullen took a mortgage on a small one-story in the steel suburbs of Phillipsburg, New Jersey. The house was cramped and dark and in need of paint. One side faced a billboardlike supporting wall, and the backyard bordered a weedy lot, but the price was within the range of their combined incomes. Adrianne had a new job as a computer programmer—entry level, but at least in a business office rather than a fast-food chain. Their reversed schedules, with her on long days and Charlie working long nights, surely contributed to Adrianne's sense of isolation, but that was only a piece of it. Increasingly, she felt alone, with or without Charlie.

Self-deprecating vulnerability had been part of the charm package Charlie had presented as a suitor. He was so forthright and often funny about his personal problems—particularly his history of depression and alcoholism—that Adrianne had quickly come to believe that she knew this man and, more important, that he knew himself. His perspective on himself made him seem not so much damaged as experienced, mature even. It gave Adrianne the illusion that Charlie was in full control of his demons; in fact, he was only now coming to know them. Adrianne sensed that a strange new chill had set into her life, an early autumn in their emotional life together. She chalked it up to the heart-rending nature of her husband's work and decided this was simply the lesson every medical spouse learns: love can't compete with death. She didn't imagine that her husband was drinking again.

Drinking had been the one aspect of naval tradition at which Charlie excelled. He drank to get drunk. He liked red wine, or tropical drinks—even Listerine, in a pinch—which had landed him repeatedly in the military's infirmary and psychiatric hospital, and introduced him to Antabuse and Alcoholics Anonymous. Adrianne had no experience with this side of her husband. She had never once seen him have a drink. When they were dating, he'd always said that he simply "couldn't." Adrianne considered his abstinence a sign of his conviction rather than a warning of his appetites. When Charlie had moved into her apartment in Union, she even threw away the dusty bottle of Baileys Irish Cream she'd kept for fancy guests.

In Phillipsburg, Charlie kept his booze in his Navy foot-locker, kept the footlocker in the boiler room, and kept a lock on the boiler room door. He drank alone in the basement, avoiding his wife. He liked it there. There was only one way in, nobody below, bedrock all around, always dark. The boiler room was a place to drink and think and watch the pilot light dance within its metal prison.

That first year of married life was a whirlwind. Charlie had been exceptionally busy. He'd received his New Jersey RN license a month after starting at Saint Barnabas, and a month later he started on another degree program at Kean College. Between school, work, and the commute, Charlie was seldom at home. Adrianne watched Dick Clark rock in the year 1988 alone with a minibottle of Chardonnay. By February she was pregnant. This was family life, the real thing, the point. But she felt her husband becoming increasingly cool with her, almost professional, as if she was one of his patients. Adrianne felt him cool down another click that fall, when their daughter Shauna[1] was born. Now any attention Charlie had previously given his wife was shunted exclusively to the baby. Adrianne didn't understand the reaction—it was as if her husband had to choose between his wife and his child, as if he couldn't broaden the focus of his affections to cover them both. Charlie was overly enthusiastic about new things—their relationship, their house, their life—but as the novelty faded, so did his affect. She had seen him lose interest in a similar way with her dogs, first with her Yorkie, Lady. Adrianne adored Lady, and had believed at first that Charlie did, too. He petted her mechanically, groomed her little ears, watched intently as she gobbled her food. Then he seemed to change the channel, and the dog no longer interested him.

He was, however, interested in the new puppy—at least, Adrianne had thought so when they'd picked it out. This was her second Yorkie terrier, a companion for Lady. She had left for work Tuesday morning, leaving Charlie with the baby and the puppy, their usual changing of the guard on his day off. When Adrianne returned from work that evening, the puppy was gone. Charlie didn't seem to care, and he didn't want to help her look for it.

Charlie said that the puppy had run away. Or, that he assumed it ran away—he'd been out taking a walk while the baby was sleeping. Adrianne had to make him repeat that one—taking a walk, *without* the baby? Well, Charlie said, looking away. All he knew, he came back from his walk and the puppy was gone. He didn't seem worried about it. He didn't seem anything at all.

Adrianne didn't understand—Charlie had left their infant daughter alone? And with the front door open? It wasn't open, Charlie said, ajar, maybe, and anyway he knew the baby wouldn't wake up. Adrianne didn't like the way he said that. *Knew.* Had he given something to the baby? She'd had suspicions he gave their daughter cold medicine as a liquid babysitter, they'd had fights about it. He always denied it, and the discussion would go nowhere. Eventually, this argument went nowhere, too. Charlie simply stopped bothering trying to convince her of his side; he just let it drop and disappeared back into the basement. Adrianne was left alone again, feeling crazy. She didn't understand where the man she married had gone, or why he had lost interest in all but the most perfunctory duties of their relationship. Even when Charlie was physically home he was emotionally absent. She would catch his eye by the coffeemaker, study his expressionless morning face, and wonder if her husband was still somewhere in there, hiding like a child in a darkened room. He appeared to be permanently preoccupied, fixed upon some secret scene to which Adrianne's every syllable was merely noise and distraction. Her friends told her to be strong. Her parents advised her that marriage was a marathon, not a sprint. He's your husband, they reminded her. And so Adrianne chalked it up to the psychic demands of mediating life and death for an hourly wage. She went to work, paid the bills, took Shauna to day care, came home. Only the car in the driveway told her whether her husband was home. Charlie was now spending most of his time in the basement. She'd tried going down there a few times. She was afraid to try again. Finding him in the half dark, she had seen something. Something disturbing about her husband's eyes. Adrianne didn't know quite how to describe it—a cool blankness, a look that belied any feelings of love she might have imagined her husband still harbored for her. Sometimes Charlie's eyes would drift apart, watching two separate directions, as if each eye belonged to a separate being. In those moments, Charlie was not Charlie. Adrianne told her friends, "You know? I think maybe there's something seriously wrong with Charlie." Then one afternoon, proof arrived.

Adrianne answered the doorbell to find her neighbor crying. Every few weeks the neighbor's ancient beagle, Queenie, would get out and wander down the block, and for some reason she usually ended up in the Cullens' yard. Adrianne had brought sweet old Queenie inside dozens of times. It got to be a sort of running joke, and when Queenie went missing, the neighbor came straight to them. But this time the neighbor found Queenie's body in the alley next to their house. The vet said that she had been poisoned. Did Adrianne have any idea what might have happened?

Adrianne didn't know what to say. She went inside to the kitchen, where the photos from PhotoMat lay on the counter, photos Adrianne had taken at day care, cute shots of Shauna with her little friends. Adrianne had come home a few days before to find that Charlie had taken a pair of scissors to each one, carefully cutting out the little boys like paper dolls in negative space. The pictures had frightened her; she tried not to think about them. Now she couldn't help it. The empty people shapes reminded her of her husband. She thought about the pictures and her puppy, about Queenie, and her neighbor crying at the front door. Then Adrianne started crying, too.

4

On February 11, 1991, pharmacy nurse Pam Allen had brought a suspicious IV bag to the desk of Saint Barnabas's risk manager, Karen Seiden.[1] The port on the bag looked used, but the bag itself was full to the point of leaking. It didn't look right to Seiden, either. Seiden got in touch with the hospital's assistant director of security, a former cop named Thomas Arnold. Arnold sent the IV bag to the pathology lab. The bag was supposed to contain only saline and heparin; the lab test found that it contained insulin as well.

Three days later, on Valentine's Day, a Saint Barnabas Critical Care Unit patient named Anna Byers was placed on an IV drip of heparin. Within a half hour she was in a cold sweat, confused, nauseous, and shakingly weak. A blood lab showed an insulin level off the charts. She was given orange juice—a simple remedy of sugar and one of the fastest ways to normalize a crash if you catch it early enough. It didn't work. The nurses were forced to give Byers an IV of dextrose, dripping sugar directly into her bloodstream. It kept Byers from dying, but she was so loaded with insulin that she crashed right through that as well. She stayed like that all morning, all afternoon, all night. Byers had a surgery scheduled for the next morning—a catheter was to be put in her heart. She was probably now too unstable to handle the procedure, but just in case, her physician ordered that her heparin IV drip be removed.[2] As soon as Byers's heparin drip was unplugged for surgery, her insulin issues abated, and she started to feel better.

By 2 p.m. she was back in her room, stable and well. Her blood sugar crash issues had vanished. Her surgical wounds were clotted. She was ready to be put back on the heparin drip. An IV was started. And soon after, Anna Byers was back on the same unstable ride again. By now her nurses were mainlining the sugar water, trying to outfeed the fire. She'd stabilize and crash, wooze in and out. By 11 p.m. there wasn't enough sugar left in her blood to even get a reading. Her body had burned it all, leaving nothing for her brain. She was ready to code.

The nurses unhooked her IV lines and rushed her down to the ICU. But within twenty minutes of being off the drip, Anna Byers was feeling better again.

Down the hall, a patient named Fred Belf was on the same ride. His heparin went in at 7 a.m. By noon he was throwing up onto his own chest, unable to keep the orange juice down, and the doctors ordered dextrose, to be delivered intravenously with his heparin. The two drips ran a race, side by side, one unhinging the other, all day and all night, like a metabolic teeter totter.

By 7 p.m. the next night, the connection had been made between the bags of heparin and the side effects on the floor. Belf's nurses unhooked his heparin drip; Belf quickly began to feel better. Gloved nurses removed his IV bag, placed it in sterile plastic, and sent it for testing.

The bag came back positive for insulin. A microscopic analysis of the exterior revealed a peculiar landscape studded by tiny needle sticks, including three on the edges of the bag. This was extremely unusual. Bags of saline sometimes get stuck by needles in the course of being connected to the stopcock and, in turn, the patient, but they never get stuck on the perimeter. It didn't look like an accident. It seemed possible that someone had been intentionally and repeatedly poisoning IV bags in the Saint Barnabas Hospital storage room. Arnold and Seiden had two bags as evidence, and the anecdotal examples of Byers and Belf. Now they dug back through the patient records in the CCU, to see if anyone else had experienced similar unexplained insulin crashes recently.

Though they had no causality, they discovered that patients were in fact crashing with regularity. For months, codes had become so frequent that they overlapped; the CCU nurses would need to leave one to attend another. The information was anecdotal and confusing—the incidents weren't confined to any one unit, or any one shift. But across the intensive care, critical care, and cardiac units, Saint Barnabas patients were magically going hypoglycemic.

Laboratory work[3] showed that not only did all of the "magic hypoglycemics" have exceptional and unprecedented levels of insulin in their bloodstream, but also that much of this insulin was "foreign"—it had not been produced by the body. The insulin had been given to them.

The first assumption was that a mistake had been made—a nurse misreading a doctor's order, for instance, or a mislabeled vial. Such mistakes happen in hospitals all the time. Arnold and Seiden studied the patients' charts but found neither a doctor's prescription for insulin nor a nurse's notation that it was given. This meant that either it was a double mistake—patients accidentally being given a nonprescribed drug, and the nurse then accidentally neglecting to complete the chart—or it wasn't a mistake at all. Either way, they had a problem. Arnold took his findings to his boss, the head of Saint Barnabas security and SBMC vice president, Joe Barry.

In his previous life, Joe Barry had been a decorated and much respected thirty-year police veteran and former major with the New Jersey State Police. Now as senior vice president in charge of security at Saint Barnabas, Barry was charged with the delicate investigation into the potential murder of patients. With their combined experience, Arnold and Barry were uniquely qualified to conduct a sophisticated investigation such as this. After ruling out the patients' own visitors, the only possible suspects left were the hospital staff. Arnold and Barry compared the nursing work schedules with the times and dates of the patient codes. Only three nurses were working every code. And of these, nurse Charles Cullen interested them the most.[4]

Arnold had already interviewed several Saint Barnabas staffers about the insulin incidents.[5] Each nurse had seemed nervous, concerned for her job and reputation and the patients involved. Only nurse Charles Cullen didn't appear worried at all. In fact, he was pointedly *not* worried, about anything. To Arnold, it didn't seem to just be a "Who, me?" act. Cullen genuinely didn't seem to care. In fact, he was defiant. Arnold had tried several times to schedule Cullen for a sit-down meeting, but the nurse was employed by a staffing service, rather than the hospital. His shifts were erratic and varied, making Cullen difficult to pin down. When pressed, Cullen always made it clear that he was busy nursing, a responsibility "more important" than Arnold's crass intrigues. When Arnold and Barry finally got Cullen into a conference room for the sit-down,[6] the nurse refused to answer any questions. He sat there in the rolling chair, arms crossed, studying the linoleum. The attitude alone was a red flag to the ex-cops, and Arnold told him so.

"I know you're putting something in those bags," Arnold told him. He was shooting from the hip, but his gut told him, absolutely, this guy was dirty. "You can't prove anything" was Cullen's reply. That struck the investigators as the wrong response for an innocent man—and not very smart, either. As former cops, Arnold and Barry read it as a *fuck you*. The attitude pissed Arnold off, made it personal. Cullen didn't seem to care about that, either. "I don't need to talk to you," he said, and walked out of the interview.

Arnold and Barry had seen this type of behavior as cops on the street, but never at the hospital. Parking lot dings, gift-shop shoplifters, or unruly responses to the posted visiting hours—those were the norm. Sometimes they had a nurse on the hot seat, but usually it was a secret doper pocketing Percocet or Vicodin, then cheating the charts on the tabulation. Addicts were the same everywhere, their motives simple and direct. But something darker seemed to be at play here. There was no imaginable motivation for the randomly poisoned bags of saline in the storage closet or the misadministration of insulin. Nor could Arnold come up with a reasonable explanation for Cullen's reaction—the guy didn't seem at all rattled by the accusations. Or even surprised. He had a dead look in his eyes that Arnold recognized and didn't like. The most disturbing part was that Charlie was correct; he didn't need to talk to them. Arnold and Barry's investigation would need to do Cullen's talking for him.

Arnold and Barry tasked the staff with helping create time lines and mortality rates during the window of nurse Charles Cullen's employment as he floated between the ICU CCU and Cardiac Care units. It seemed like the deeper they dug, the more questionable cases they found.[7] But what they didn't find was absolute, case-making certainty. The patients all had a complicated symphony of diseases and symptoms, and there was no way to connect their unexplained spikes in insulin directly to one event, or to Charles Cullen, or, in several cases, to their eventual deaths. It was entirely possible the facts were coincidental. And because Cullen was a floater, and many of his shifts were unscheduled call-ins at the last moment, cross-indexing Cullen's actions with the problems on the unit was all the more difficult. If they were going to take the investigation to the next level, they'd need outside help. It was time to alert the police.

Arnold and Barry had a regular monthly sit-down with the Livingston chief of police, Don Jones. The meet-up was purely a matter of practicality; Saint Barnabas was the largest employer in Livingston, the bedrock of the township's tax base. It was unrealistic to separate the medical center's private corporate concerns from those of the municipality.

Chief Jones was a familiar character in Livingston, with a reputation for supplementing his salary with the sort of overtime hours usually doled out to low-wage rookies or cops expecting a new kid. With retirement on the horizon, crossing the line into the private sector for a lucrative security management position with the Saint Barnabas Corporation was a far more appealing opportunity. If Jones hoped to prove himself to the Saint Barnabas administration, one of the first chances to prove it came on March 5, 1991, when Barry and Arnold met Chief Jones at an Italian restaurant and presented their case over lunch.

They had all the fundamentals of a solid police investigation: a crime, victims, evidence, and a suspect.[8] They had probable homicides on at least two units. They possessed physical evidence of criminal IV tampering involving deadly drug dosages, and their investigation had yielded a strong suspect in one of the Saint Barnabas staffers. To an ex-cop like Arnold, it seemed clear that Saint Barnabas Medical Center had a serious criminal issue on its hands. But Chief Jones didn't want to touch it. He told Barry and Arnold that he didn't think he could do anything with the evidence they had so far. It would be best for the hospital to handle the matter internally. Barry and Arnold didn't know whether Jones simply thought he was doing the hospital a favor, or if he truly felt incapable of attempting a complicated medical investigation with the evidence on hand. Arnold couldn't blame the man for that—they couldn't prove it themselves yet. Either way, the problem was still theirs.

Arnold and Barry threw every trick they had at catching Cullen in the act, even installing stop-motion cameras in the med storage room for a few weeks. They interviewed a cross-section of the physicians, staff, and even families who coursed through their patient wards, and initiated a new drug sign-out protocol for the nurses, which treated the usually common stocks of insulin with the same stringent regulation given to dangerously addictive drugs like morphine. When two more patients were discovered crashing with inexplicable hypoglycemia in the Saint Barnabas CCU that October, and found connected to IV bags that had been tainted with insulin, they had their suspicions, and even more frustrations, but still nothing they could prove.[9] They were still trying when, all of a sudden, Charles Cullen simply went away. The problems with the insulin spikes disappeared with him.

Charlie assumed his world would fall around him like a cardboard stage prop. He felt that the Saint Barnabas people knew what he had been doing there[1]—the hospital investigators had left him little doubt of that during their interview. Whether he'd spiked one or one hundred, or even more, it didn't matter. They knew. They hadn't even looked at his time working the burn unit, but they still knew. For months they'd been focused on two patients, both of whom had crashed and coded. It was easy to get confused about the other patients, and hard to sort their unusual symptoms from the usual cacophony of ailments, but these two were clear-cut. Charlie was aware that they'd cross-indexed the nurses on duty for the evenings of those two incidents, and discovered that he was the only nurse working both shifts. And then there was the matter of the IV bags he'd been spiking with insulin in the storage closet—they'd found them, analyzed them, saved them as evidence. He'd been spiking the bags at random sometimes, sending them out like grenades. Charlie was certain that his fingerprints were all over the tainted IV bags—he hadn't bothered to wear gloves. He figured that if they wanted him, they had him.

He enjoyed the waiting, the little death of that caesura,

the special tension it lent to the dark hours. It pulled everything into sharp focus, imbued every snap of a glove or sip of
coffee with tragic portent and meaning. He waited all spring
for a conclusion to the affair, then fall and winter, right into
the New Year. When no conclusion came, he decided that
either the hospital was stupid or afraid, maybe both. Charlie could only imagine the epic liability issues that rippled
from his pinpricks—the big-money lawsuits like you see on
TV, the sort that humble even corporate Goliaths. Whatever
it was a hospital worried about, Charlie didn't think it was
patients. They lied, the way they'd lied to him when he'd
looked for his mother's body. They covered up. They hid.
And nobody ever truly treated your pain; he'd learned of that
hypocrisy, too, when no one had treated his. Professionally,
he found the legalistic attitude utterly galling. As a lapsed
Catholic, he found it ironic; Saint Barnabas, Son of Encouragement, patron saint of the bottom line. The hospital's failure to stop him seemed like a sort of absolution from blame.
And so, when Saint Barnabas[2] finally stopped calling him in
for shifts, Charlie couldn't help but feel genuinely surprised.

6

January 10, 1992

Charlie explained it to Adrianne as an internal political issue at the hospital, some trouble that didn't really involve him, or shouldn't have. He was being targeted by the nursing administration, he said, a vendetta, out of spite. Charlie told Adrianne the reason was a pending nurses' strike. There had been talk of it on the unit, and Charlie had been one of the few voices against it. Patients would suffer, he said. It was a principled stand—Adrianne could see some of the old Charlie flaring back to life as he spoke. Charlie made it clear he'd prioritize patients over paychecks and break the picket lines if it came to that. It wasn't a popular opinion and, as a result, he became the target of a revenge campaign within the unit. They had made him the scapegoat.

Now Adrianne was really confused. Scapegoat? A scapegoat for what? Charlie perched high on his chair like a cat, attentive and regal. Well, Charlie said, it all revolved around some strange occurrences at Saint Barnabas. There had been incidents, and an investigation into them. The incidents—well, someone had been spiking IV bags in the storerooms. Spiking them with insulin, which was dangerous,

as Adrianne might imagine. It was a shocking story. Charlie laid it out calmly, explaining with great technical flour-
ish how the IV ports on the saline bags are designed to
be injected so you can add drugs into the mix, how it was
impossible to tell an injected bag with the naked eye. Under
the microscope, he said, you could see it; the plastic port
punctured like a used cork, some of them punctured dozens of times. There had been crashes and codes on his units,
Charlie said—that's the only way the administration had
finally figured it out. It was impossible to know exactly how
many patients were affected, and which had died as a result,
but possibly a great many, a truly impressive number.

It was a mystery as to who was behind it, Charlie explained,
real spy stuff, the hospital had done a huge investigation but
they couldn't figure it out. Charlie thought that the whole
affair had made the Saint Barnabas bosses look stupid. That
was why they needed a scapegoat, a martyr. Charlie had been
crucified because he had done the right thing, with the nurses'
strike. He had been made the focal point of the internal investigation at Saint Barnabas. That was why he had been let go. It
wasn't fair, Charlie said, but that was his life, unfair.

Adrianne hadn't seen her husband so excited for a long
time, and the spark in his affect somehow neutralized the
horror of what he was describing. The whole story didn't
make sense to Adrianne. She let it not.

———————

Charlie waited for his world to fall, the crash and the ham-
mer of air behind it, but the blast never came. Cause and
effect: the cause was buried in the euphemism of "issues";
the effect was only movement and change. There were no
policemen, nobody followed him, nobody called. Instead of
being cast into the void, Charlie found himself two weeks

later in Phillipsburg, New Jersey, sitting in a chair opposite the HR department desk at Warren Hospital,[1] filling out the application for another full-time position.[2]

Under "Work History" he listed his Navy nuclear submarine tech duties, three years cutting boxes in the stockroom of the West Orange Caldor, and nearly six years nursing at Saint Barnabas. His indicated "dates of employment" from May 1987 to January 1992 were technically true: he'd been fired from Saint Barnabas in the first days of January. It was still January now.

Do we have permission to contact your current employer? Charlie circled Yes.[3]

Professional References: Charlie listed the Saint Barnabas phone number.

And when the lady recruiter asked why the young nurse wanted to leave his long-standing job, Charlie took a deep breath, and told her it was the commute. Warren Hospital was twenty minutes closer to his home and family. Changing jobs was a family decision, that was the sort of person he was. It just plain made sense.

Charlie wanted all the work he could get, nights, weekends, and holidays. Warren would pay $14.84 an hour, $18.30 if he stayed on Adrianne's medical insurance, with an extra 23-cents-an-hour bump if they moved Charlie to the ICU. Charlie called Adrianne from the pay phone in the Warren Hospital main entrance, eager to tell his wife he had the job. If Charlie had done anything wrong, would he have been able to find a new job so easily? Adrianne put down the phone and silently thanked God. To be honest, with two kids and a mortgage, it didn't really matter whether Charlie was right or wrong, just that he was working. And what her husband was saying finally made some sense. If you couldn't trust a hospital, what could you trust?

7

Adrianne hoped for the best. Charlie's termination had seemed so damning that she'd at first considered it a validation of her personal concerns about her husband's character. But then, when he'd found new work so quickly, she doubted herself again. Charlie was a union member, had been educated and tested, received degrees that required regular recertification, and was governed by state nursing boards, hospital ethics boards, supervisors, and staffing departments. If there had been no repercussions from such serious accusations, if he had been fired and quickly rehired, then this must simply be the process. It was inconceivable that at an institution entrusted with human lives, the staff weren't at least as carefully regulated as the stocks of morphine. Adrianne didn't know the business of medicine, but she did know the business of business; all signs indicated that Charlie's termination and rehiring had no more moral undertone than any other corporate restructuring.

The change of jobs seemed to rejuvenate her husband. His career had a new direction and a higher rate of pay. He seemed excited by the new routine, the new technical systems to learn and new patients to master them on, and that excitement carried over into an attitude in his home life which was, if not positive, at least more animated. Charlie even agreed to start working days, so that their schedules weren't at such absolute odds. That put added pressure on their day-care needs, but seemed like a hopeful sign for the relationship. It was only a week before their troubles began again.

She didn't think Charlie had been a good husband for a long time, and soon after their second daughter, Saskia, was born in the middle of December 1991, she decided she didn't like him as a father, either. Charlie's secret drinking had finally become impossible for even Adrianne to ignore. There was no avoiding the topic. First he denied it. Then Adrianne broke into his footlocker while he was at work, and confronted him with the bottles. Charlie made her violation of his privacy the issue, or tried to—Adrianne didn't go for that one. Finally, he acknowledged his drinking but insisted it wasn't a problem. He was depressed, he said, but no, he didn't want to go on antidepressants. It was obvious to Adrianne that her depressed husband only became more depressed from his drinking, that he was caught in a spiral with her family in the center. Confronting Charlie while he was drunk was pointless. They'd fight and say things, and Adrianne would suffer a night that Charlie either didn't acknowledge or didn't remember the next day. Each time she tried confronting him when he was sober, Charlie would flee to the basement. Adrianne finally decided she needed outside help. The family health benefits from her employer would pay for five days in an alcohol treatment center. But Charlie didn't actually want to stop drinking. Adrianne tried leaving his old AA books out for him on the counter, hoping maybe he'd remember his former resolutions. But the books backfired. Charlie would get angry, or ignore them, or put them away as if straightening up. Then he'd sit and drink

Coke and eat potato chips until it was time for him to retreat to the basement.

Charlie saw no benefit to be gained from talking. He liked drinking. It lifted his spirits, at least initially. It drowned out the noise. It transformed slippery minutes into a constant Now. He felt at once more distant and more focused. That focus was dedicated primarily to himself. He felt wronged, and deeply misunderstood, and considered it criminal and tragic that his own wife didn't appreciate his frailty, the verity and intensity of his internal suffering. Because Charlie *was* suffering, deeply and daily. Adrianne never appreciated that, not that he didn't try to show her. He staged demonstrations of his pain carefully, making sure that, for example, Adrianne would walk into the living room while he was on the phone with the local funeral parlor, inquiring about their burial rates.

Charlie's demonstrations did little more than further annoy his wife and confirm his own sense of futility. And so, he tried again. He waited until he heard Adrianne walking from the kitchen, then flopped dramatically off the couch onto the living room floor—tongue out, prescription pills spilled like blood spray from the amber bottle, suicide in flagrante. Surely, Charlie thought, this bit of stagecraft would demonstrate the sincerity of his pain. But Adrianne only heaved a great annoyed sigh, stepped over him, and grabbed a magazine from the coffee table, leaving Charlie lying there, unsure how long to hold the pose. Crouching on the rug, picking up the pills one by one and placing each carefully back in the bottle, he allotted himself an extra dose of sympathy, knowing how very wrong it was for his own wife to ignore the obvious agony that he had demonstrated. He'd hang on to that hurt for a few days, then devise some other way to elicit the proper sympathetic attention. But the more he tried to show Adrianne how he needed to be taken care of, the more Adrianne hated him for it.

Finally, in November 1992, Adrianne decided she'd had enough. She didn't tell Charlie, but she did tell a lawyer; she was worried that what happened to Queenie could happen to her kids. Afterward, driving home in the early dark, Adrianne felt fortified by her secret decision. The only problem was that Adrianne needed to go in for gallbladder surgery that coming January, and that surgery had been scheduled to take place at Warren, where Charlie worked. The lawyer said the paperwork wouldn't be ready, but Adrianne insisted. There was no way she was going into that hospital— Charlie's hospital—without a piece of paper declaring her intent to divorce and the reasons behind it. If Charlie was working, she said, something might happen to her, as it had with Queenie. She didn't articulate exactly why she felt this way and she didn't dare to. All she told the lawyer was that she needed it done. Adrianne's father escorted her to the surgery and waited for her to emerge from the recovery room. She told him not to allow any other visitors, especially not her soon-to-be ex-husband.

Charlie was working in the Warren ICU that afternoon when the legal paperwork for the divorce was delivered. The man had tricked him, it seemed, into identifying himself, then put the envelope directly into Charlie's hand, and in public. He was humiliated at having such a personal thing served to him there, in his hospital, but when he tried to find Adrianne in the post-op recovery ward, he found his father-in-law and a closed curtain. And when Adrianne was sent home from the hospital, her father went with her, and he stayed on the foldout couch like an implied threat.

Charlie became indignant, then pathetic. And gradually, Adrianne began to feel some of the old sympathies for her husband. The man was suffering. He was the father of her children, after all. He was no longer fighting the fact that their lives would be separated—did she need to punish him as well? It was agreed: Charlie would move out as soon as he could afford it, but they would continue to live in the house together until they could figure out the details. Adrianne regretted the decision almost immediately.

8

It was night when the police arrived, the two young patrol-men toting heavy Maglite flashlights, the cop car parked conspicuously outside. This was new for Adrianne, taking it beyond the house, putting it on paper.[1] She told the troop-ers that her soon-to-be ex-husband was a dangerous drunk, and accused him, vaguely, of domestic violence. She'd found her husband loaded in front of the fireplace, staring dead-eyed at the AA books, poking the pages to fresh flame. She told them everything she could think of, including about the investigation at the hospital, and how Charlie had once bragged about poisoning his pregnant sister's abusive boy-friend's drink with lighter fluid as a child. She hadn't yet connected the dots herself, but she wanted to make an offi-cial statement linking those stories to his drinking and to her fears for her children and herself. Maybe bringing in the cops would force the issue. She was flexing a little, but it felt good.

Adrianne told the officer every odd thing about Charlie she could think of. The domestic abuse call quickly became a monologue about the strange occurrences surrounding the

Cullens' pets. So much wasn't adding up—at the hospital, at home, in their marriage—but the animals were something she could put her finger on. It wasn't just the missing puppy—at various points there had been ferrets, hamsters, goldfish, and, of course, Lady, her maiden animal. She told the officer how Charlie used to keep the Yorkie chained to a pole in the yard while Adrianne was at work, how it barked and turned around its worn track until the animal cruelty people took it away. Adrianne had to drive to the ASPCA and beg for her back, a truly humiliating experience. After that, they kept the dog inside, and then the noises started coming from the basement. Sometimes the thumps and yelps would wake her up. Charlie maintained he was training the dog, but to her it sounded like punishment. Adrianne would pad over in her robe and slippers and crack the door, afraid to go further. She would yell down from the top of the stairs, "Leave her alone!" Charlie wouldn't answer, but the noises would stop. Adrianne would stand there, listening to the silence, waiting him out. She could tell he was down there, standing frozen like a child playing invisible under a blanket. Finally she'd close the basement door, pad back to bed, and put the pillow over her head.

Charlie was livid. It was simply inconceivable, not to mention totally unfair, that his wife would tell these stories to the police. There wasn't a good reason for her to have called them in the first place. Charlie was a lot of things, but he wasn't a wife beater. She was playing a game for the lawyers. She was making him out to be a bad guy, crazy even, creating a paper trail for the divorce settlement. Forget about the reason she had called the police, once they were there, *whammo*. She'd even told them about his feigned suicide attempts. Charlie replied by washing down twenty pills with a bottle of supermarket Cabernet. Showing her what it looked like, for real this time.

Charlie had often imagined his own death, even as a child in West Orange. In the dream, his hair was parted by a bullet. He was a war hero, a cop, a popular and important senator giving speeches that would ring forever in marble halls. And he was dead. Martyred. Heroic and noble. But it was always a dream. He would open his eyes, alive, a child, a nobody. This wasn't the life he was intended for. At Catholic school he felt incompetent and humiliated; in the world he was disconnected and alone. He was often so depressed that he refused to go to school or even move. All he wanted was to stay in the house with his mother.

His first suicide gesture had come at nine years old. Charlie had mixed the contents of a chemistry set from the church charity box with a glass of milk, but the chemistry set wasn't that good, and he succeeded only in making himself sick. His second came one afternoon in December 1977. Charlie was home in bed, playing sick from high school, when the phone rang; his mother had been in a car accident, with his epileptic sister at the wheel. They didn't tell Charlie that the collision was head-on, or that his mother was already dead. Charlie tried to find her at Mountainside Hospital, but the staff told him his mother's body had already been taken away. He would never see her again.

Charlie felt that they'd lied to him at Mountainside Hospital,[2] a crime he would come to believe was characteristic of hospitals in general, and one that he would never forgive. He was angry and beyond consolation, and turned again to the relief valve of suicide. This attempt yielded his first hospital stay and his first psychiatrist, but Charlie wasn't willing yet to talk to anybody. He didn't want to say, yet, *Nobody treats my pain. Only I treat my pain.* The psychiatrist sent him home again, back to the hole where his mother had been.

Charlie hadn't wanted to go back to school, or to the dank wooden house and the men who arrived at all hours with who knew what on their breath or their minds. The only option he saw was the Navy. The recruiters had promised an identity and a uniform: white shoes, white pants and belt, even a white hat, whites that hadn't gone gray on another boy's life. It felt to Charlie like the most passive branch of the armed services, heroic but safe, like his childhood dreams of death. *I won't die,* Charlie thought, *but I could.* He pictured the immaculate silence he'd seen in submarine movies, that regular, pinging heartbeat, the amniotic red lights, and he signed on for training as an electronics technician, servicing the sixteen Poseidon nuclear missiles on the USS *Woodrow Wilson*.[3] But Charlie soon tired of the routine, and realized that he didn't like electronics anyway. And he didn't like taking orders, or being stuck for months under the ocean surrounded by strange, rough men. Tour after tour, the pale young seaman they called "Charlie Fishbelly" was the punchline for even the most novice seamen. He tried repeatedly to cancel his six-year Navy contract, but succeeded only in being repeatedly busted in rank and pay for refusal of orders[4] and his increasingly bizarre behavior.[5] His final year[6] would be spent above the waves, mopping out latrines and getting hammered as often as possible.[7] When the booze ran out, he turned to Listerine[8] or cleaning fluid. On January 13, 1984, Charlie downed a bottle and reported to the USS *Canopus*'s sick bay. "I drank some poison," he told the medic. "I don't feel well." This was already his third suicide announcement since joining the service, and his third ambulance trip to the Charleston Naval Hospital's psychiatry ward.[9] But for all his suicide gestures, the fact was that Charlie wouldn't kill himself, not really; the nuns in Catholic school had taught him that suicide was a sin, and Charlie didn't want to end up in purgatory.[10] But he could make himself sick, and in many ways, sick was better. Nobody loves you the way they do when you're dying.

————————

Charlie was still recovering[11] in the ICU from his last suicide attempt when Michelle Tomlinson came to visit. Michelle was a fellow nurse on the Warren Hospital Telemetry unit, a friend, and, Charlie hoped, maybe more. He knew they had a connection. There were always moments during a shift when all the patients have been looked in upon and the orders are filled, a downtime which Charlie and Michelle filled with conversation. Charlie thought that he and Michelle were very much alike. Michelle was depressed as well. She appreciated him. They might even be soul mates.

Michelle saw Charlie as he felt he should be seen. She felt sorry for him. She saw his depth and pain, and responded with maternal attention. He was a wounded baby bird. Michelle came with the eyedropper of attention. It was her suggestion that Charlie get himself transferred to Muhlenberg, a psychiatric unit across the state line, in Bethlehem, Pennsylvania. Michelle knew people at Muhlenberg, she said. It was good. Charlie would like it. Charlie requested the transfer, took another ambulance ride, and settled in. Michelle had been right. He did like Muhlenberg. Michelle visited there, too, bringing flowers. She'd pull up a chair and sit by his bedside. Even in bed, even suicidal, Charlie could make Michelle laugh. He was self-deprecating, funny, and charming—she found him charming, at least, and the thought of that, the promise of it, became a solid thing in his mind, enough that he felt well enough to check himself out of Muhlenberg on his own recognizance, just in time to meet his wife's divorce lawyer.

Charlie was determined to represent himself for the divorce.[12] The divorce itself was already going to cost him enough money, so there seemed little point in paying a stranger to lord a degree over him just to speed his blood-letting. Charlie was actually looking forward to stepping into this new role as pro se advocate, showing that he could do the lawyer-speak and jump through the hoops. He was a quick learner and had no doubt that he could perform against Adrianne's professional lawyer, a local attorney named Ernest Duh. It seemed strange to Charlie that what was knit together under God in a fancy rented hall could be dissolved by a lawyer on office furniture. Duh presented a checklist for splitting conjoined lives into equal parts. She got the house, he got the Honda and the Ford, they'd sell the Oriental rug and the Royal Doulton china. The rest fit easily into the back of Charlie's Escort station wagon for the ten minute trip down US 22 to his new apartment on the other side of Phillipsburg.

Charlie had circled the ad in the newspaper, a private basement apartment in a seventy-year-old stone house,[13] and rented it over the phone, sight unseen. The landlady was cautious, renting to a strange man without seeing him, but responded well when he listed his qualifications as a gain-fully employed nurse, a father, a nonsmoker. Charlie had only left out one detail: her potential tenant was calling from a psychiatric unit. He'd tell Michelle about that one when he got back to work at Warren.

When Charlie returned to work he seemed as bonded to her as a puppy. Michelle was a newly single mother with a full time job, a dragging divorce, and a volatile relationship with her on-again, off-again boyfriend, Jerry. Charlie was relief. Whatever absurd nugget Michelle might mine from her pathetic life, Charlie could match, then trump. He was always willing to offer up another chapter of his sometimes ridiculous life. They called it a pity party, making the joke but knowing that was exactly what it was. So when she and Jerry split up for a week she figured, yeah, what the heck, and broke her rule about dating coworkers. She'd let him take her out to dinner, just the once.

9

Charlie had been excited in preparation, shaving, showering, then shaving again. He felt handsome and charming as he looked at himself in the rearview mirror on the way to meet her at dinner. By the time Michelle had ordered her brownie sundae, Charlie had fallen in love. He watched her across the booth, twirling fudge with the special long spoon, and knew it: Michelle was his soul mate, period. So Charlie turned up the charm.

The way he'd read it, Michelle liked brownies. So Charlie started bringing brownies every day, even on his days off. When Michelle didn't touch them he'd plate up a square and place it by her charts, sometimes along with other gifts, little romantic somethings for her to find. When Michelle didn't respond to these, either, Charlie assumed he wasn't trying hard enough. They were on shift together at least three nights a week, but Charlie wanted more. When he couldn't get shifts, he'd come in anyway. On those nights he could follow Michelle full-time, cranking up the charm to high. One day he came in with a ring.

He told her, I love you. I'm in love with you, Michelle. But this didn't have the effect he'd imagined, not at all. Suddenly, she was busy with her patients. She avoided the nurses' station for the rest of the shift, didn't say good-bye. He'd tried calling her house but only got the machine. *Maybe,* he thought, *I'll see her at work tomorrow.*

All that March he hurried through his routine, delivering death notices to family members with a told-you-so air. The clock turned, the sun rose, night shift handed over to day. Charlie grabbed his coat and sulked back to the car, the highway, squinting through a smudgy little hole in the frosted windshield and thinking only about how Michelle had turned off. A light had gone out in her; it wasn't shining on him. The darkness in his soul mate could only mean one thing: she was depressed. He knew it. That was why they were soul mates. Life had become too much for her. She still needed him, but was too far gone to say so.

Back at his apartment, Charlie dialed Michelle's number without even taking off his coat. It was the machine, so he tried again, then again. He stopped after a few hours. Then Charlie's phone rang. It was Jerry, Michelle's on-again off-again sometimes-ex, telling Charlie, "Lay off, leave her alone."[1]

"Look," Jerry continued. "Michelle is really upset—she's hysterical after this."

Charlie stuttered something and placed the wall phone back in the cradle. What had Jerry meant by "hysterical"? Michelle was hysterical? Charlie knew Michelle, he understood her, better than Jerry ever could. The phone call had been from Jerry, yes—but this whole thing was a cry for help, from his Michelle. She was in trouble, suicidal maybe. He could save her. He was a hero to her, Charlie knew that, even if Michelle had forgotten.

10

March 23, 1993

Michelle rented a condo. Charlie knew the address. He slowed at her address to scan her windows and, seeing nothing, took a left then another, boxing around and cruising the building again, then boxing it the other way, checking from different angles in case he'd missed something before driving back home to leave another phone message. Then, back in the car and over again, cruising slow, and this time seeing one light on and her car in the drive but nobody in the window. He looped her neighborhood again to be sure. Nothing. Just the car, no life inside. Then he had a chilling thought—what if she was trying to call him? Now? Each trip was forty minutes, at least. He should drive faster. How many times had she called?

Back home he stared down at the machine, still not blinking. He played the tape anyway, in case the light was broken. No message. He called again, dialing the glowing numbers in the dark, left a long message, telling her everything in his heart, then hung up and got back in the car. Drove back to Michelle's apartment, saw the car still there, the light still on, nobody at the window. Why wasn't she answering? He drove back to his apartment. The light wasn't flashing but he checked the messages in case. Picked up the phone to call but then realized how late it was. He called. No answer. He drove back to her apartment, the rain precipitating out of the fog now as he killed the lights by the curb, stepped across the lawn, his white work shoes whipping wet through the grass. He stepped carefully on the gravel by the foundation and cupped his hands to the porch glass. No movement in the dark kitchen, only the steady red flash of a message machine. The glass door was locked, so Charlie tried a brick. He waited for something to happen from the noise. When nothing did he stepped inside.

The kitchen was lit only by the luminous moon of the stove clock. He wiped his sneakers on the kitchen rug, shedding bits of tracked glass, then stopped, listening. Just the tiny marching of the stove clock, the blood in his ears. No other sound. Not even his footsteps as he climbed the stairs. The bedroom door was closed. Charlie opened it.

Inside, the raw human smell, sound of sleeping breath, rough and regular. Charlie stood in the doorway, bathing in the intimacy. It is a tender thing, to watch over the sleeping. More tender still because the sleeping are unaware, like children blind to God's attentions.

———

Afterwards, Charlie drove to the minimart. He bought a jumbo coffee against the morning cold, and waited by the pay phone until the sun rose and he could call again. This time, Michelle answered. She sounded frazzled—somebody had broken into her apartment. They'd smashed the glass and come inside, with her and her son there, asleep. It felt like a sort of rape.

Charlie rested his arm on the metal cord. He said that he

wanted Michelle to know—so much to tell her—first, that he had talked to Jerry. So he knew she and Jerry were back together, and that Charlie wasn't supposed to bother her anymore. He'd gotten that straight, he was cool, no probs. Then Charlie told Michelle, "I was the one who did your house."[1]

That stopped her. "Did" her house? She didn't know where to go with that. What else had he done? Had he come inside? Well, yes, Charlie said, he had. "I wanted to check on you," he said. "You know, to make sure you were okay. That you didn't try anything—like suicide."

Michelle did not say anything. "You know, I'm, um, feeling a little crazy right now," Charlie said. He'd told her he'd totally understand if she wanted to call the police or something. He meant it as a gesture, showing her his sincerity.

Charlie knew he had unleashed yet another torrent, one already sweeping him forward like a leaf to the gutter. He crawled back into the car, feeling silly. Back home, he pulled a Coke from the fridge, found a half bag of chips, and sat in front of the TV until the phone rang again. It was an officer from the Palmer County Police. They'd issued a warrant for the arrest of C. Cullen, five foot eight, 150 pounds, brown hair and mustache. Yes, Charlie said, that was him. He promised to drive himself straight down to the police station and give himself up.

Normally, this would be the perfect moment for a suicidal gesture, but the necessity of showing up at the police station complicated things. With the proper timing, it was still possible to do both; in fact, as he thought it through, it was actually better this way. He'd collapse and fade, right in the jail cell, where he was sure to be seen and saved. He would be simultaneously both the criminal and a victim. Charlie popped a handful of the .05 mg Xanax the doctor at the psychiatric ward had prescribed for him, and added some narcotic Darvocets he had taken from his wife after her gallbladder operation, twenty pills in all. Then he drove straight to the police station.

This was him, an earnest health-care professional, love-sick and concerned, the sort of foolish heart who had told the policeman that he'd drive right over and did just that, on time. He figured that later, when the pills kicked in, he'd be Romeo, overwhelmed with love and poison, right on stage.

The drugs worked as planned. Xanax is a fast-acting antianxiety drug and kicked in first, delivering wave upon wave of *So What* while his wife's opiates put a little gravity in his feet. Charlie answered the policeman's questions, feeling high and loose. He offered his fingers, and the sergeant rolled each on an ink pad, then onto a corresponding square. They took his picture and sat him at a desk with a typewriter. But the Palmer police had no intention of holding Charlie in a jail cell. A complaint had been filed, and they had his address and number. They knew where to find him if he failed to show up for his court date.

Charlie was almost floppy by the time they released him back into the parking lot. The late winter sun was almost gone now, and a cold rain fell from a dirty nickel sky. He found his keys, sat in the driver's seat, stared out the bleary windshield. He couldn't stay here, with nobody to see. He skated out onto the main road, heard a horn, traced the white line. Brake lights blossomed across the glass, rain pounded the roof. He needed a pay phone. He pulled off the strip at some motel lights and opened the door, slid halfway out, stopped. The rain was cold needles on the back of his neck, soaking his knees. Who to call? Michelle wasn't an appropriate choice at this point, and this clearly wasn't a call he could make to his ex-wife. The only other number he could remember was the babysitter. Charlie made the call. Then he sat on the curb and waited for the ride to the hospital.

11

The ambulance proceeded up the drive lined with leafless trees toward a fortress of ash-colored rock. The New Jersey State Lunatic Asylum at Morristown had changed little in its 150 years, except in name. These days, it was the Greystone Psychiatric Hospital at Morristown. Most folks called it simply "Greystone."[1] It was an impressive if intimidating facility of stepped domes and Empire colonnades, a classic of 1870s Kirkbride design as ornate as a tiered wedding cake. The name referred to the rocks themselves, gneiss slabs quarried directly from the seven-hundred-acre estate and stacked into a fortress sufficient to separate the townsfolk from the inmates. The day after tax day,[2] 1993, Charlie Cullen was transferred here for intensive inpatient treatment. He was taken through a plank oak door studded with iron spikes into a banal modern office, to be processed.

Greystone was a decrepit and outdated facility only a few years away from being permanently shuttered, with grooved linoleum halls and peeling paint. The asylum was understaffed and drafty, and the beds—which had once housed some seven thousand inmates—were now used by only a few hundred patients and supported by a skeleton staff. But the old stones still retained a manorlike majesty, and Charlie was flattered by the placement. The asylum had been constructed under the psychological philosophy that architecture was an essential component of mental hygiene, and Greystone's bucolic view was as integral as the violent insulin shock therapy or the quieter psychosurgery in their approach to the rehabilitation of the depressed and suicidal.

His room lay in one of the dormitory wings, which fanned from the main buildings like spokes from a wheel. Each room had a barred window framing calming pastoral views of hills and trees. A stately carriage road trailed gently into the wooded foothills of the real world. Such a setting, coupled with an abundance of light and exercise, might allow an inmate to unknot the tightest monkey's fist of bad ideas, circular thinking, and other spasms of the mind that the increasingly industrialized world inflicted upon a fragile human psyche. The hope was that the disease of the mind arose from the environment, not the individual; change the environment and you change the man. At least, that was the idea.

Certainly, during his stay Charlie felt less stressed. He was, in a manner, happy. Whether this constituted merely a temporary vacation from his old self, or some new discovery of his true nature, the question didn't occur to him; happiness was a bubble that rough thoughts could prick. Greystone's thick stone walls were like a basement built aboveground, providing insulation from the pressures of work and romance and an asylum from his triggers and compulsions.

In therapy sessions, Charlie never had to fight to be recognized and validated. He learned to contain his known demons within pat psychological phrases. Talking about himself was encouraged; in fact, his personal issues were the only topics. He enjoyed his April. Each morning, Charlie would rise and look out over the asylum campus, taking in the rapidly greening lawn, the bare woods already hazing with the first buds. These were wet days filled with a cozy, gauzy weather, the light rain falling from a herringbone sky, the cardigan chill of the stone manse. There were no surprises, no triggers, no mail or calls. He felt calm. Maybe because of the attentions, maybe the meetings, maybe the meds—but April was good. And then the calendar turned a page, and vacation was over.

The skies brightened, the clouds burned off, and the heat arrived early. Each day set a new record, as if God was cranking up the volume. The second week of May hit ninety degrees. The dormitory became an oven, the windows were hot squares, wince-inducing. Weather was the first topic at the group meetings now, weather actually worth talking about. But the focus had splintered. It was another stunningly hot day when Charlie saw the note waiting in his cubby hole.

Patients didn't have telephones at Greystone; all calls came in through the antiquated switchboard, with messages relayed by pencil on small white pieces of paper. Charlie recognized the familiar 908 area code and the Warren Hospital switchboard exchange, and he knew, *Okay, this is it.* He'd actually wondered if they'd bother with the formality of firing him, or whether this was something more serious.

He hadn't exactly presented his best face at Warren Hospital. Charlie wasn't particularly concerned about blowback from patient deaths. The two that came immediately to mind had been quiet and largely unremarkable. But Charlie's own emotional breakdown had been anything but subtle; his private business had been entirely public at Warren. The staff knew all the juicy details of his stalking episode, they'd seen him wheeled into the ER by the babysitter. Charlie knew what that looked like: Michelle's stalker, fresh from another failed suicide attempt, halfway between jail and the nuthouse. At least they were paying attention. He'd return that call.

When he cradled the phone five minutes later, Charlie wanted to laugh—not out loud, of course; laughing to oneself was discouraged in a psychiatric facility—but it *was* funny. The call had been from Warren Hospital, all right. They wanted to know when he was available. As long as a Greystone physician cleared him for work, Charlie was headed back to the night shift.

12

The basement apartment had been shuttered while Charlie was away. Now he reclaimed his space, applying the Kirkbride style to his own private asylum. The lot directly adjacent to his building was empty; Charlie put his between-shift energies into converting the weedy plot into a garden. He soaked up sunshine while his store-bought seeds did the same. The flowers needed him. Here between his hedgerows, Charlie was in charge.

At Warren, he'd sometimes catch a glimpse of Michelle Tomlinson between the closing doors of the elevator, or a flash of her hair glossed by the yellow lights of the parking lot as she walked to her car, and each time he had to strangle the impulse to call out to her. But Michelle either never saw him, or pretended not to. It didn't matter. Even if she *had* seen him, the restraining order prevented them from working together on the ICU, a point needlessly explained by Charlie's new nursing supervisor, Connie Trembler. Charlie didn't need someone telling him what he could and couldn't do. He was determined to be good. Connie had gone on and on about the new rules but Charlie had kept his expression blank. He knew he'd messed up with Michelle. Silence was the best penance he could offer. And anyway, Connie had moved Charlie to a great posting next door, in Telemetry, which had its own secret rewards.

Telemetry was a halfway ward, a sort of purgatory between the eyes-on intensity of Intensive Care and the hotel-like existence of a regular hospital inpatient. The ward was primarily reserved for heart patients—not the critical ones but those on the mend, whose stability might suddenly nosedive. Such patients needed to be carefully watched.

Of course, from a patient's perspective, purgatory was extremely annoying. They were strung with wires and IVs like marionettes, tethered to a beeping, flashing, and sometimes sighing machine, like the beeping thing in soap operas, the one that flatlines in the dramatic parts. As telemetry patients were not heavily sedated, the association made them nervous, which did nothing positive for their blood pressure, and sent the machine beeping double, which was where Charlie came in. His main skill was Patient Education, a one-on-one scripted pedagogy he enjoyed. Charlie was encyclopedic in his iteration of the technical details, and he had effective means to explain the devices. He explained that, Yes, fearful patient: you are hooked to a lie detector test, at least aspects of one.[1] But when you understood how it worked, a polygraph wasn't really all that frightening. And Charlie certainly knew; at this point, he understood how they worked better than most cops.

The electrocardiogram (EKG) contains an incredible amount of information. Blood comes in the top of the heart and flows out the bottom, pushed by the squeezing of the chambers, atria to ventricle. The squeeze is triggered by an electric impulse. The EKG translates those electrical pulses into a picture, drawn by an inked needle jerking across rolling graph paper.

Usually, Charlie explained all this as he applied the electrodes to the taut rib cages of the elderly, the dry eraser nipples, the merkin of hair.

In the healthy heart, the muscle rippled, moving blood through the heart like a farmer's hand moves milk through a cow's teat. On the EKG, the stages of a normal pulse looked something like a mountain range. The information lay in the size and spacing of the peaks. Some looked slurry or slouched or notched, others read as irregular as an earthquake. Looking at the paper, a nurse could tell which; beneath the johnny, behind the ribs, the heart was trembling like a bag full of mice.

Charlie's pending divorce had led to two polygraphs that spring. The first was precipitated by Adrianne's allegations that her husband was a dangerous alcoholic who drank while watching the children. This, and a restraining order, requested in the wake of her domestic-violence call to the police, formed the core arguments in her request for full custody of their children. The polygraph was Charlie's idea. Arrangements were made on June 18, two months after Charlie was released from Greystone. According to the machine, Charlie passed the test; he was telling the truth. But this was only a small victory within the bizarre war he had been waging in the courtroom, and twelve days later Adrianne was granted a final restraining order against her husband.

The divorce proceedings in the Warren County family court system were not going well for Charlie. Neither was his case in the Northampton County Court of Common Pleas. Charlie had been charged with stalking, breaking and entering, and trespass and harassment. This was a criminal situation, far more complicated than his divorce, and pursued by an aggressive and intimidating government prosecutor. Charlie had initially decided to represent himself but quickly realized that he was in over his head.

Charlie needed to demonstrate financial need in order to qualify for a public defender. But while his application listed his necessary outside expenses, such as $1,460 a month in child support, psychological counseling fees, and credit card minimums, he neglected to list his most basic personal, day-to-day living expenses such as rent and food. It wasn't a chance oversight—the droll expenses of his physical sustenance simply were not the needs that mattered. Charlie did not list them, because they did not exist for him. He was flat broke, but his net income appeared too healthy for the court, and his application for public counsel was denied. Now Charlie needed to pay for a defense lawyer, too, putting him further into debt.[2] He picked one from the yellow pages and paid the retainer. The relationship lasted three days before the lawyer quit, claiming that Charles Cullen was "too difficult" a personality to represent as a client. With no outlet to vent his frustrations in the courtroom, Charlie directed his rage against his former lawyer instead. He wrote long, ranting letters to the court, comparing the legal profession to his own. Would a nurse simply walk out on a patient? he asked. No, he would not. Why not? It was unethical, and therefore unprofessional. The venting didn't improve his situation. Now he had no choice but to represent himself.

Charlie was nearly incoherent in court, and he knew it. On August 10, he gave up and simply pleaded guilty to the lesser charge of harassment and defiant trespass. He was given a fine and probation but no jail time. He was free to go home, where he tried suicide again, this time with pills and wine, driving himself to Warren Hospital and admitting himself to the emergency room. The familiar combination of his own willful actions and his resulting helplessness relieved some of the stress, like a sneeze or a compulsion acted upon, but the relief was short-lived, and the next evening Charlie was released to drive back home in the fog.

The basement apartment was oddly cool, even in August. The only sound was the soft *tchuckk, tchuckk, tchuckk* of the stove clock, counting the seconds. Michelle had a phone, and he knew where she lived, but using either was a violation of his probation. He had been squashed and silenced, but still needed to speak. He was clicking in time with the clock again, teeth edges together, *tchuckk. tchuckk*. Winking one eye then the other, watching the wine bottles in their parallax dance, left, right, his elbows hard on the kitchen Formica as he put the words down on paper for the judge.

"Their was a sexual intamate [*sic*] relationship between Michelle Tomlinson and myself,"[3] he wrote. This judge didn't see him, not as Charlie wanted to be seen. But Charlie had seen judges. They had been his patients in the Saint Barnabas Burn Center—fragile men stripped of their robes, reduced to probabilities, breathing by the grace of a machine. He wrote until the sky was inky with morning. He brushed his teeth, spitting red into the sink, drove to hand-deliver a fat stack of handwritten motions. Then he went to see George, the court-appointed family services counselor who would determine Cullen's future with his children.

Charlie very much wanted to keep his kids, especially now. His young children were the unquestioning fans of a certain select version of himself. They were dependents, just like the patients under his care in the ICU. He believed that in time he might actually become the man that his children imagined him to be: A caring father. A good friend. A compassionate caregiver. Some people saw him that way. Some of his fellow nurses saw him that way. His mother had seen him this way. Adrianne had, once, and so had Michelle.

Maybe, he thought, if he kept his kids, he could make them love him; they'd seen him this way, too. If Charlie was satisfied by their attentions, he might not be willing to risk losing them again. Maybe he'd have no reason to keep dosing patients at the hospital, such as Ms. Natoli. Charlie would be the good father and the good nurse, an outcome he believed George and the family court should want. George's recommendations held the key to this potential future, and so Charlie was always sober for their mandatory interviews.

Of course, George had no idea that Charlie was killing people. But he was very much aware that Charlie was regularly attempting to kill himself, or at least making grand gestures at it. George noted in Cullen's file that suicide was "the most severe and ultimate form of abuse/neglect, rejection, and abandonment one could inflict on one's children." Later that week Adrianne's lawyer used the report in family court. Combined with a host of other evidence regarding Charlie's drinking, the police calls, and Adrianne's concerns that if Charlie was left alone with their daughters, he would "impulsively take his life and theirs," Charlie had no standing in the courtroom. The only arena in which he still had gravitas was in the hospital.

13

September 1, 1993

He didn't know what he'd do, exactly. It wasn't a decision, but he had been visiting the ICU lately, and he was zeroing in. A Mrs. Helen Dean was scheduled to leave the hospital the next day. She was an elderly woman recovering well from breast cancer surgery, and she had an adult son, Larry, who seemed never to leave her bedside. Something about that detail forced Charlie's decision.

The digoxin was in small glass ampules in the hospital drug closet, loaded into a plastic drawer called a cassette. Digoxin is a common drug on the ICU, called "didge" by the nurses, and written quickly on charts as "dig." A pharmacopeial relative of the Foxglove extract digitalis, dig was used in the hospital to slow the firing mechanism of the heart muscles. Charlie loaded three amps, thinking, *Three times point-five mills, that's a milligram and a half; intermuscular, it could be enough.* He palmed the syringe as if he were doing a magic trick, and walked into the room.

———

The way Larry Dean remembered it,[1] he was sitting at his mother's bedside when the male nurse entered. Immediately, something struck him as odd. Larry had been at the hospital every day since his mother had come in. He knew all the nurses, at least by sight, and would especially remember a male nurse. He'd never seen this guy. That was strange, but stranger still was that this nurse was dressed entirely in white, like an ice cream man. Every other nurse he'd seen at Warren was dressed in blue.

The nurse in all white told Larry, "You've got to leave the room." The nurse said this without eye contact or facial expression. So Larry did what he was told and headed down the hall for a coffee. He returned ten minutes later to find his mother, alone and angry. "He stuck me," she said.

Helen Dean pulled up her johnny and pointed to a spot on her inner thigh. Larry had his Swiss Army knife, the deluxe kind with the little magnifying lens, and sure enough, there was a pinprick. So Larry called the doctor.

"It could be a bug bite," the doctor explained. But by the next day, Helen Dean was violently ill. She was sweating, exhausted. When her heart stopped, she could not be revived, and Larry could not be consoled.

Larry Dean knew right away that something wasn't right and took it upon himself to investigate. He complained to his mother's oncologist, who confirmed that Mrs. Dean hadn't been scheduled for any injection. He complained to his mother's other nurses. They told him that the male nurse his mother had identified was Charles Cullen.

Larry Dean's next call was to the Warren County prosecutor. He said his mother had been murdered, and told them who had done it.[2]

After injecting Helen Dean, Charlie had driven home and thought about his actions of the evening. He didn't much dwell on it; he simply assumed that this time they'd figure it out. Wouldn't they? Maybe it depended upon whether Mrs. Dean was dead. He went in to work the next day, and he was surprised it had taken twenty-four hours[3] but, yep, she was dead. And yep, they were figuring it out. His work schedule was crowded with meetings about the incident. He was questioned by the doctor, the Warren administrators, his nurse supervisors, and two people from the Warren County Prosecutor's Office, Major Crime Investigation Unit.[4] Each wanted him to run them through the scenario aloud. Charlie denied everything, of course, including the injection. He watched as they searched his locker. Meanwhile, Helen Dean had been wheeled into cold storage, then thawed. A doctor from the Medical Examiner's Office sampled the tiny injection site on her thigh. The medical examiner would test for nearly one hundred potentially lethal chemicals. But for some reason, they neglected to test for digoxin. Helen Dean's death was determined to be of natural causes.[5]

Charlie's supervisor informed him that he would be put on indefinite paid leave, effective immediately. That didn't sound so bad, being paid not to work, until he sat home in his basement apartment, thinking, depressed, wondering if they'd come for him or if he should set it up so he could be a tragic suicide in jail, as he had after breaking into Michelle's apartment. He had nothing to do and all day to do it, sitting on the couch until the TV numbed him, moving to the kitchen table, the bed, the couch again. The stove clock piled up the seconds: *tchuckk tchuckk*. The ambulance arrived just before 11 p.m. This time, Charlie left the door unlocked for them.

14

Charlie tumbled through the suicide cycle: emergency room to inpatient Psychological Hospital[1] to outpatient counseling program. He popped out the other side to find the Warren County Prosecutor's Office waiting. They did the usual interview. He denied everything. When the questioning ended, they brought in a polygraph.

The wires connected his body to the machine. Inked needles scribbled the results on the graph paper, showing the spiking of the QRS complex and frequency of the P wave. Charlie knew that the spikes could be moved up or down, even stopped altogether. Changing those spikes was what he did for a living.

The police didn't know medicine and didn't care about what the spikes and troughs really meant. They were only interested in the most basic changes, like pulse, rhythm, and pressure. On the basis of this, they accessed what they called the truth. Charlie called it something else. Charlie knew these were changes you could control with digoxin, beta blockers, nitroprusside.

The polygraph made gross assumptions. It ignored the most fascinating arenas of the EKG. It connected the truth in a man's head and the action of his heart, running a string from one to the other like a child's tin-can telephone. It was a stupid test, and Charlie passed it with flying colors. But personally, Charlie was pretty sure they knew the truth.[2]

———————

Charlie's paid leave from Warren Hospital lasted him into the New Year, but he'd already decided not to go back. He would need another job if he was going to make his child support payments, especially at the high sum the judge had based on his eighty-hour-a-week work schedule. Charlie found it at Hunterdon Hospital, a pretty little nonprofit medical center in the boutique town of Flemington, New Jersey. The numbers of both Warren Hospital and Saint Barnabas Medical Center were provided as potential references.[3] By April 1994, Charlie was making $23 an hour plus overtime in the Hunterdon Hospital ICU, and living up to his recommenders' reviews.

His October 1995 performance report from Nurse Supervisor Marjorie Whelan called him "a patient advocate... cares about his patient's welfare... organized, very giving of his time, so much to offer, very bright, witty & intelligent." He started dating Kathy, another nurse on the ward, unhappily married, apparently available, three kids. He was sated by her attentions, rather than those of the hospital, and that winter he received a photocopied certificate filled in with his name in magic marker from the Hunterdon ICU. "To Charles Cullen, in appreciation for 'Grace Under Fire,'" it read. "For all the night shifts you helped out on, thanks!" Marjorie Whelan went further. "Charles is always positive and polite! An excellent patient advocate! Helpful!" she wrote. "He has no medication errors."

But in fact, he did.

The change came as imperceptibly as twilight becomes

night. It wasn't a conscious choice—he couldn't say exactly when or why—but as 1995 wore on, Charlie went dark. By November, the man who showed up to work each evening bore little resemblance to the dream nurse Hunterdon had imagined they had hired.

He didn't really remember the names of those he injected and killed,[4] no more than he cared about the reprimands and write-ups now thickening his once-perfect personnel file.[5] Some nurses complained that Cullen was "over-lubricating his patients," turning them into "grease buckets" after he bathed them alone with the blinds drawn. The practice struck his coworkers as unprofessional, bordering on creepy, but his litany of medication errors was far more serious.[6] Charlie was caught administering unprescribed drugs to some patients and withholding essential prescribed drugs from others. Nurse Supervisor Whelan couldn't explain this sudden turn in her star employee or his new, bizarre behavior, but she grew concerned enough to pull Cullen's patient charts. These weren't normal mistakes. Whenever Nurse Cullen gave the wrong drug to a patient, he also failed to record that drug on the chart. The nurse was playing doctor as no doctor would. Nurse Cullen was even ordering his own lab tests. The requests were bizarrely specific, as if he was looking for something in particular.

On the morning of July 19, ten days after Charlie had killed the elderly Jesse Eichin with a dose of digoxin, Whelan pulled Charlie into an empty room for a conference. She couldn't make sense of the disturbing pattern she saw, so she presented an ultimatum. One more incident, Whelan said, and Charlie would be terminated.

For the past two weeks, Charlie had been fueled by the hurt delivered by Kathy, who had gone back to her husband. Now, he turned all his attentions to this threat from his supervisor. One more? It was unfair. It wasn't just Whelan, Charlie felt, it was all of them, the whole bunch. And so he'd told Whelan, said it right in that closed office: if they really thought he was that bad, he'd just quit. He'd quit right now, he said, if that would make them happy. Is that what they wanted? Charlie left in a hurried sulk, slamming himself into the car for an angry drive home. He pulled out the type-writer again, to make it official, and really gave the keys a workout, employing whole sentences of all caps and lines of solid "!!!!!" and "??????" for emphasis. It felt good to vent, to tell them that he had 170 hours of paid vacation time coming and he didn't care, they could keep it. It felt good to say that: Keep it! 170 hours because of his perfect attendance. He told them to use the money to find somebody else. It was a grand gesture, a sort of suicide. Who but a righteous and wronged man, a good man of pure intent, would be willing to throw away paid hours? Especially one who needed the money as desperately as Charlie Cullen did? Charlie drove to a mailbox, intoxicated by the promise of its dramatic impact. He pulled back the metal handle, stuffed the letter into the chute, slammed it home, and opened it again to make certain it had really gone. Then he realized exactly what he'd done. He went home to quickly draft another letter, hoping to catch the first, nullify it somehow—but it was too late.

Whelan received Charlie's resignation. It was gratefully accepted. He would be allowed to pick up odd shifts, but strictly as a freelancer, on a per diem basis. Charlie grudgingly accepted. His name went back up on the Hunterdon schedule. But Charlie never showed up. He sat in his rented basement room, listening as the phone rang and rang. He felt powerful again, ignoring them, holding his breath, really showing them, all of them: his ex-wife, his family, Michelle, Kathy, Whelan. Then his phone stopped ringing.

God had turned off the spotlight. It was just him in his basement apartment, checking his empty mailbox. The final letter from Hunterdon arrived, wishing him "Good luck with his future career." Charlie pulled out the electric typewriter again and grabbed one of the letters on the stack from his wife's lawyers, copied the threatening official style of date and address, then dove directly into the unfairness of his situation:

> They had been interviewing others in house,I have been told before Loretta got back to me that when one of the interviewrs went up to LOretta and asked "Why are we even interviewing when no decision has been made about Charlie?"
> The respose was "THat's not even a consideration, he too un-stable."
> If Loretta who so freely told my co-worker that I was unstable, she should of also felt free to explaime if true why did they not insist that I be examined or at the very least not let this "UNSTABLE" co-worker continue to work, and tell this co-worker but we might offer him per diem.[7]

Charlie didn't see that he was in fact making an argument against himself, only that he was making an argument. The syllogism went something like this:

> A "dangerous" and "unstable" nurse should not be on the nursing schedule.
> The hospital administration put Charlie on the nursing schedule.

Therefore: Charlie wasn't dangerous; the complaints against him were unfair; Charlie was the only victim here.

Of course, Hunterdon never wrote back. It cost him six weeks of unemployment and 170 hours of paid vacation, but the incident taught him a valuable lesson: Never put it in writing.

15

After his resignation from Hunterdon in October 1996, Charlie had simply driven straight up the road to apply at Morristown Memorial Hospital. Morristown HR rigorously vetted Cullen's background through a professional service,[1] but despite several discrepancies in his stated dates of employment, they hired him anyway. After all, *nobody* remembers their exact dates of hire and fire, not even an accomplished and accredited nurse with nine years' experience at Hunterdon, Warren, and Saint Barnabas.[2] Morristown needed staffers to fill the hours. In Charlie's case that was seventy-five hours a week, plus whatever shifts he could grab, at a new rate of $23.27 an hour, working 7 p.m. to 7 a.m. on the Cardiac Care Unit. But Charlie was still reeling, and failed to give one of his better nursing performances at Morristown.

The morning shift would arrive to find Charlie's patients cowering in pools of their own blood, twenty-five washcloths in the sink, and junk all over the counter. They'd written it all up in the patient incident reports,[3] which Charlie considered astonishing reading—he couldn't believe how petty nurses could be, counting washcloths like that. One patient told Charlie's supervisor that he "wanted to call the police," but the police weren't called, and Charlie got a lecture instead. They were watching him. He knew it, he'd seen it before. Morristown had it in for him. They'd noticed the pattern, especially with the drugs he was administering. He appeared careless, several times loading patients with the wrong dose of Diprivan[4] or heparin. He was there for less than a year before Morristown fired Charlie, not for killing patients[5]—as he was certain he must have done, not many, just one or two, he couldn't say—but for "poor performance" and what they called "nurse practice issues." His superiors were concerned about their patients and their reputation. There were too many incidents to ignore.[6] Even the patients were complaining.

The final straw involved a male patient—Charlie didn't catch the name. The patient had a surgery scheduled for the following morning, for which he had been prescribed regular doses of heparin. As his nurse, Charlie was supposed to administer the heparin; he didn't, and the patient died. Naturally, the physician on call was furious, and Charlie got an earful, which he didn't like. He told the doctor, and everyone else afterward, that it had been an accident. It was a weak excuse, but as far as he was concerned, he hadn't been actively attempting to kill this man. More like, he wasn't trying *not* to.

Charlie's mistake and the patient's death were never explicitly linked, but the potential harm to the patient was gravely obvious. The administrative director, Lisa Gannon, called his actions "inexcusable."[7] Her concerns were validated by the chief of the Department of Cardiovascular Medicine, Dr. John Banas. Gannon wrote she was "concerned about Charles' competence and ability to provide safe care." He was moved to harmless busywork for the remainder of his shift, then sent home for a week. Charlie felt deeply wronged, but he didn't confront them directly, not at first. He just drove home, flopped on the couch, and waited for the phone to ring. When it did, it was the administrative director's secretary, calling to schedule a meeting. Charlie didn't want to come in. He told the secretary, "If they want to fire me, they can call me on the phone," and hung up. An hour later, Gannon called back. But now, it was Charlie who wasn't picking up, figuring, *Hey, now they call?* He let it ring. Gannon kept calling, leaving messages on the machine. "Charles," she said, "we need you to come in. We need to speak with you." *Yeah,* Charlie thought. *Now they need something.* That was August 13. He was angry, and determined never to go in again. After several more messages, Gannon finally sent Cullen an edgy certified letter demanding his hospital ID and all other hospital property, "since your employment is terminated effective today." That was August 14. A few days later, Charlie came in anyway, early for his usual Saturday night shift, and found his name crossed off the shift whiteboard.

Without hospital work, he had no way to blow off his stress as he had before, taking it out on the hospital, showing them. Instead, he drove to the corner mart, loading up on Coke and chips and a thick pack of kid's notebook paper. He spread out at the kitchen table and wrote a long letter to the Morristown director, Kathleen C. Chumer. He demanded to have his case reviewed. It felt good but it wasn't enough, so he wrote again, typing this time, remembering that illegible handwriting was one of the reasons he'd been let go in the first place. His typing wasn't particularly good, either, so Charlie corrected in ballpoint.

The responses from the director and the Hospital Review Board arrived a week later; each concluded Charles Cullen had been terminated appropriately. Charlie wrote again, demanding outside arbitration. Paperwork flowed back and forth for a month, certified mailings, faxes. The process was too slow to provide Charlie with any satisfaction, so he tried suicide instead, telling 911 he'd swallowed a handful of pills, and knowing the ambulance would be required to bring him to nearby Warren, where, at least, he was known.

Usually, suicide cleared the air like a summer storm. The attempt was an assistance bell, always at the ready. When nobody else cared enough, the ambulance crews always did. The ER attendants always took him seriously. The little penlight in the pupils was a tiny spotlight not only on him, but *right into him*. The pressure cuff hugged his arm like a friend. Each assessment of his vital signs was a kindly and sincere nudge of his very existence. Charlie told the paramedics that he was an RN, as he always did, and made a point to call the things around him by their special names, *johnnies, codes, stim-pack,* so they'd know he was an insider. The ride to the hospital was a special time. But once he arrived, it was a different matter. Charlie Cullen was rolled into the ER as a familiar character at Warren Hospital, an eye roller, the former employee turned suicidal stalker freak. *Did you hear? Charlie's back.* They wheeled him into a little area, drew the privacy curtain halfway, watched him. Charlie knew how they whispered at the nurses' station, the gossip that went on there, the rubbernecking at this accident dragged in off the human highway. He could almost empathize. But Charlie was stubborn when he had a goal. He wanted to go back to Greystone. It had been so pleasant there. Only a hospital could admit him. Warren had done it the last time he showed up in their emergency room—wouldn't they just rubberstamp him forward again? But the ER doctor required a blood sample first. What he was checking for, Charlie wasn't sure—perhaps he suspected that Charlie hadn't really been trying to kill himself, that he was simply gaming the system. The doctor would screen Charlie's blood for drugs and make a recommendation of care based on what he found. He might not recommend Greystone.

Charlie refused the blood test. He made it extremely clear to anyone who came into his curtained area. He had given blood plenty of times, dozens of times, hundreds of times, over twelve gallons of blood, by his own count, but this wasn't him giving—it was *them taking*. Once decided, Charlie shut down. There would be no negotiating. Doctors and nurses approached, he pushed them away and started to leave, and when they tried to stop him he slapped them away again until finally someone at the desk called security. Charlie could only imagine what the nurses were saying about him now—*And we even had to call security!*—but at least he got his way.

———————

Ah, *Greystone*, ever so much grayer in October, as if the sprawling stone estate sucked color from the clouds themselves. Charlie arrived back at the haunted-looking mansion on the hill the day before Halloween. He'd have months. The familiar driveway was a salted seam of asphalt through bare poplars, and from his dormitory window Charlie watched snow muzzle the distant fields, followed tender plumes of wood smoke rising from invisible hearths. The outside world held its breath. There was nothing but time here, enough for a new drug routine to kick in, for the therapy sessions to get traction, time enough for a patient to clear his mind and refresh. But Charlie wasn't interested in new thoughts, and when he was discharged on December 11, he drove straight to the police station to press charges against the Warren Hospital ER physician, the one who had tried to steal his blood. Charlie stood before the bewildered desk sergeant, making sure the man had it all written down before hopping back in the car to pick up his held mail. Most were bills for alimony and child support, and letters from the Morristown Memorial Hospital lawyers. After months of preparation, his review had been forfeited, because he hadn't paid his side of the arbitration fees.[8] In January 1998 Charlie wrote back: he had been in a mental institution and had no employee handbook, so the delay was not his fault. He was a victim. In March he wrote again, threatened to sue Morristown Memorial Hospital unless they granted his extension.[9] They sent Charlie yet another employee handbook, this time by certified mail, and granted his extension. But Charlie never wrote back. The matter at Morristown, once so desperately important, no longer seemed even to exist. He had already found a new outlet for his frustrations.

16

The Pennsylvania border was just a line on the map to most people, but extremely important to a nurse like Charlie. Pennsylvania required a different nursing license—a simple application. It meant a clean start.

His application to Liberty Nursing and Rehabilitation Center of Allentown, Pennsylvania, was made through a staffing agency called Health Force[1] and required references. Morristown Memorial Hospital, from which Cullen had been fired for incompetence, patient complaints, and grave medication errors, simply confirmed his former employment. Charlie's reference from Hunterdon Hospital was Marjorie Whelan, who had threatened to terminate Cullen for his multiple medication and patient-care issues. The Liberty HR reference form would record that Charles Cullen was "an excellent nurse, gave good care, was excellent with patients," and that Whelan would recommend Charles Cullen for employment. Nobody at Liberty questioned why a nurse with ten years of hospital experience would downshift to a nursing home and a $5-an-hour pay cut. They needed the help, and Charlie needed the money.

After months without work, Charlie was $66,888 dollars in debt. The interest on his maxed credit cards grew, as did the money he owed for alimony and child support. If Charlie didn't pay, he might be characterized as a bad father, which was not acceptable to him. It might seem like he was abusing his kids. His inability to pay would give Adrianne an opportunity to poison his children's minds, characterize their father as a bad guy—Shauna was already nine, old enough now that she might even get the idea herself. And that wouldn't help him at all. Each evening he packed into the aging Escort and took his troubles to the Liberty night shift.

———

Francis Henry[2] was an elderly resident who needed extra attention for a broken vertebrae. Doctors had stabilized his neck with a halo device—a Frankenstein-ish rig of shoulder supports supporting a metal ring screwed directly into the skull. Nurse Cullen believed that Mr. Henry should be in a hospital rather than a nursing home.

It was Charlie's diagnosis, his alone. In this matter, there would be no arbitration board, no letters of rejection. Instead, he simply loaded a syringe with insulin, and injected it directly into Mr. Henry's IV.[3] It was a whopping dose. During his overnight shift on May 6, 1998, Mr. Henry quickly spiraled into diabetic shock. The results were almost unimaginably violent; Charlie Cullen had put an elderly man with a broken neck into violent seizures. That night, Francis Henry finally devolved into a coma,[4] and by morning, Charlie's "diagnosis" had been proved correct; Henry did, in fact, need a hospital. Henry was returned to the nursing home the next day, and died soon after. Three days later, on May 13, Charles Cullen filed for bankruptcy.

Mr. Henry's death was not quiet, and suspicion was inevitable; Charlie knew that this time, he'd pretty much asked for trouble. Liberty initiated an internal investigation and discovered the massive levels of foreign insulin in Mr. Henry's blood. Insulin appeared nowhere on Mr. Henry's medical chart—he had not been prescribed insulin at any dose. His charts had no record that any staff member had administered it to him. It was extremely unlikely that an immobilized, elderly patient had overdosed himself, and suspicion quickly fell upon the night shift for what was assumed to be a medication accident. Charles Cullen had already been written up for several nursing issues during his short tenure at Liberty; he was ready for the axe to fall again. Instead, Liberty fired a senior nurse named Kimberly Pepe. Nurse Pepe's lawyer immediately hit Liberty with a wrongful termination suit, going so far as to suggest Charles Cullen was more likely responsible, and that Liberty Nursing Home had suspected as much.[5]

According to Pepe's suit, she had first been asked about the incident by her nursing supervisor several days after Mr. Henry's death. "They were not looking at me at that time," Pepe claimed in her lawsuit. "They were, in not-so-many words, looking at my co-worker, Charles Cullen." Liberty would go on to vehemently disagree with Pepe's accusations[6] and deny that they had any suspicion of Charles Cullen.[7] Liberty and Pepe later settled her suit out of court.

It's impossible to say with certainty why Pepe had been targeted; perhaps it was simply a mistake. But *somebody* had poisoned Mr. Henry, and they were either still working at Liberty or had been moved on to another hospital. But there would be no criminal investigation. Liberty and its parent company, HCR Manor Care, maintained they were unaware of this being a criminal matter.[8] Pepe and her lawyer were asking for more than $50,000 in damages, but the exact amount of Pepe's settlement was sealed, along with her nondisclosure agreement.

Whatever Liberty did or didn't know, they moved Nurse Cullen out of their Intensive Care Unit. Reassigned to work shifts on the psychiatric wing, Charlie quickly discovered that some of the patients were downright feisty. On October 1, Cullen was seen with syringes entering the room of an elderly woman who was not his patient and delivering her drugs that weren't prescribed.[9] A scuffle ensued, and the patient ended up with a broken wrist. Finally, five months after Mr. Henry's death, his killer *was* fired, for failure to follow drug protocol.[10] Charlie was only on the couch for two days before a staffing agency[11] found him nursing work. It was always easy to get extra hours during the holidays.

The week between Christmas and New Year's Day was a stressful time for Charlie, but he was happy to be in uniform. The commute to the new job was only a couple miles down the road from Liberty, at Easton Hospital in Easton, Pennsylvania. He'd be happy with whatever shifts they'd give him, racking hours in whatever ward needed the help. Mostly, that meant working overnights in the familiar confines of the ICU, where death on the night shift was never totally unexpected.

———

At first, Kristina Toth didn't make much of the strange man with the syringe;[12] she wasn't even certain he was a nurse; all she noticed was that he was male, another uniformed stranger now responsible for keeping her father alive. Ottomar Schramm's strokes had started a year before, each clot annexing another small quadrant of his body, and though he was now unable to put on his socks or navigate stairs, he was still Dad, even when unconscious in a nest of tubes and wires. Kristina comforted herself knowing that Ottomar had been a practical man, with savings and a living will and a knowledge of what life brought; he was not surprised that it was his turn to suffer the same pedestrian indignities of old age that had afflicted his friends years before. He was now in the hands of the professionals at Easton.

Kristina remembered the man saying that he needed to take her father out of his room for "some tests." The syringe, he said, was "in case her father's heart stopped." Kristina didn't believe her father had any issues with his heart, but then, she wasn't the professional here. At the time, she just accepted it.

The next time Kristina saw her father, during visiting hours the following morning, December 29, 1998, he looked waxy and unwell, far worse than when he'd arrived at Easton Hospital.[13] According to the doctors, Mr. Schramm's deterioration appeared to be unrelated to his stroke. His heart rate wavered, his blood pressure plummeted. Mr. Schramm appeared to be spiraling downward, and Kristina began the mental preparations for her father's imminent death. It seemed to be some sort of medical miracle when she arrived at the hospital the following morning to learn that her father's condition had stabilized. In fact, she was told, her father was improving. With each passing day he was more responsive. Her visits were happy events. Otto's wife and daughter would come nearly daily with cookies and a hot thermos, and he was always pleased to see them, even more for the kiss Kristina planted on his pate before she left for work. She allowed herself to feel the first ticklings of hope. The worst seemed to be over.

On the third afternoon, Kristina Toth received a strange call from her father's longtime GP, Dr. Robert Silberman. Silberman told Kristina that somebody in the hospital—Silberman didn't know who or why—had ordered a series of unauthorized blood tests for her father, which had turned up equally mysterious results. Ottomar Schramm's blood contained digoxin, a drug he had never been prescribed. Silberman described the digoxin levels as being "off the charts." Dr. Silberman couldn't explain any of this, but promised to call back with the results of a follow-up test. At 1:25 a.m., Dr. Silberman called again, in shock. The new tests were consistent. And Kristina Toth's father was dead.

"Please, listen to what I'm about to tell you," Silberman said. "When you get to the hospital, they will ask you if you want an autopsy performed," Silberman said. "If I were you, I would say yes." Kristina didn't understand. *"Because of the digoxin,"* Silberman said. He didn't think he should say more.

Kristina's family arrived back at her father's Easton hospital room the next morning, finding it empty except for Charles Cullen, still on his night shift. Kristina got the sense that the male nurse had been waiting for her. He led Kristina's family down the hall to another room. Otto Schramm's body was there, cleaned, combed, and unhooked from the machines. The sight of him, truly dead, shocked her. "I'll give you some time," Charlie said. Something about that rankled Kristina—as if time with her father was a personal gift from this nurse—but she let it pass. Cullen returned a few minutes later. He wanted to know if the family planned to request an autopsy.

Kristina remembered what Dr. Silberman had told her. "I think so," she said. "We were thinking about it."

Nurse Cullen didn't seem to like the answer. "Why would you want an autopsy?" he said. Cullen reminded her that Mr. Schramm had a living will which had specified against the use of extraordinary measures such as life support. An autopsy would be even more intrusive than life support—didn't she see that she was violating the spirit of her father's wishes?

Kristina didn't bother answering. She simply told Nurse Cullen to leave the room.

Another nurse entered only minutes later, a woman this time. She too asked Kristina whether the family would request an autopsy.

Kristina didn't understand. Was she being tag-teamed, or were the nurses not communicating? Hadn't she already told her father's nurse everything necessary? "We're not sure," Kristina said. The nurse nodded and left the room, and Kristina returned to her family.

A few minutes later, a third nurse arrived, and again asked whether they'd be requesting an autopsy. This time, she'd had enough. "Yes, we want an autopsy!" Kristina said. "Of course we do—somebody here gave my father an overdose and—"

"I wouldn't say anything more," the nurse said.[14]

17

There had been an internal investigation after Ottomar Schramm's death, and when the presence of a potentially lethal level of unprescribed digoxin was discovered in Schramm's system, his autopsy was turned over to the county coroner.[1] It would be ruled an accidental death, though Charlie didn't really know about the outcome, and it didn't much affect him. He'd never intended to stay long at Easton, anyway. It didn't suit him. By the time questions began to circulate in March 1999, Charlie already had a full-time position down the road in the burn unit at Lehigh Valley Hospital.

At Lehigh, burn nurses still scraped patients on a metal gurney, and they still used pressure suits, but burn wards were no longer the scream wards in which Charlie had come of age. The new drugs saw to that—the new "benzo" class of antianxieties that had accompanied a new understanding of the relationship between stress and pain. Morphine, the traditional therapeutic drug, seemed rather primitive next to the new classes of pain killers, especially OxyContin, which had entered the pharmacopoeial marketplace only three years earlier.[2] Now there were drugs to effectively block the pain of even the youngest patients.

Along with the new drugs came new ways to track and distribute them, in the form of computerized cabinets called "Pyxis MedStations," which were manufactured by an Ohio company called Cardinal Health. The Pyxis machine itself was essentially a great metal drug cash register with a computer screen and keyboard affixed to the top. Not all the nurses were comfortable with the new computerized element of nursing care, but Charlie actually enjoyed it. He'd always been good with the technical devices, and he appreciated how the machine efficiently tracked a nurse's drug withdrawals the way a bank ATM machine traced cash withdrawals, linking each with the account of a particular patient and nurse and creating a record. The Pyxis simplified billing and provided a means for the pharmacy to know exactly when any given drug was running low, and to send a runner for restock. It was a useful system, but hardly perfect. Ultimately, it was just another tool in the service of an intimate art, practiced by real people with flaws of their own.

Charlie considered himself to be a veteran burn nurse, particularly in light of his time in the esteemed Saint Barnabas Medical Center's Burn Center. But here at Lehigh Valley, Charlie felt like he was back in the Navy, treated like a freshman "new fish." He didn't like their attitude toward him or toward the patients. Their professionalism struck Charlie as heartless and unempathetic.[3] He called them cruel and cold. They, in turn, called him a weirdo. And so, during the long overnights that winter, Charlie felt himself compelled to do what he had always done, not remembering the specifics of whether the patients he'd intervened with had come in from car accidents or house fires, not remembering how many he did[4] over the sixteen months he worked the overnight. Most died during his shift, coding right there in front of those "cold" nurses. It was something he could do, an act of personal will in a tyrannical work situation.

On the burn ward, most of the young male patients were either drunken campfire burns or car accidents. A patient named Matthew Mattern was one of the latter. He had been trapped in the burning wreck, and rushed into Lehigh with burns over 70 percent of his body. His was a grim case, even for the most hardened nurses. The presence of such a young, critically injured patient on the ward brought a wave of fresh emotion and an uncharacteristic outpouring of distraught young visitors. The older nurses were reminded of sons or grandsons, the younger nurses of friends or lovers or even themselves. And while none of the staff had mentioned it, at least not in front of Charlie, many had privately done the math. By the rule of 9s, the twenty-two-year-old Mattern was 92 percent dead. He might make it, there was a chance of that, but eventual death was far more likely.

Mattern was what nurses called a "slow code"—a Code Blue in slow motion. Charlie had watched his progress, knowing that even if Mattern survived, if the transplants took, he would be forever damaged, an amputee bound in a cocoon of scar tissue and locked in a pressure suit. Meanwhile, the surgeons were amputating him, piece by piece. Butchering him, the nurses thought. Mattern had been charred through to the bone; his extremities were gone.[5] Eventually the surgeons would take everything. Many of the nurses prayed for the inevitable.

Charlie recognized the helpless feeling. He'd felt it when dealing with the veteran nurses, felt it the same way in the house he grew up in, from the strange and sometimes violent men who wandered the halls while his brother dealt nickel bags upstairs, from the boyfriends who continued to live in his sisters' rooms even after his sisters had run away; and later, after Charlie had run away himself, he'd felt it again, in the submarine, when veteran sailors hazed the new fish for a tour until even newer sailors would come aboard and it was their turn. He's been a quiet kid, solipsistic and friendless, and ill-equipped to decipher the social dynamics of Navy culture. He couldn't take teasing, and soon it snowballed into more. The other sailors saw how he bristled too hard, how he'd drop his eyes and mutter under his breath then shoot a look, like he'd kill you in your sleep. They called him fucking psycho, fag psycho spaz. He was "fishbelly," pale as death, except when snagged with the rat tail of a wet towel, when he went welt-red and batshit. Even his ears went red. Even the other new fish picked on him. Tour after tour, Charlie Fishbelly was always good for a laugh. But Charlie had left the Navy. He was in charge now. On August 31, 1999, Charlie loaded Mattern's IV with a bolus dose of digoxin. The slow code was over before sunrise, some of the nurses thanking God for His intervening grace. Charlie merely headed back to the parking garage.

Stress-relieving impulses like these had driven most of his actions during the previous year. His intervention on behalf of his patients was a compulsion that had little to do with the patients themselves; often, in fact, he failed to notice the patients at all, only their outcomes. Each spasm of control offered a period of relief and afterglow. This lasted through the summer, and into the fall and winter, through the recurrent stress of the holidays. Finally, it ran out, and Charlie found himself just after sunrise, driving through a cold rain in the new millennium and pulling into the parking lot of his local Gas-N-Go minimart.

The hibachis had been stacked by the door by the wiper fluid and Styrofoam coolers. The one he bought was cheap and disposable, essentially an aluminum roasting pan with a grill top, but small enough to fit in the basement apartment's clawfoot tub. Charlie squirted on the lighter fluid, struck a match, and dropped it on the wet coals. He watched the fire flash and dance for a moment before remembering his glass, walked out of the bathroom to the kitchen counter, poured another drink, and carried it back to the bathtub.

The patrol car swung into the driveway of the Shafer Avenue apartment a few minutes later. An Officer Duddy spoke with the landlord, Karen Ziemba, who had placed the call to 911. She told Duddy about the smell and the ambulances Ziemba had sometimes seen carting away her troubled tenant. Duddy trudged back down the stairs to the outdoor entrance to Charlie's basement apartment. The storm door was locked, and rolled towels had been stuffed into the jamb between the doors. Duddy banged hard, identifying himself as police. Soon the deadbolt clicked, and the door cracked open. Charlie looked out sheepishly.

"Sir," Duddy said. "Are you having problems with the kerosene heater?"[6]

"Uh, no," Charlie said. But with the door open, the fuel smell was overpowering.

"Well, I'd like to check it for myself, if you don't mind."

"Well, um, it's fine," Charlie said, not moving.

"You might as well let me," Duddy said. "Fire department's on its way."

Charlie sighed and opened the door. Duddy stepped in. The fuel smell was stronger now, and something was definitely burning. Towels and raw insulation had been crammed into the vents of the heating ducts. The smoke alarm lay on the kitchen table, stripped of batteries. Duddy looked back at Cullen. Charlie was looking at the floor. Duddy moved past Charlie, following the fuel smell toward the bathroom. The mini hibachi sat in the bathtub, burning. Charlie explained that he had placed it there, of all places, careful not to start a house fire—he was, after all, a nurse who worked in a burn unit. He had seen what fire could do. But Duddy radioed for an ambulance. Charlie sighed and went to look for his shoes.

When the ambulance arrived, Charlie asked the EMTs if they could take him somewhere other than Warren Hospital. He didn't want to be seen as some kind of freak.[7]

18

April 2000

Charlie was increasingly aware that his time at Lehigh
Valley Hospital was running thin. The Burn Unit
senior staff no longer disguised their contempt of Nurse Cullen.[1] Charlie tried to transfer, but the Cardiac Unit wasn't
interested in inheriting the problem. Charlie continued at
Lehigh for three months, ameliorating the hurt by killing
patients[2] and slowly canceling his shifts as he sought out
work nearby.

Luckily, the past decade had seen a double-digit population influx into the Lehigh Valley. Hospitals blossomed along
the old coal seams like mushrooms in rot. A coffee stain on
his glove box map covered at least half a dozen Pennsylvania
health-care employers within a half hour of Charlie's rented
basement, each with more shifts than nurses. Charlie turned
to the word processor and sent off an updated résumé. He
had thirteen years' experience at six different hospitals
and—despite having left under claims of incompetence, and
suspicion of worse, at nearly all of them—he could count
on former coworkers to confirm his dates.[3] He had a valid
Pennsylvania nursing license and references still willing to

describe him as an "excellent team player" with a "calm, gentle" demeanor, an employee who was "always willing to come in" for extra shifts. Communication skills? "Good." Quality of work? "Great." One of the first to receive Nurse Cullen's résumé was St. Luke's Hospital in Fountain Hill, just down the road from Lehigh.

The hospital had been growing steadily year by year, bolstering core life-saving services while diversifying into new income streams like weight-loss surgery and sleep disorders.[4] They were willing to train on the job, but experienced critical-care nurses were an especially prized commodity; when Charlie signed, St. Luke's threw in a $5,000 hiring bonus.[5]

For Charlie, this was a prestige appointment. St. Luke's was ranked by *U.S. News & World Report* as one of the country's best medical facilities, and the nine-room Coronary Care Unit was one of the jewels of that crown.[6] He was going to be a star player in a star ward. Cullen dove right in, tidying his new work environment like a bird in a spring nest. "First appearances matter," he told his coworkers.

Not all the nurses noticed at first.[7] People die, that's what happens in a hospital, especially the CCU, and sometimes those deaths seem to come in clusters, but something seemed to have changed. The veteran nurses felt it, a new night wind blowing their patients away. It seemed to some that the codes were almost constant now. And they weren't ending well.

Some nurses enjoyed the action of the life-saving event, the immediacy and adrenaline, rushing in the door when the patient's life force was rushing out. Some nurses even became addicted to it. Charlie Cullen didn't strike his colleagues as a code freak, but when a code was called, Cullen was often the first into the room. They couldn't help but note Cullen's habit of hopping onto the bed, straddling the patient, and pumping away at the chest. There was little doubt about his enthusiasm. Cullen's attitude seemed overly dramatic, but oddly without emotion.

Sure, the new hire was different, but how could you criticize a nurse for caring too much? You certainly couldn't accuse Charlie of being inattentive, only of obsessively attending to the wrong things—such as the chairs in the nurses' station. Every night, he'd wheel a couple of these chairs down the hall into a spare room. Every night, Charlie's supervisor, Ellen Amedeo, would ask him to return the chairs.[8] He'd sigh and roll his eyes and head off down the hall to wherever he'd squirreled them away, but the next morning he'd do it again. He seemed to be intentionally testing their patience. It was only after the shift change that anyone would notice, and by then Charlie was gone. The nurses would have to search all the rooms and look for the missing chairs so they could wheel them back again. The staff found the ritual ridiculous.

There seemed to be no sense to it. It was almost as if Charlie was playing a game.

19

It had been thirteen years since Charles Cullen had been a former Navy man in an all-girl nursing college, and the world had changed. Now there were women serving in the Navy, and many men working in the nursing station. Charlie didn't like this dynamic. He found the male nurses mean, uncaring, cold. Charlie rarely spoke to them, and he doubled his attentions toward some of the young female staffers at St. Luke's. Julie,[1] in particular, he liked a lot. Charlie started leaving her little presents at the nurses' station, "from a secret admirer." It was cute at first, but as the gifts piled up daily, the "secret admirer" thing got creepy. So finally, Charlie signed a card: "To Julie, from your admirer, Brian Flynn." The nurses ate it up. Who the heck was Brian Flynn?[2] It was all they talked about at the station. Charlie was being the anonymous center of attention. Overhearing the gossip, he burst with pride. Finally, when he could contain himself no longer, he admitted it was him. But the revelation didn't elicit the reaction Charlie was looking for. The men laughed at him, and the women seemed afraid. All the highs he'd experienced as Brian Flynn were mirrored in the lows of being himself. Charlie felt rejected, humiliated. He was so much more being anonymous. There was power in that role. Anonymous could deny; anonymous could disappear. Anonymous was an unapologetic mystery, godlike in control.

————————

On many of his shifts Charlie was teamed with three other males, Joe and Brad and the other one, Charlie wasn't sure of his name. He disapproved of their working styles, like the way they put diapers on the patients rather than walk them to the toilet. It was unprofessional. He preferred, whenever possible, not to be scheduled with the men at all. But this night, they called him at home. A new patient was en route, a transfer, and they needed Charlie to come in. So he slipped into his scrubs and hit the highway. By the time he arrived, the new patient was in bed, and his male coworkers were complaining.

She was an elderly woman, very sick, transferred from another facility. She'd arrived by ambulance. It was the sort of patient the nurses called a "dump." She was going to die. She'd already coded twice during the ambulance ride over. It was only a matter of time. Charlie knew that the dump was a tactic—offloading the terminal patients was one of the means a hospital or nursing facility could use to keep their mortality rate low, one of the ways you get into *U.S. News & World Report*'s list. St. Luke's was Top 100 material;[3] the CCU nurses were proud of that. But dumps screwed the numbers.

He later remembered the nurses laughing at this old woman, like it was a party. He remembered how her doctor had come to the hospital, trying to justify to the family why they'd transferred her at all, why they'd put her through the ambulance ride and the code, what they could possibly do for her at St. Luke's that they couldn't do at the previous hospital, which, Charlie thought, was nothing, nothing at all. This was what they called the Code Conversation. Charlie knew it cold, and he was good at it. Families didn't want to face reality. But they needed to.

Meanwhile, the guys had started playing Hacky Sack with a ball of tape.[4] He understood the need for gallows humor—that's normal on a unit. You don't cry over the dead. But you don't play Hacky Sack, either. For that matter, you don't play with the nitroglycerine, which the unit stocked to be used for patients as a heart drug, not so these male nurse fools could goof around and smash the stuff outside against the parking lot to see if it explodes.

Charlie saw two potential paths for the dump. Tonight, he took what he thought of as the direct route, injecting digoxin right into the piggyback port of the old woman's IV. The piggyback is just an extra onramp into the IV line; nurses inject into it all the time, usually sterile saline, what they call "flushing the line." Injecting into the line was a totally legitimate action, not suspicious at all. If someone were to walk in on him, that was what he'd say he was doing. The dig is clear, same as saline. But nobody comes in. The rooms are private. One-on-one care is one of the selling points of this Top 100 unit.

Afterward, Charlie placed the vial and the used needle in the sharps box and left the room for the nurses' station. Straightening. Hovering. Busying himself. Putting the chairs away. Until the code finally came, and he was right on it, a captain, the code leader, trying valiantly for the save.

Later, after the woman has expired and her family has gathered to mourn, Charlie can still hear the guys carrying on with the stupid tape ball. But for now he's done.

She was his only patient. He's allowed to leave. He headed home. He'd been working on a project—a hobby horse he was carving for a pregnant nurse named Jane. The guys on the unit had been picking on Jane, too, Charlie felt. Charlie wouldn't do that. He wanted her to know. Maybe he'd even present it to her anonymously.

20

It was spring when the St. Luke's nurses noticed that their meds were missing.[1] Not all the drugs, of course, just one which for some reason they stocked heavily, but hardly ever used: Pronestyl. Every afternoon they restocked it in the med room. Every night it was gone. For six months it was a head scratcher. The nurses joked about it—somebody must be using the stuff as fertilizer![2] Nobody knew what was going on, but neither did anyone investigate it.

Which was a disappointment to Charlie, because he'd been sending a message. For months he'd been throwing the drug away, every day he worked. He had decided that he truly didn't like St. Luke's Hospital. Charlie had always considered it to be a Catholic institution. It wasn't—in fact, St. Luke's had no religious affiliation at all, but Charlie thought of it that way. It shared a name with a saint of his childhood, one the nuns had taught him. Charlie felt St. Luke's should be more saintly behaved. It was still a world-class institution, a good place to be if you had to be in the hospital at all, but Charlie didn't like the attitude. He kept putting the chairs away and they kept bringing them back. And the lotion—he used it heavily here, too, and his supervisors wouldn't leave him alone about it. It was his way of needling them. He'd go into a patient's room, use the lotion, see the bottle of talc on the sill, and throw that away, too. They'd give him hell about the lotion, so he had his war with their powder. He sometimes saw the absurdity of all this. He saw himself as a lapsed Catholic at a Catholic hospital.[3] He had renounced the religion of Christ for marriage and children, then lost the marriage, then lost the children. So where did it leave him? As an Irish Catholic Jew working for Saint Luke, the first Christian physician. Patron saint of doctors and surgeons, bachelors and butchers, painters and sculptors, too. Throwing away medicine, costing the hospital money—by his calculations hundreds, maybe even thousands, of dollars—was simply something he could do. It was his means of communicating, taking another indirect route. Part of Charlie figuring, *They'll know, they'll figure it out, they've got to,* like it was a test, an act of faith. But part of him they wouldn't see. Until, suddenly, they did.

———————

Thelma Moyer, the day charge nurse, noticed that the Pronestyl seemed to be running out "in spurts."[4] In April 2002, Moyer mentioned it to her supervisor, Ellen Amedeo, and the hospital pharmacist, Tom Nugen. Nugen checked his records but couldn't account for the disappearance. Amedeo took all this in, but didn't do more.

June 1, 2002, was a Saturday, a day that could run hot or cold for Charlie, depending on his mood and the custody arrangement. Good weekends were when the kids were visiting and glad to see him. He was happy poking around the little garden plot out back and selecting flowers for his girls' hair, or spending an afternoon working through the Dairy Queen menu, anything they wanted. This happened to be one of the bitter weekends. The afternoon was humid, and the forecast called for rain. He'd waited for it all day and it never came. Which was typical. They say it's going to rain and, of course, it never does. They don't say anything and it rains for a week. He dressed for work not even knowing whether to bring a rain slicker or not.

The drive to St. Luke's was a straight shot west on and off Route 22. He was in the lot by 6:15 p.m., in the unit by 6:20. Night shifts didn't start until seven o'clock, but he liked to be early. He dropped his coat and changed his shoes in the men's locker room. Nobody else used it at that hour—another reason for being early to work: you could urinate without anyone hearing you or looking at your privates, no boyish chitchat, no locker room hazing. Outside the doors, the CCU was humming with activity, visitor hours still in effect, the unit full, the nursing station abandoned.

Charlie went into his routine, messing with the chairs, but keeping his eyes on the monitors. Each monitor corresponds with a name, a room number, a bed, a life. He'd been watching. But Charlie wasn't exactly sure of tonight's program. Then he gathered up the medicines the pharmacy runner had dropped off for the night shift, walked them down the hall to the med supply room, punched his code, and closed the door behind him. He was alone. There was peace in enclosed spaces: basements, boiler rooms, bathrooms. The sudden dark smarted with sparks. Charlie flipped the light and got to work, only then deciding he'd take the indirect route.

The indirect route was impossibly subtle. Nobody questions. All the other nurses see is that Charlie is being helpful, stocking the drugs in the med room. Later, he'll be helpful in setting up the lines for his fellow nurses, assisting the start of a new IV. Later, they see him helping again, with the code. They never connect the three. There was no rational reason to connect them. He didn't have to hide, he didn't need gloves. He just pulled a 10 ml syringe, popped it from its candylike wrapper, unsheathed the hollow little needle, *pop-pop*, in and out of the saline. Then, switched bags, *pop-pop*, into the IVs. He dumped the now-empty vials and the used syringe into the metal sharps container, then gently laid the finished antibiotic cocktails into the named patient trays. Charlie was about to flip the light again when he noticed the Pronestyl, on the shelf above. It was back, stocked full. Back like the chairs.

Charlie couldn't believe it. They push and he pushes back. It's like yelling your throat bloody and nobody's listening. So he'll keep yelling. Not really yelling, of course. He wouldn't yell. But he will be heard. He flipped off the light and hurried back down the hall. And when the next shift came on at 7 a.m., there would be a couple hundred dollars' less medicine in the med supply closet, and fewer patients breathing in the CCU.[5]

21

June 2002

The rain came finally with morning. It stayed through the shift change and kept on through the afternoon, when a thirty-one-year-old CCU day nurse named Kim Wolfe stepped into the med storage room to draw her IVs.[1] She finished with the needle and stuck it into the sharps box, same as always. Usually, the needle clinks on the bottom of the box. This time there was no clink. The used needle wouldn't even fit into the trash.

Nurses don't have much reason to open the sharps bin, digging into dangerous drug garbage. Since AIDS had upped the ante on hepatitis, risking needle-sticks was strictly a job for Environmental Services—biohazard garbagemen who collected the needles and other medical waste[2] and whisked it off to another piece of New Jersey for incineration. But Kim was curious. She lifted the lid and peered into the hole. Instead of used sharps, she saw white cardboard boxes.

Wolfe left the closet to find Gerry Kimble and Candy Wahlmark at the nursing station. Gerry was the veteran here—he'd been in that unit sixteen years. He marched down to the med room expecting that the younger female nurse was eeking at a mouse but, yep, there was something in there. Gerry got on the phone.

The sharps box is like a drop mailbox; only Environmental Services had the key. They unlocked it, and Gerry upended the box into a bedpan. He and Candy brought the pile into a spare room, on a mission now. They carefully picked the drugs from the needles, lining them up on the counter.

For a nurse, it was a stunning sight. The drugs are poison. They're also money, and the job. Instinctually, the pair began to catalog their discovery on a legal pad. Among the finds were six bottles of vecuronium bromide, or "vec." There was magnesium sulfate and phenylephrine, Levophed and dobutamine, nitroglycerine and labetalol, and forty boxes of the missing Pronestyl.

Gerry and Candy had zero context for any of this. It didn't fit any of their whispered scenarios, which revolved around drugs being stolen, for sale or use. This is a common hospital problem for drugs like ketamine, OxyContin, Vicodin, Percocet, Darvocet, Demerol, morphine—anything escapist and everything addictive. But who would want forty-eight boxes of phenylephrine? There was nothing vaguely recreational about elevated blood pressure or altered heart rhythm. They couldn't figure it. The dumped bottles full of Pronestyl was one issue, weird and wasteful. It bothered them. The empty vec bottles were what scared them. Vec was what they called an unreconstituted drug. It came in a powder form, sealed inside a glass vial with a permanent rubber stopper. The only way to get the drug out of the bottle was to reconstitute it—like making Kool-Aid in a sealed container, using a syringe. This required loading a needled syringe with saline, stabbing the needle through the rubber stopper, injecting the saline, shaking vigorously, then withdrawing the reconstituted contents into the syringe. The empty vec bottles suggested that the drug had been withdrawn into a loaded needle, and in staggering quantities.

Vec is an exceptionally powerful paralytic.[3] Overdose by vecuronium bromide would be much like drowning or slow suffocation. The musculature of the body shuts down but the person inside remains intact, at least until the heart muscles and lungs fail. Worse, the patient would suffer all of it—vec would keep you from moving or screaming, but it would not stop you from feeling pain.

Prolonged or excessive vec dosing had caused brain damage in comatose patients, and the possibility of hugely negative side effects made vec an increasingly unpopular drug amongst doctors. The rare prescriptions called for only small doses, usually around 5 mg.[4] And none of the patients currently on the St. Luke's CCU had been prescribed vec during the entire four-shift weekend. Yet someone had apparently reconstituted 60 mgs of the dangerous paralytic into needled syringes and injected it... where?[5]

Gerry Kimble stepped back into the hallway, suddenly uneasy. Patients lay unconscious in every room around him. The hospital itself was full of staffers, visitors, specialists, new hires, cleaning temps. He and Candy and Kim decided to keep an eye on the medical storage room, taking shifts between patients. Kim, going first, had a clear view from the nursing station. She didn't recognize the first guy who stopped at the med room. She watched as the guy punched the code, worked the handle, and wedged a sneaker in the doorjamb to prevent it from closing as he restocked. She had him in direct sight the whole time. A half hour later she watched the pharmacy guy punch the code and enter. He too left the door open. Kim and Candy exchanged a look. It was getting silly. And they still had a day of patients before the shift change.

At 6:20 p.m. Charlie Cullen walked into the unit, early as usual. Kim Wolfe was glad to see him—she liked Charlie. They'd been crossing shifts for over two years, not friends but friendly, saying hello and good-bye when their schedules happened to mesh. Sure, he was a little different, but Wolfe didn't judge him for his quirks. He was helpful and generous with his time for anything another nurse needed. Kim and Candy kept their heads in their charts while Charlie made his ritual rearrangement around the nursing station.

The chairs were these alien OfficeMax things with spider-leg wheels. Charlie wheeled the extras to a dead office down the hall, did two, then came back for another two. He took those, then stopped along the hall at the med room door. He punched the code and slipped inside. The door locked behind him. Kim ran over to tell Candy, but Candy was already watching.

It was a full five minutes before Kim and Candy saw the door open. Both women looked down as Charlie stepped out of the room and walked the other way down the hall. Kim ran over to the med room door, punched the code, and peered inside. The sharps box was full again. The ICU floor manager, Ellen Amedeo, needed to be alerted immediately. They found her at home and breathlessly told her they knew who'd been using the deadly vials of vec.

A half hour later, the day shift left, Gerry and Sue and Candy with it. Charlie stayed on. He had twelve hours. The first code came less than halfway through it.

———————

The sharps box wasn't opened again until the shift change Monday morning, June 3. Day nurse Gerry Kimble and manager-supervisor Terry Koehler donned sterile gloves as a hospital security officer watched them upend the contents onto the counter. This time they discovered several dozen bottles, many of them empty, including nine spent vials of vec.[6] Though they didn't know it yet, the drugs had already been used on patient Edward O'Toole seven hours earlier.[7]

By now, Ellen Amedeo had arrived on the unit, and administrative wheels were turning. Janice Rader, St. Luke's Hospital's risk manager, set a protocol: for the remainder of the day shift, the charge nurse was to regularly check the sharps box for additional stashed meds. Cullen wasn't working; the sharps box remained empty.

Rader had no choice but to contact Ken Vail, St. Luke's risk management director. Dangerous heart drugs were missing, massive quantities of a paralyzing agent had been activated and disappeared. Together, Rader and Vail strategized on what would be "best for the hospital,"[8] given that nurse Charles Cullen was scheduled to be back on shift again in less than eight hours. The decision was to consult St. Luke's in-house counsel, attorney Sy Traub. Traub called in the Stevens and Johnson law firm,[9] corporate specialists in criminal law and malpractice defense. One of their young Turks was a former Philadelphia assistant district attorney named Paul Laughlin.[10]

By 2 p.m. Laughlin was sitting in the administrative offices at St. Luke's. He was briefed, then went home to wait. The call came just after midnight. It was the CCU nursing floor. Charles Cullen was back on shift, and another cache of drugs had been discovered in the sharps box. It couldn't wait. Laughlin drove back to the ICU and parked himself in an empty room at the end of the hall. A few minutes later, a male nurse named Brad Hahn delivered Charles Cullen. Charlie hadn't seen it coming. He cut Brad a look, telling him, "You know, you could have given me a heads-up."[11]

22

The young lawyer asked Charles Cullen to take a seat. He started off friendly, asking Charlie about his background, his work habits.[1] Charlie answered each question in order, pretty sure where this was headed. He told the lawyer he liked to get in early, about 6:30, and stock the drug totes. He'd done that today, it had taken about ten minutes.

And after that? Laughlin asked.

"Yes," Charlie said. "I'd been, you know, in the med room after that."

And why, Laughlin wondered, would Charlie be in the med room again?

"I don't know," Charlie said. "Maybe somebody asked me to. If someone had asked me, I would have gone in for that."

"Okay," Laughlin said. "So—did that happen? Did anyone ask you to go in?"[2]

Charlie looked at the ground. "I can't remember," he said. "I'm working on no sleep here, so, you know, I don't really remember anything specific about the shift." He was almost mumbling.

"Did anyone talk to you about drugs being found in the sharps bin?"

Laughlin brought the sharps bin over and opened the lid, showing it full of boxes and vials. Maybe Charlie was supposed to show surprise, but he didn't. He didn't care enough to remember what emotions people were supposed to have in these situations. What did it matter? He looked back to his spot on the floor. The linoleum was mottled like lunch meat.

"So, let me ask you again: have you heard anything about medicines going missing?"

This time Charlie said, "Yes. I'd, you know—Nurse Moyer, Thelma. She mentioned something about it."

So, Laughlin asked, who put them there? Did he have any idea?

The man kept talking. Charlie heard him listing all the shifts when the medicine had been found, the hours that corresponded to Charlie's shifts. The man talked about the vec, demonstrating his understanding of how it was a dangerous drug that had to be reconstituted, mixed up, withdrawn by syringe. Who was on all those shifts but him? Anybody? Charlie? Charlie?

Charlie glanced around the office, the desk, the chairs, the lawyer's lap. He had the patient records, their blood work, the lab reports of the vec overdoses. They had the vials.[3] To Charlie, this all added up to bullying. They knew already; the questions were simply cruel. "You've already made up your mind about it," Charlie said. What did they expect him to do now?

Charlie knew he had a choice[4]—well, it wasn't really much of a choice.[5] If he resigned, St. Luke's would give him neutral references, and the incident wouldn't show up on his records. Charlie watched the floor. He was getting shuffled off, a dump. He figured this was how you stay on *U.S. News & World Report*'s annual list of America's Best Hospitals. Charlie couldn't believe it—a saint-named hospital, of all places. What would the nuns from Catholic school say? Saint Luke, patron saint of liability. He'd take the deal, but he knew he was the righteous man here. Security frog-marched him through the unit like Christ to Calvary and left him standing in the cool of the parking garage.

23

On June 8, three days after Cullen was escorted to his car by Saint Luke's security, he was pulling into another lot just ten minutes down the road in Allentown, Pennsylvania, early for another night shift in another CCU. The transition to Sacred Heart Hospital was especially simple, as he'd been able to truthfully list his dates of employment at St. Luke's CCU as "June 2000 to present," and count on St. Luke's[1] for neutral references.[2] His transition seemed normal. Charlie hadn't realized that several of the administrators at St. Luke's had been calling around to their colleagues at other hospitals. And anyway, it didn't matter—they hadn't called Sacred Heart. Charlie was steered straight into his orientation on the ward. He would start right away.

Cullen sensed he would like working at Sacred Heart. He already liked his coworkers, especially a young mom named Cathy Westerfer. Like him, Cathy was a new hire, single and working nights. He hadn't been there a week before they were dating. As usual, Charlie attached himself quickly. Two weeks later Charlie got the familiar call, telling him not to bother coming back for shifts, but even that had an upside; Cathy felt sorry for her new boyfriend. The whirlwind arrival and departure seemed romantic, somehow.

A few months later, Charlie would load up the Escort and move into Cathy's rented house in Bethlehem.

The blank on his Sacred Heart termination notice had read "interpersonal conflicts." Charlie figured that basically meant some senior nurse had heard rumors about him. In fact, one of the Sacred Heart nurses had formerly worked at Easton Hospital, where the suspicious digoxin death of Ottomar Schramm still echoed. She'd heard the stories. Soon, her Sacred Heart coworkers heard them, too, and petitioned the administration. They threatened to quit en masse if Cullen wasn't fired. Charlie didn't know the details and didn't need to. The bottom line was that he'd need to move further afield. A clean start was only as far away as the state line. Charlie was going home.

———

Charlie still had the benefit of neutral references from St. Luke's. The hospital would later assert that Laughlin's investigation, the chart reviews by Risk Manager Rader and Nursing Supervisor Koehler, and additional inquiries by St. Luke's general counsel Sy Traub all failed to identify any suspicious deaths related to the empty bottles of vec, or any other actions by Charles Cullen in their hospital. But St. Luke's administrators didn't want Cullen working in their health-care system. And they apparently believed that other hospitals would have reason not to want him working in theirs, either.

In August 2002, Charles D. Saunders, St. Luke's senior vice president of medical and academic affairs, had called his colleagues in the local Bethlehem area, asking whether they had experienced any unusual incidents with a nurse named Charles Cullen, and telling them that Cullen was beyond consideration for rehire. St. Luke's executive vice president (and former St. Barnabas Medical Center president) Vince Joseph[3] and Attorney Paul Laughlin were calling their colleagues too.[4] But Saunders, Joseph, and Laughlin apparently weren't passing these warnings on to the public,[5] the cops, or the State Nursing Board.[6] And unfortunately for the patients of Somerset Medical Center, they weren't on the call list, either.[7]

24

September 2002

The recruitment flyer was a high-quality mass-marketing mailer, a full-color appeal for qualified nurses. Charlie studied the brochure over the kitchen sink, turning it over in his hand. "Join the Team!" it said. Should he? His life's path had been shaped by doors that opened at just the right time, fate showing him the downhill path. Charlie didn't know Somerset Medical Center, or Somerset County, New Jersey, but it was obvious that after five medical centers[1] in less than four years, his name was burned in Pennsylvania.[2] He'd had problems in New Jersey, too, but it had been four years since he'd worked there, and New Jersey was a big state.[3] Although Somerset County was only a fifty-minute drive from the house he'd been raised in, socially and economically, it was as far as Charles Cullen could hope to venture from his West Orange roots.

————

Somerset was one of the oldest and richest counties in the United States,[4] a fertile farming settlement set between wooded hills and the overgrand country estates favored by financiers and industrialists.[5] John Dryden, a founder of Prudential Insurance, built his Versailles-like mansion in Bernardsville in the 1880s; a generation later, Brooke Kuser—soon to become Brooke Astor—would live in a manor called Denbrooke. In the boom years following the Civil War, these were the wealthiest citizens of the wealthiest nation on earth, and they could have anything they wanted. In 1898, what they wanted was a hospital.

One death had done it, that of a sixteen-year-old boy with a blow to the head. Even in 1898, this was a far-from-fatal condition; drilling holes in the skull to relieve the pressure was a simple surgical procedure older than the Lenape arrowheads that still littered the Raritan River clay. But during the long wagon journey to Newark, the boy's traumatized brain continued to swell like a baking loaf, crushing itself against the confining skull. By the time he reached Newark, the boy's pupils had bloomed dead, and the cry for a local hospital was taken up.

With an initial donation of $5,500, a house on East Main Street was outfitted with electricity and running water and the latest technology of modern medicine, including a German machine that could photograph the human interior by means of "unknown" or "X" rays, and a surgical theater sunned by a new electrical bulb recently invented by Thomas Edison of neighboring Menlo Park. It started with ten doctors to attend twelve beds. As the county grew, the hospital expanded in step, adding wings and annexes until the simple wood-framed town house had molted into a redbrick city catering to dozens of specialized medical procedures, with over 350 beds for overnight patients and thousands of highly paid professionals to attend to them. It was blessed with abundant parking and a convenient location between the highways, and prosperous enough to offer a $10,000 bonus to experienced nurses willing to sign on for a six-month hitch.

On August 15, 2002, Charlie sat down at the desk of Somerset Human Resources and filled the familiar blanks.[6] Nurse Cullen presented a tempting hire. He indicated truthfully that he was a certified and registered nurse, lied righteously about not having a criminal conviction, and wondered not at all whether they bothered researching those answers. He preferred Critical Care but would work in any ward, and was open to all hours, rotating shifts, on-call shifts, nights, weekends,[7] and holidays. For references, Charlie listed St. Luke's, indicating that he had left only because he "needed change," which was true enough. He also listed his years at the Lehigh Valley Hospital Burn Unit, which "did not work for him," and Liberty Nursing and Rehabilitation Center, where "there weren't enough hours available." All were, in a fashion, true; it would be up to the Somerset Medical Center HR department to try and color in the details.

Cullen's former supervisor at Warren Hospital confirmed that Charlie had indeed worked there, and extolled Charlie's work ethic, conscientiousness, and intelligence. And as promised, the St. Luke's HR gave his dates of employment and verified his former position.[8] In September 2002, Charlie was offered a job working full-time with some of the most vulnerable patients on the Somerset Medical Center CCU.

———

Charlie quickly became a popular night nurse at Somerset. Usually, the hand-off between the day and night shifts could last an hour, depending on the nurse, but Charlie was quick, he didn't ask questions, and the day nurses were always thrilled to see him on the schedule. They could give him a quick report and go home, knowing he was already off down the hall with his little Cerner PowerChart, the mobile computer database of patient charts. His fellow night nurses appreciated Charlie even more; he started early, worked efficiently, and was always the first to finish. His colleagues would return from their initial patient checks to find Charlie already standing by the Pyxis machine, helping lay out their IV bags for the evening. Later, they would see him again, helping out at the code.

Each night shift nurse had an independent schedule, and each night saw a different composite crew. Charlie was quickly singled out by one of the nurses he was often on with, a tall, pretty blonde named Amy Loughren.[9] She was a self-proclaimed "pain in the ass," which meant she was outspoken and honest, the kind of person who cast a shadow Charlie could shade himself by. Charlie was quiet around her at first, but over the long overnight shifts Charlie began slipping in wry comments about hospital bureaucracy while waiting for the Pyxis machine, or sending a dramatic eye roll across the room during a particularly labored evening report. Late at night, after all the drips had been hung and their respective patients tended, Charlie offered up slapstick tales of debilitating depression, bad luck, and bullied victimization with a wry honesty he believed Amy would connect to; she'd reply with laughter and the maternal attentions Charlie needed. As the weeks passed, they graduated from familiars to friends.

––––––––––

Amy Loughren had emerged from an abusive childhood with a bold defiance toward the fundamental bullshit of life and a mystical conviction that the universe owed her one. Thirty-six hard, impulsive years had brought Amy ten boyfriends, two daughters, an RN degree, and a leased white Jaguar, but behind the blonde highlights lay a void she struggled to name. Her off days were punctuated by panic attacks that sometimes kept her from even leaving the house, and her nights were spent either working or drinking wine. She split her time between her house in upstate New York and her job in New Jersey, her personality between home and hospital, and she worked hard to maintain the shelter of that division. She didn't share herself fully with her daughters or boyfriends, or most of her coworkers. Only her new friend, Charlie Cullen, made her feel totally safe. Charlie seemed to need her protection, too.

———

When Charlie had first started working at Somerset that September, Amy knew, almost right away, that she liked the new guy—not "liked-liked," she was single but not that single, not in a million years, and she sensed the new guy knew his limitations. Amy was blonde, nearly six feet tall and conspicuously curvaceous, even in scrubs, and accustomed to unwelcome attentions. But Charlie seemed safe to Amy. He paid attention without an obvious agenda, and he never hit on her. And if he didn't always keep eye contact, at least it wasn't because he was trying to steal glances down her scrub tops. He was quiet, too, at least at first, and Amy was instinctively drawn to quiet people. *This guy,* she thought, *has secrets, just like me.*

The new male nurse also seemed as serious about the job as Amy was, maybe more so—efficient and attentive to the point of obsession. Charlie tended his patients alone, with the door closed and the blinds drawn. He stripped them naked and bathed them before lathering them comically pearlescent with moisturizer. Amy called them his "Butterball turkeys," too greasy to turn. His other eccentricity was an obsessive use of the Cerner machine. Charting was the necessary paperwork of nursing but Charlie took it to an extreme, spending hours tapping away on the mobile unit far from the scrutiny of the nurses' station. Amy teased him that he was writing a novel. Uncharacteristically, he welcomed her teasing, recognizing it as guileless affirmation.

Like many nurses, Amy saw herself as a hero defending humanity's most fragile, an advocate and facilitator for the voiceless and immobile. With his question mark posture, soft gray hair, and ratty old-man cardigans, the new nurse struck Amy as another sensitive soul in need of defending—a sad Mr. Rogers type, both drippy and depressed. His nurse whites had the dingy air of bachelor washing, and behind his greasy drugstore glasses his eyes held a darkness and desperation that Amy recognized as masked anger. It took only a couple overnights together before Amy realized that Charlie Cullen was also one of the funniest people she had ever met. At 4 a.m. Charlie could make her laugh with a story that put her own crazy life in perspective. Humor and gossip provided a buffer against the suffering and grief that came with the job, and Charlie always delivered. Several stories centered on the absurdity of his Navy years, his assignment to guard nuclear missiles with a billy club, or the indignities suffered when he refused to pee into a cup in front of another man, but most involved Charlie's girlfriend, Cathy, and her sporadic attempts to get Charlie to move out of the house. Amy called it "The Charlie and Cathy Show," and she tuned in nightly. Eventually, she reciprocated with confessions of her own.

Each night, Charlie would zip through his responsibilities with patients and then cruise the block of rooms until he found her. Amy was a procrastinator, always running late, and she appreciated his technical proficiency, born of fourteen years' experience[10] at nine other hospitals. Soon, she came to rely on it. Her position at Somerset was the best Amy had held in her nearly fifteen years of nursing. The $20,000 bonus on salary for a seven-month contract plus $1,700 a month for local lodging was "crazy money." She wanted to keep it, even if it was killing her.

———————

Midshift that October, Charlie found her listing against the hard white wall of the nurses' station. He helped her to an empty room and shut the door. Amy sat on the bed, gasping until she could explain. It was a funny story, at least to the gallows sensibilities of a veteran nurse; she was working in one of the nation's top cardiac care units, and secretly, slowly, dying of heart failure.

Amy had diagnosed it herself as advanced atrial fibrillation brought on by prolonged chronic sick sinus syndrome. The condition was at least partially responsible for her crippling panic attacks and the reason those attacks were so unsettling. The synaptic wiring in her heart muscle was misfiring. The result was an erratic heart rhythm insufficient to cycle oxygenated blood between her lungs and her body. Amy felt herself drowning in her own stagnant bloodstream. While her personal medical theory was that her heart muscle had been ravaged by a virus from, perhaps, one of her patients, she wondered whether the real problem wasn't something more mystical: an emotional virus of some kind, psychological shrapnel from the monsters of her childhood, the damage of memory. Amy's failing heart wasn't the only secret in her life. Those were killing her, too.

Charlie listened, nodding like a doctor. Then he left the room, returning a minute later with a mint-green oval in his palm—diltiazem, 0.5 mg. Amy popped the pill and pulled herself upright with an empty IV tree. It was just 2 a.m., and she still had work to do.

"No, listen," Charlie told her. "You rest. Doctor's orders." He showed the hint of a smile. "I'll handle your patients tonight."

"Charlie...," Amy started.

"Don't worry," Charlie said. "I can keep a secret."

———————

Charlie never knew how many he did at Somerset, only that it started around when Amy got sick, and once it started it did not stop.

Amy's cardiomyopathy went unchecked until February, when she collapsed at work and was rushed to the ER. She would require a pacemaker and a leave of absence. Charlie was alone on the overnight. He replaced her attentions with his own compulsions.

The specific ones, the very old, the very sick, the special and the memorable, seemed to begin mid-January[11] with digoxin and a sixty-year-old homemaker named Elanor Stoecker. Two weeks later, Charlie worked the night of his forty-third birthday, and used Pavulon, a strong paralytic similar to vec. It was an effective drug by itself, but Charlie had incorporated it with others, and at the end of the night he wasn't exactly sure who had died as a result of his actions, nor what, precisely, had killed Joyce Mangini and Giacomino Toto. He was, however, quite certain that it was norepinephrine that blew out John Shanagher's heart on March 11. His reputation as a code genius grew, and by the time Dorthea Hoagland's hammering heart stopped beating and Code Blue bleated through the speakers that May, Charlie once again seemed to have the answers. Charlie's knowledge of which drugs might reverse the patient's sudden failure seemed, to the other nurses, almost magically prescient. Even the young residents on call stepped back to let Charlie take charge. Each patient had complex and interlacing issues with their organs or chemistry, and each responded uniquely. It was a busy spring, and Charlie was less interested in names than in causes and effects.

Michael Strenko was young for the unit, and his illness was particularly upsetting to the younger nurses. Michael's parents believed their child was on the road to recovery at Somerset, having increasingly better days, but the twenty-one-year-old Seton Hall computer sciences student had a genetic autoimmune disease, and his care was complicated. Amy, back on the unit from a pacemaker surgery and bed rest, worried that young Michael wouldn't survive. Charlie was sure of it.

In the end, it had been digoxin, or epinephrine, or some combination which had put Strenko over the edge—the sick were so precariously balanced, it only took a little push, a sigh that floats a feather, a nudge so subtle and dispersed that nobody noticed the cause, only marveled at the effect. The codes that night were multiple, and not pretty. After the second, Charlie shuffled out to the waiting room to find Michael's mother, giving her a graphic and technically accurate word picture of what was happening, at that very moment, inside her son's body, the drugs used and the measures taken by the medical staff to preserve her son's life. "Michael is gravely ill," Charlie told her. "People don't always make it."

Michael's parents were overwhelmed by this rendering. "That's enough!" his mother said, and told Charlie to leave. But Charlie was right. And at approximately 2 a.m. on May 15, when Mrs. Strenko finally waved off the last shock paddle from her son's exhausted body, the flatline proved it.

———————

She didn't set out to make a stink, but Amy questioned everything. Amy figured, if sometimes she went too far, then fine. At least she wasn't cattle. That was her, she always said so, a hotheaded, reactionary bigmouthed girl with a temper, but not cattle. She wouldn't just go along. They heard about her all the way down in Oncology: Amy, the ICU nurse who refused the exasperating new safety protocol, the one who wouldn't put her name on their new insulin sign-out sheet. That told her what a big deal she was making—you practically needed a shuttle bus to get from the ICU to Oncology.

They were calling the new drug protocol an "insulin adjustment form." Her manager, Val, had explained it, trying to convince Amy to sign. Previously, the insulin had always just been there in the little fridge. But now for some reason they were changing the protocol, making the nurses more accountable by forcing them to put their electronic signature on their guess as to how much was left in the vial. Amy thought it was inaccurate and stupid. How could she eyeball exactly how much was left? They were asking her to bet her nursing license on a jellybean counting contest. Amy demanded to know what was going on, but her supervisor wasn't about to tell her. Why treat insulin like a narcotic anyway?

When her manager wouldn't answer, Amy refused to cooperate. Val said "Sign," and Amy said no. "Just do it," Val said. Amy wouldn't.

Now Val was angry too. Amy didn't understand the reaction. Why the hell get so worked up over a simple piece of protocol—what, did somebody die?

Val was practically screaming as she finally told Amy, "Look, just sign it—this whole thing isn't about you, anyway!"

What did that mean? Who was this about?

At the time, Amy did not connect the new protocol requirements with the sudden frequency of codes. All she knew was she was wrapping so many bodies now, probably more in the past half year than during her entire career. She had no idea there was a problem, much less imagine that Charlie was the cause. Charlie was a good nurse, extraordinary even. She was always glad to find his name on the whiteboard schedule. Her doctors had told Amy to take it easy, but with multiple patients under her care, easy wasn't always an option. Often she had to choose between being careful of her own heart or tending to theirs. With Charlie on shift, she had a third option. He was never too busy to help.

On June 14, 2003, Charlie was early by a full half hour—he couldn't wait. He checked the computerized Cerner charts of various patients and decided on the Oriental lady.[12] Mrs. Jin Kyung Han wasn't his patient now, but she had problems. Han had come into the hospital June 12 with Hodgkin's lymphoma and heart disease. Her cardiologist, Dr. Zarar Shaleen, had Han on digoxin already, small doses, usually 0.125 mg, keeping her at the therapeutic level of around 0.63. Her doctor had ordered another dose of digoxin for Han on June 13. Then, when he studied her EKG, he discovered that dig wasn't helping her new cardiac arrhythmias. In fact, it might kill her. He ordered that the drug be discontinued.

At 7 p.m., the nursing shifts went through their handoff report. Charlie was free again by 7:30, going straight to the Pyxis drug computer and calling up digoxin. He placed an order of the drug for his own patient, then quickly canceled it. The drug drawer popped open anyway. It was that easy. The new security protocols were stupid. Charlie pulled out two units and closed the drawer.

Charlie entered Han's room; the woman was asleep. He took the direct route, injecting the digoxin dose as a piggyback into the IV line snaking between the hanging bag and her vein. The IV bolus that Charlie injected represented a dose eight times what Han had ever received.[13] Then he ditched the needle in the sharps bin and left the room. It was nearly dawn; the dose would take full effect only after his shift was over. The anticipation echoed across his day off, blurring thought. Charlie reported back for work on the evening of the sixteenth, early, to check. But Han was still there.

Charlie took the Cerner and went back through her chart. Han's heart rate had plummeted, she'd been throwing up on the morning shift, and a blood screen found the dig in her system, which had spiked from her normal level of 0.63 up to 9.94. Han's cardiologist immediately ordered an antidote, and Han settled down. Afterward she teetered through the day shift and into the night, not well, but surviving.

———

Amy waited for Charlie. He was especially good at after-death care, helpful and quick. He had a serious routine, and he didn't like to talk as he did it. He would wash the body, pull the IV needles from the veins, wrap the lines, unhook the catheters and feeding and vent tubes. Then he gathered the death kit and the shroud. *Shroud*: to Amy the word conveyed a holy thing, solemn and homespun and grave, but at Somerset the shrouds were thin sheets of cheap, clear plastic that ripped easily and were never large enough. They reminded her of generic Saran Wrap. Working alone, her dignified attempts always devolved into macabre slapstick. Wrapping a body required working multiple pieces of this plastic material under the dead weight of the corpse without ripping or wrinkle. It was like making a bed with someone lying in it. Amy's pulling, lifting, and tugging generally made a mess of the job. She'd tried fitting the four-foot squares so they overlapped, but there was always a gap in the middle that exposed the belly. Adjusting them this way and that she'd end up with the feet hanging out, then the head uncovered. Eventually she'd just wind rolls of tape around the crinkled gob the way a child wraps a birthday present. Or, better yet, she'd call Charlie.

Charlie had it down. He squared the sheets neatly and with just the right overlap, angling and creasing and fixing the deceased into a professional polymer cocoon, head and feet and all. Charlie was good. She told him so. He told her it was easy. He'd had plenty of practice.

———————

The Rev. Florian Gall had arrived by ambulance before being delivered to the Somerset Medical CCU, nearly nine months to the day after Charlie's own arrival on the unit. His fever was three-digit and his lymph nodes were swollen to stones, both symptoms of an overwhelming bacterial infection, and probably pneumonia. His lungs, sodden as wet facecloths, labored to deliver oxygen to his heart and brain. A machine would have to breathe for him. Gall's chin was raised, his mouth opened, and a plastic tube was shoehorned into his windpipe, fitted into an accordianed length of plastic ductwork, and attached to a ventilator. Meanwhile, Gall's overwhelmed kidneys began to fail. They would recover if he did; until then, a machine would filter his blood as well.[14]

The reverend's sister visited his bedside daily. Lucille Gall was a former senior nurse at a nearby hospital, which allowed her to stay at his bedside late, a professional courtesy. The sister had opinions about her brother's care.

Charlie wasn't always assigned to the reverend, but he always checked up on him, and he didn't appreciate the sister's proprietary attitude. She had argued with him about which drugs he was giving her brother and why—acting, he felt, as if she was in charge. She didn't, for instance, think Tylenol was a good idea, considering the reverend's failing liver. Her attitude bothered him, to the point that when he thought about Gall, the image in his mind was not him, but her. It was only when she left that Charlie could get down to business.

Gall's real problem was his heart—atrial fibrillation, probably, meaning that one of his heart chambers was contracting too rapidly to effectively fill or pump. The cardiologist on call prescribed digoxin. It would slow the atrium, and oxygenated blood would once again circulate through the reverend's body. At least, that was the idea.

At that point, and for that whole first week, it was impossible to know whether the Reverend would live or die. His family consented to a Do Not Resuscitate order; if Gall's body did quit on him, at least he would pass unto the Lord without the earthy indignity of dramatic and "extraordinary measures." But then, gradually, the reverend started to improve. His heart rhythm stabilized, and his digoxin was discontinued. At the doctor's suggestion, his sister rescinded the DNR order and kindled a renewed hope. The reverend was getting better. Eventually, if he continued to improve, he would leave.

————

Charlie would study the man at night, his bald head glowing in the light of the machines, his clerical vestments exchanged for a disposable frock. He looked nothing like the priests of Charlie's youth, nothing like God's man on earth—he looked sick, and very human. That was his prognosis. Charlie knew the charts, he'd pulled the little computer cart to the corner of the Cardiac Care Unit to pore through the drama of numbers.

Rev. Florian Gall coded at approximately 9:32 a.m. the morning of June 28. He went unexpectedly into cardiac arrest, and heroic measures were undertaken. They were unsuccessful. His time of death was noted in his chart: 10:10 a.m. Gall's bloodwork showed that his digoxin levels were off the charts. The Somerset Medical Center administration had a problem. It was not a natural death. And Gall wasn't the first. They called him "Patient 4."

The plan was to deal with it internally,[15] and as quickly as possible. Pharmacy would examine the Pyxis around the dates of the digoxin deaths. Assistant Pharmacist Nancy Doherty was assigned to contact New Jersey Poison Control Center. The question was, how much dig would have been required for the numbers they saw in Gall's blood work. The only part they needed help with was the math.

25

July 7, 2003

The hold music is lite jazz, upbeat and hopeful. The recorded voice said, "Thank you, a poison specialist will be with you shortly, please..."

Then: "New Jersey Poison Control Center, can I help you?"[1]

"Uh, yeah." The caller identified herself as Nancy Doherty, calling from the pharmacy department of Somerset Medical Center. "It's actually not something that's happening now—we're trying to investigate, um, a 'didge' toxicity that occurred in a patient and I don't know if you have somebody that I could discuss it with..."

"Okay," the operator said. "So this is a case that happened..."

"It happened...um...a couple...well, the person is actually..."

Dead. But Nancy stopped herself.

"Six twenty-eight, it happened," she said.

———

New Jersey Poison Control pharmacist Dr. Bruce Ruck[2] called back to Somerset Medical Center ten minutes later.

He was put on hold and listened to Vivaldi behind a professional female voice: "At Somerset Medical Center, patient safety comes first…"

"Nancy Doherty." Nancy's rounded Jersey vowels were a shock after the clipped broadcaster English: *Nyancy Dowyty.*

"Nancy, hi, it's Bruce Ruck." *Broose* shared Doherty's accent and much of her training. He knew that Nancy was only a messenger, but one tasked with handling a serious internal matter at Somerset.

"Yeah," Nancy said. She exhaled into the phone. "It's… getting real…complicated."

Doherty was calling on the instruction of her bosses, to get help figuring the probable drug dosages in two patients. She told Bruce that the first patient coded in their Cardiac Care Center three weeks ago, on June 16. A blood test revealed the patient had excessive levels of the heart drug digoxin. In small doses, "didge" helps stabilize heart rhythm. But Nancy was not calling about small doses.

"Then on the twenty-eighth, on the same unit, we had *another* dig toxicity…."

"Wait," Ruck said. That couldn't be right. Two patients, same drug, different nights? "And this was in the *same unit*?"

"Yeah."

Ruck asked about the first patient, Mrs. Han—had she come into the hospital with dig toxicity?

No, Nancy said. "We called the lab. She had normal dig levels when she came in."[3]

"Oh my," Bruce said. "Nancy, what hospital are you in again?"

"Somerset Medical Center," Nancy said. "I feel like I'm a detective."

"Well, it sounds scary to me!" Bruce said.

"Yeah," Nancy said. She sounded relieved, hearing another pharmacist acknowledge that.

Nancy put Ruck on hold, so she could explain the rest from the privacy of her office. "Patient 4, the Reverend Gall—" Nancy read his dig numbers from the lab reports: 1.2. on the twentieth, 1.08 on the twenty-second, 1.59, 1.33,...and then, just after dawn on the twenty-eighth, it suddenly jumped to 9.61.

"So after the twenty-seventh, before he spiked—when did he get his next dig?"

"He never got another dig," Nancy said. His digoxin levels spiked a full day *after* doctors took him off the drug.

"First thing I think of is lab error..."

"Well, they're telling me they retested it."

"Mmm," Ruck said. "Then it couldn't have gone up to nine-point something..."

Bruce wasn't getting it. "He coded," Nancy said. "He died, okay? All right?"

Ruck was struck silent. "Okay," he said finally. "Let me slow myself down. I'm going to take a deep breath."

"I know...," Nancy said.

"I apologize. Okay."

"All right."

"First of all," Bruce began, "as far as I'm concerned, on the twenty-seventh to the twenty-eighth? It's impossible for the level to go up like it did...unless he got more digoxin. Right?"

"Okay..."

"Let's take that, okay?"

"Okay," Nancy said. It was that simple. And it was bad.

"I want to run this by somebody else," Ruck said. "This—this is a huge issue."

"Yeah," Nancy said. "And Bruce?" she whispered.

"Yeah?"

"Off the record?"

"Yeah?"

"There were *two more* people. Before this."

———————

Nancy Doherty paced the pharmacy until the phone rang again. As promised, it was Bruce. "Um, can you hold? I want to take this in my office," she whispered. The line clicked over to a recording: "Our new million-dollar computer system is guaranteed to further reduce the possibility of medication errors..."

Nancy closed the office door and pressed the blinking Hold button. "Thank you," she breathed. "Okay. Hi."

"Nancy," Bruce said. "You know, you've got a real—"

"Yeah," Nancy said.

"I'm picking my words carefully here."

"Yeah."

"—dilemma."

"Yeah," Nancy said. "Dilemma. Right."

"And—I used several different calculations, okay?"

"Yeah?"

"And to get that kind of level increase, at minimum you're going to need two to four milligrams of digoxin."

"Two to four milligrams," Nancy said, jotting it down. "Okay, of dig?"

"Yeah," Bruce said. But it wasn't the math that was scaring him. "You see, the main issue, as far as I'm concerned, is the body does not make digoxin."

"Right," Nancy said.

"So, I don't know any way possible of that level going from 1.33 to 9.61 without the patient getting the drug."

"Uh-huh," Nancy said. Nancy knew this, and she wasn't

alone. She had been talked to, by her risk manager Mary Lund, and Dr. William K. Cors, the medical director. They needed some calculations done, to connect the dig spike to the nursing schedule. If Gall's heart stopped at 6 a.m., what time did he get that drug, and how much?

"What they, they were—and I don't know if it's possible, but they want to visualize, like a curve almost," Nancy said. "A curve, you know what I mean?"

"But Nancy," Bruce said. "You know, what also got me a little nervous is your two hypoglycemics you told me about."

"Yeah," Nancy sighed. "Which you're probably not supposed to know, because they're like, they're like, you know..." She and Marty Kelly, the nurse practitioner who first alerted Risk Manager Lund to the issue, had panicked[4] when they saw those numbers. They had insulin ODs and dig ODs. Calling the hotline for help with the dig math was supposed to be a neutral resource, like a police tip hotline or a crisis center. She'd tried to put the hypoglycemics behind her. But Bruce was making that impossible.

"I don't want this...," Nancy sputtered. "You know, they're not—"

"Nancy, Nancy, you know something?"

"We're not looking at them now," Nancy finally blurted.

"But we *are*, Nancy," Bruce said. "We *have* to. We *have* to look at them."

"Yeah," Nancy said.

Bruce spoke slowly, to make certain Nancy couldn't miss it. "Not only do you have to look at them," he said, "but you have a *police matter*."

Ruck waited.

"And I'm going to put it *right in your hands*," Ruck said finally. "*You now have a police matter.*"

"Okay, I, I...," she said.

"In my opinion, you have a police matter."

"Okay, you know what I see, it—"

Ruck wouldn't stop until she heard it. "Look, Nancy," he said. "I hate to say it—it's a police matter."

Nancy was silent. "Okay," she said finally.

"Whether this is a pure accident where somebody screwed up, or—"

"Right," Nancy said. She could do this. "Okay."

"That's the best-case scenario."

"Okay."

"But Nancy? On those two hypoglycemics? If they had high insulin levels, and they showed no C-pep, then somebody gave them insulin."

"Okay."

"You know what I'm saying?"

"Yeah," Nancy said. It was chemistry, not magic. No elevated C-peptide meant that the insulin wasn't human. It came from a laboratory. There was no other way to look at it: if it was in the patients' bodies, and they hadn't made it themselves, that meant somebody put it there. And that someone was killing patients.

"Yeah," Nancy said. "I hear you."

"You've got a big issue here, Nancy. And I'll tell you something, you—and I'm, again, I'm not telling you what to do, I'm not being—"

"Oh, no," Nancy said.

"I mean, maybe there's a good reason for all of this."

"Right," Nancy said.

"But you know what?" Ruck warned. "If this turns out to be a police issue, and you guys are waiting, Nancy? They're going to smear you like crazy."

Nancy sighed. "They don't know that I told you about the hypoglycemics..."

"Nancy, you're doing the right thing."

"Okay . . . ."

"You're doing the right thing."

"Yeah," Nancy said. She needed to get off the phone and deal with this. Ruck was talking about driving down from Newark and looking through the files. It was her phone call, her information, that had precipitated that. That wasn't the plan. Now she'd need to tell her bosses.

Nancy asked Bruce not to come down. She'd brief Cors and Lund herself.

Bruce Ruck gave Nancy his direct line. Nancy promised they'd call back, as soon as possible.

———

Ruck hung up and hurried down the hall. He found his boss's door open. Poison Control director Dr. Steven Marcus was leaning over his crowded desk. Ruck only got a few sentences into it before Marcus cut him off. Data are not ambiguous. His gut told him that somebody at Somerset Medical Center was "knocking off patients."[5] And the longer the Somerset Medical Center administration waited to acknowledge the facts, the more patients might suffer.

———

But a day later, Ruck and Marcus were still waiting for the callback from Somerset. Finally Bruce Ruck dialed the Somerset Medical Center Pharmacy operator again, identifying himself, and waited until the hold music clicked over to the extension. The voice that answered was male, and not friendly. Stuart Vigdor was the head of pharmacy, and Nancy's boss. Bruce decided to drop the emergency tone for something friendly and casual.

"So," Bruce said. "I was just trying to follow up with the outcome. What'd you guys decide to do?"

"Actually, Administration has kind of taken over the investigation," Vigdor said stiffly.

"Uh…"

"They've called in our attorneys. And they've asked me really not to talk to any outside agencies at this point in time, until our internal investigators—"

"Okay," Bruce said. "Just, just so they know, Stu, I'll speak to my medical director, it should be his choice—but you guys put him in a real bad spot."

Vigdor didn't say anything to that. Ruck tried again. "So, you don't know if they've gone to the authorities yet?"

"I don't know that now," Vigdor said. It seemed to Ruck that Stuart Vigdor was shutting this conversation down before it began. And Vigdor knew it would be his ass on the line, not Nancy's.[6] "I'm asked to direct all calls up to Risk Management, up to Mary Lund."

"Okay."

"I think you spoke to her?"

"Yeah," Ruck said. It was a lie, small but quick enough to keep Vigdor from closing the door. "Do you know her number? Let me call her then."

"All right," Vigdor said. He sounded relieved.

"You know, I totally understand," Bruce said, still friendly. "And, they're doing the right thing, in terms of that."

"Yeah," Vigdor continued, "because, we don't know for a fact if these patients have been…" He paused. "It's an ongoing investigation at this point," he said finally.

"Right."

"Right," Vigdor said. "We don't know that we have devious activity or—"

"Oh, absolutely," Ruck said. "But again—whose responsibility is it to investigate—"

"*We* are investigating," Vigdor started, then backed off

the defense. "We can—you know, *they* can...I'm sure *I* can give you assurance of that."

"Sure, sure," Ruck said. "Okay, so, what's the number?"

Bruce heard a rustling of papers, then silence. A few moments later Vigdor returned. He didn't have the phone number, but he'd been thinking, and he needed Ruck to know, this whole overdose thing, it wasn't a *pharmacy* mistake. It sounded to Ruck like Vigdor didn't want to be caught in the middle, the way maybe Nancy was now. This was a job for the administrators.

"And you want them to report it, too?"

"Well...yeah..."

"You know Stu, you don't have to say it," Ruck said. He'd been picturing Vigdor all wrong. Vigdor was probably just a kid. Not bad, just ambitious and scared of stepping out of rank.

"I really feel, that they feel you guys are forcing their hand, um, inappropriately. For what that's worth," Vigdor said. "And, you know, you guys..."

"Sure," Ruck said, "sure..."

"You're supposed to be there as a viable, um, you know..."

"Sure."

"Resource..."

"Sure. Sure."

"So that, you know, we shouldn't be afraid to call you guys."

"No, absolutely, I agree," Ruck said. "But Stu, when it comes to toxicological surveillance, we *do* have an obligation to report to the State."

"Right...," Vigdor said.

"So, that's one of the—that's one of the sticking points, there."

"Yeah, uh, well—," Vigdor started.

Ruck cut him off. "What's her number?"

Vidgor read it out, sounding relieved.

"That's the risk—the *quality assurance* manager," Vigdor said, correcting himself. "Mary Lund."

"Sure," Ruck said.

"You spoke with her yesterday..." Vigdor said, half asking.

"Sure."

"And I believe that was with, with Bill Cors—"

"Sure," Ruck said.

"And I know that, you know, um—upper management has come to *me*, and told *me* that it's an internal investigation at this point. They brought legal counsel in on it. They are bringing in investigators."

Ruck smiled at that one—*he* was a pharmacy investigator, here on the phone, ready to investigate. But apparently they didn't want *him* in there. "Okay," he said.

"Okay?"

"Yeah," Ruck said. "*No problemo.*"

"You know," Vigdor said, "I probably said more than I should have right now."

"Stu. What you tell me is—listen to me, Stu—"

"Yeah?"

"It's between, you know—it's just us," Ruck said. "It's *confidential.*"

But what Bruce Ruck failed to mention was that all their conversations were also on tape.

26

The conference call with the Somerset Medical administrators was set for nine o'clock, pushed by increasingly heated calls from the New Jersey Poison Control director.[1] This was Somerset risk manager Mary Lund's second call with Dr. Steven Marcus; the first conversation hadn't gone so well. This time, it was her bosses' turn to catch a direct blast.

"You see, my problem here is that you've put us in a... a ticklish bind," Marcus boomed over the conference room speaker. "And that's why my comment to you last night was that—look. If there is somebody out there, that is *purposely* doing this to individuals at your hospital, we have a *legal obligation* to report it!"

"Um, okay...," Cors said.

"And not just as an adverse drug reaction!" Marcus continued, working himself up. "I mean, this is a forensic thing. And I sure as heck don't want to get involved in—get caught with my pants down, like they did on Long Island a few years ago. Or Michigan, you know, five or ten years ago, when they had somebody that was going around, doing in patients!"

Marcus's blunt language seemed to have stunned the room. Several awkward seconds passed before Lund filled the gap.

"We're listening to you," she said finally. "We do understand your concerns. And as I said yesterday, we're struggling with these same questions and what our responses need to be."

Now Ruck jumped in. "And there's supposedly two other patients with very strange glucoses, as well?"

"Um, yes. I think *Nancy* discussed these with you?"

Ruck had promised Nancy Doherty that he would protect her, and so instead of giving up his source, Ruck answered Lund's question with a question, one he already knew the answer to. "Did you guys ever run C-peps and insulin levels and all that on these patients?"

Again, there was a protracted silence. Ruck had asked the critical question. The C-pep tests would have indicated whether the overdose insulin had come from their patients' own bodies, or from some other, outside source. If it was an outside source, they obviously had a real problem.

Finally, Cors and Lund both answered, barely audible:

"Yeah."

"Yep."

"And . . . ?" Ruck led.

Silence.

"Um, did they come back in correlation?"

"Yes," Lund said finally. "They did."

"Well," Cors began, "the endocrinologist on the case . . . he, um, felt that, um . . . at least in one of the cases . . . um. . . . I'm trying to remember which one, I don't have the charts just right in front of me, but um . . . he would be hard-pressed to explain what happened to the patient, absent an. . . ." Cors paused to think " . . . an *exogenous* source of influence."

"Well, hey!" Marcus said. Cors's own physicians had concluded that someone must have injected these patients with overdose levels of the drug. He'd said it. "That—yeah, that is our worry about this *whole thing*!" Marcus boomed. "Because my gut feeling is that, they're all victims of the same thing!"

"Well, we have gut feelings, too," Cors admitted. "And what we're wrestling with is, um, you know, throwing the whole institution into chaos, versus, you know, our responsibility to, you know, to keep patients from further harm. And, um, that's what, that's what we're, that's what we're wrestling with, right now."

The Poison Control end of the line was silent, waiting to know the outcome of Cors's wrestling.

Finally, Cors continued. "We have been trying to investigate this. To get some more information before we made any kind of rush to, you know—judgment. Part of that investigation involves an expert opinion. Which we solicited from you. And now puts you in an unfortunate position."

"Yeah!" Marcus snorted. "You see, the problem is that in *every single report* like this in the literature in years gone by, there was *significant delay* in the hospitals instituting any sort of a legal investigation. You know, physicians— I don't care how good your background is, they are really infamously poor at doing forensic investigation. And, the problem, in the past, has always been that somebody then moves on—and, and, you have trouble tracking them."

"Yeah," Cors said. "Who does do good forensic investigation?"

"This is a police matter," Ruck blurted. He'd said it a half dozen times over the past two days.

"Yes, it's a police matter," Marcus said.

"Um, oh-kay," Cors said.

"Okay, I mean, quite honestly," Marcus said, "if you *don't* report it to the police, and *somebody else* dies, and then it comes up that you *stonewalled* it—you're really going to look terrible!"

"Well, oh-kay." Cors chuckled. "We're looking at protecting *patients*."

"No no, no," Marcus said. "Obviously I'm concerned in protecting all of the patients in your hospital as well. But I'm also concerned that, that we'll all be caught with our pants down, and we'll all look like morons!"

Cors listened, then cleared his throat. "One of the reasons we called you was to determine if there's really any further benefit, at this point, with you coming in and taking a look, um, through the, the actual records," he said. "And, maybe we should defer... maybe what we should do is maybe kind of, *end this call* at this point, so that we can confer with our legal counsel and, uh, get some advice—just lay out all the facts and, um, make sure we do the... right thing."

Marcus sighed wearily. "Well I.... sure. We'd be more than happy to come look at it. My gut reaction, having been doing this for, you know, a number of years, being involved with the police investigation of several, other... *situations* over the last twenty years, is that, yeah, you need to get your legal people on board—but I would *not waste time*."

Marcus knew of several cases in which hospital staff members had poisoned patients. They called these killers "Angels of Death." All of those cases shared a simple but disturbing pattern; each time, the doctors treated the rash of crashing patients like a disease to be studied, while the administration and the lawyers treated them as a potential lawsuit. The institution dragged its feet before calling in the cops. And while they dragged, people died. That was the pattern he saw repeating itself at Somerset.

"I would make sure you go to the authorities, and make sure that they know that there is this question," Marcus said. "And then it's in their hands. And if they decide not to do anything, then that's their problem."

"Oh, I understand," Cors said. He sounded tired of being scolded, and ready to end the call.

"We *do* hear you," Lund added.

"And also including the Department of Health!" Ruck reminded them.

"I mean, this is certainly a sentinel event," Marcus said.[2] He knew the effect of those words on a hospital administrator. A sentinel event is any which threatens patient safety. Marcus had thrown the gauntlet; by law, Somerset had to report such an event to authorities. "They need to know about it."

"All right," Lund said, using the sing-song tone that signals the end of a phone call.

"Well, we surely appreciate your input," Cors said. "And, we will, um, indeed get back to you . . . so . . . you'll hear from us one way or the other . . ."

"Hopefully it was nothing *inappropriate*," Ruck said, trying to lighten the murder thing, keep them moving. "Hopefully just an error or whatever."

"I know!" Cors said. "I just wish somebody would come forward and say, 'Hey, I screwed up.' I'd sleep a lot better."

"Well, you've got two patients with dig and two patients with insulin," Marcus said. "That doesn't sound to me like it's going to be a simple screwup."

Bruce Ruck knew he was pushing his luck, especially after the bomb Dr. Marcus dropped in the last phone call, but he needed to check on Nancy. He dialed the number for the

Somerset Medical Center pharmacy again, figuring if he got Vigdor, he'd make something up. A female voice answered on the second ring. This time, he didn't identify himself.

"Hey," Ruck said. "I'm trying to get in touch with Nancy—"

"Yeah, hold on, she's right here." The phone at the other end was muffled. "That's for you."

"Nancy Doherty, can I help you?"

"Nancy, it's Bruce."

"Um, hi," Nancy said quickly.

"Look," Bruce said."I know you can't talk about the case, and that's fine..."

"Um-hmm," Nancy said.

"Nancy," Bruce said, "the only thing I want to tell you is, if they're going to try and get you in trouble in any shape or form..."

"Um-huh."

"The medical director, he and I have talked about it. We will back you five hundred percent, 'cause you did nothing wrong."

"Okay," Nancy said.

"Are they giving you a hard time?"

"Ah, there's some..." Nancy picked her words. "There's a lot of...*issues*. Floating around..."

"Okay."

"A *lot* of issues," she said.

"Okay," Bruce said. "But Nancy, Nancy."

"Yeah?"

"You did nothing wrong."

"Yeah."

"And that's why him and I sat down and discussed it."

Nancy sounded like she was trying hard to keep it together. "Okay..."

"Because if, God forbid, Nancy, if they try to do anything to you, professionally?"

"Yeah?"

"We will one hundred and fifty *percent* back you up."

"Okay."

"I put it together," Bruce said. "You? You just called for information."

"Yeah."

"On how to increase dig levels, or whatever."

"Okay," Nancy said. She sounded grateful at Ruck helping her, getting the story straight.

"You should *not* take the brunt."

"Yeah," Nancy sighed. She sounded on the edge of tears. "You don't know how much that means to hear you say that right now."

There would be only one more conference call between Dr. Marcus at Poison Control and the Somerset Medical Center administration. Once again, Marcus told the Somerset administrators that they were obligated to report these incidents to the state within twenty-four hours of their occurrence, and that they were already out of compliance with their obligations. And again, Marcus was told by Somerset that, until they'd mounted a thorough investigation, they were not planning on reporting these patient incidents to anyone: not the New Jersey Department of Health and Senior Services (commonly known as the DOH), and not the police.[3]

But this second conversation differed from the first in two crucial aspects. The first was raw volume, most of it from Dr. Marcus. He was, in his own words, "extremely concerned" and "frustrated"; "rude, confrontational, and adversarial in his dealings with Somerset Medical Center employees," was how Dr. Cors would later characterize Marcus's phone manner. The poison control director was furious and unmuzzled. This was a police matter, he insisted, a matter of patient safety. He gave them twenty-four hours; if Somerset refused to act, Marcus had an obligation to report their problem to the DOH personally. And, he added, "it will look a lot worse if I do it."

In fact, Marcus had already reported the issues at Somerset.[4] Earlier that afternoon he'd called Eddy Bresnitz, MD, the state epidemiologist and assistant commissioner of the DOH, pulling him out of a meeting. Marcus would recall[5] telling Dr. Bresnitz of "a cluster of illnesses in the hospital which may be based on a criminal act." Marcus then dashed off an e-mail to Amie Thornton, the assistant commissioner of health, summarizing both "what appears to be a cluster of four untoward clinical events" at the hospital,[6] and Somerset's unwillingness to report them until after they mounted a thorough investigation themselves.[7]

The second crucial difference came twenty minutes into the call, when Marcus informed the Somerset Medical Hospital administration that all their conversations had been recorded.

———

A few hours later,[8] Mary Lund contacted the Department of Health and reported their four patient incidents, Gall and Han by digoxin and the others by insulin.[9] The report, by fax and e-mail, explained the steps thus far taken to account for these incidents.

They'd checked for manufacturer's recalls and adverse drug interactions. They'd ensured that IVs and bedside monitors were serviceable and accurate. It couldn't have been a lab error—they'd already rerun all the lab tests. They were running out of alternate theories. As a caution, Somerset tightened pharmacy controls on digoxin, as they had on insulin, making their nurses now accountable for these commonly used medicines; if the drugs were being used to harm their patients, the least they could do was make them more difficult to get.

The most likely scenario to account for the incidents was human error of some sort—medication errors were always possible in a hospital, as mistakes are possible anywhere. Proof of an innocent mistake would probably show up in the paper trail. The Somerset Medical administration assured the DOH they were already reviewing all their documentation systems. Somerset Medical Center employed two major computerized documentation systems; the Pyxis MedStation 2000 for the drugs, and Cerner, which stored computerized patient charts. So far, their review hadn't found any innocent mistakes.

But what else was possible? Something unusual, and far more sinister than error. "Human resource factors are being evaluated," Lund's July 10 letter informed the DOH. "Independent investigators are conducting interviews of involved staff."[10]

————————

On July 14, attorney Raymond J. Fleming, of the West Orange law firm of Sachs, Maitlin, Fleming, Greene, Marotte and Mullen, drove out to Somerset Medical Center. Fleming was briefed on the situation by Mary Lund, then set up in a room to meet with Charles Cullen.[11]

Charlie found Fleming seated at a conference table wearing the telltale dark-suit/bright-tie combination that distinguished corporate lawyers from undertakers. Charlie knew this had to be about the recent deaths on his ward; he'd been through this sort of thing plenty of times before. He was ready for the questions.

Ray Fleming seemed to already know a bit about him. He knew that Charlie had worked at Somerset for less than a year, and that he had left jobs at many other hospitals in the past. To Charlie, that suggested that the man had looked at his application. Charlie hadn't listed the proper dates there. Maybe this lawyer knew that, too. Maybe that mattered, maybe not. Charlie didn't think it did. It never had before.

Fleming also knew about the Reverend Gall. That seemed to be the point of the meeting. He knew, for example, that Cullen was not Gall's nurse the night the reverend died, but that Cullen had worked with him before, and that he was familiar with Gall's medical history. Fleming knew that history, the medical issues Gall came in with, the time line of his illness and apparent recovery, and the spiking of his digoxin levels just prior to his code. He also knew that Charlie had been assigned to Reverend Gall for three nights, June 15 to 17.

Charlie had ordered digoxin for Gall on his first night, the fifteenth. He'd then canceled the order. It was on his Pyxis. Charlie was also working on the night Gall died. On that night Charlie had again ordered, then canceled, digoxin. It was one of his two cancellations that night.

Neither of these cancellations made much sense as mistakes—if Charlie had typed in the wrong code, or pressed the wrong button in the process of entering a drug order, then you'd expect him to follow up with another, presumably correct, order. But the Pyxis orders were time coded, and there had been no immediate follow-ups. Apparently, Charlie had taken the time to enter his name, patient, and specific prescription drug order into the Pyxis keypad, confirmed his order and, as the drug drawer popped open, decided only then that he needed nothing from the machine, and canceled the transaction. It was a bizarre and unlikely scenario, but one Cullen apparently repeated several times a night.

Fleming had another interesting fact at his disposal. He'd checked with the pharmacy and discovered that a number of vials of dig had been unaccounted for that month. Fleming didn't put any of this in a particular order as far as Charlie could tell, and he didn't accuse Charlie or threaten him or offer to let him resign, as other interviewers had done before. It was a curious interview, Charlie had to admit, and it got stranger when Fleming asked him a question:

Was Charlie aware that if he ordered a drug, and then canceled the order, that the cancellation still showed up on his computerized Pyxis record?

"Yes," Charlie told the lawyer. If he didn't know it before, he certainly did now.

27

Charlie was pretty certain they were just looking at his digoxin, as if dig was the problem. But the night before Fleming's interview, Charlie had killed a man with dobutamine,[1] a chemical relative of adrenaline. It worked fine.

———

His shift hadn't started yet, but Charlie was already in his whites when he walked into James Strickland's room to watch him breathe. Then Charlie felt a presence, someone at the door behind him. He tucked the sheet, as if finishing up nurse work, then ducked toward the door.

"Charles?" It was Mr. Strickland's daughter Janece, a middle-aged blonde woman with an oversized purse denting her shoulder. The daughter noticed things, used his name, asked questions. It was uncomfortable for Charlie, like walking too close to a strange dog on the street.

He'd seen her several times during her visits to her father. They'd interacted and, gradually, fallen into roles Charlie was more comfortable with. He liked to explain the technical aspects of her father's medical condition, and she seemed to listen. She also sometimes brought her younger son along, an autistic boy, a child Charlie thought of as vulnerable, though tonight, she was alone.

"Charles?" the woman said again. "Charles, are you my father's nurse tonight?"

Charlie didn't want to talk. He kept moving, pretending he hadn't heard as he turned down the hall into another room to wait until the daughter left. Then Charlie pulled the Cerner cart to the end of the hallway and called up Mr. Strickland's charts. No, he wasn't Mr. Strickland's nurse, not technically. He shouldn't even have been in Strickland's room. But Mr. Strickland was still within Charlie's sphere, and he had decided. *Insulin*.

Unlike digoxin, insulin was a hormone, a drug the human body produced naturally. In the hospital, it dripped into the patient from an IV. In the body, it dripped from the pink waterlogged pinkie of the pancreas, radiating from special cells the textbooks called the Islets of Langerhans. The name made it sound like it came from pirates. When Charlie was in nursing school, the foreign insulin, the drug diabetics used, all came from animals, pigs or cows, usually, as if it were a by-product of hot dogs. They'd all laughed about that in class, letting out a collective *eew* after they'd been so tough about so much else.

Insulin was like a volume control for sugar. Not enough and you were diabetic. Too much and you were hypoglycemic. It wasn't a poison—you can't eat insulin and get sick; the stomach juices would gobble the bonds like hamburger. But injected overdoses happened, sometimes on purpose.

First the lips and fingers go tingly and numb, then it's the brain. The flood of insulin gives orders to the cells, makes them hungry. The cells take up the glucose; the blood is left barren and the extremities starve. The human brain, surviving on oxygen and sugar alone, begins to shut down,

resulting in a confused stupor that occasionally lands hypoglycemics in the drunk tank by mistake. It's a space-out, a
fuzziness. The body goes insubstantial, the personality light,
and individuals become either cranky or giddy, depending
on their nature. Then the stomach sinks. Sweat beads form
on the scalp. The head pounds, the heart skips, concentration evaporates. Vision slurs and pixilates. Moments pass,
unfiled in memory.

All this happens quickly. With a patient who is unwell,
or already zonked on a tranquilizer or paralytic agent, these
intellectual and perceptual effects may go unnoticed by the
outside observer. The next stages will not, as the convulsions
start.[2]

Some of the most extensive research on insulin overdose
was undertaken by Nazi scientists. At some concentration
camps, children were injected with graduated doses of insulin to measure their endurance to extreme hypoglycemia.[3]
The bell curve on these so-called terminal experiments
tapered at death. But the use of intentional insulin overdose
had its origins as therapy. The intentional induction of a
coma, or shock, was considered the ultimate sobering slap for
certain maladies of mind, a treatment started in Switzerland
soon after the discovery of the hormone in the 1920s. Like
electroshock, insulin shock therapy was used throughout
the 1950s in the treatment of paranoid schizophrenia, before
being discontinued due to the violence and occasional brain
damage that were the occasional side effects of the brain-
starving procedure.

Surviving an insulin coma is like surviving a near drowning, and the extent and permanence of the injuries are related
to the length of time that the brain was starved of nutrient.
Continued starvation damages the cerebral cortex. The
microscopic chemical architecture of the brain collapses,

the surface area smooths, and crenulations simplify, much like the brains of patients with neurodegenerative disorders. The effects range from Parkinson's-like symptoms of rigidity and the choreiform, or jerky, movements of a damaged motor cortex, all the way to permanent intellectual retardation.

But of course, the ultimate effect was death. The only trick was figuring the right dosage.

28

Charlie always preferred the hospital at night, without extras: the candy stripers, administrators, and visitors. The gift shop was closed, the public bathrooms locked. Even the janitors were gone, their whirring machines lassoed with yellow extension cord.

Overhead, the mercury vapor lights hummed like neon. The vending machines murmured down the empty hall. The break room tables showcased teeth-marked Styrofoam cups, lipsticked bendy straws, still lifes with Snack Mix and mini-donuts. Some of the other nurses ate this crap all night, but not Charlie. Charlie never ate on shift. He waited.

He watched the silhouettes through the Levolors, waiting for the small hours. Then he waited on Mr. Strickland. He checked his chart on the Cerner, made coffee, checked again. He was still there. Charlie always made the coffee. Some people were so inconsiderate about that; they used the coffee but they never refilled it, which was okay, but he was always taking care of it, helpful in that way, secretly helpful. He watched the nurses at the station, stirring their coffees, his coffee, helped by what he did, dependent really but not even knowing it.

He pulled a 10 cc syringe from his scrubs pocket and

injected four ampoules of insulin into the port of Mr. Strickland's IV, throwing the syringe and ampoules in the sharps bin. Then he signed out and went home. He never saw Mr. Strickland go through his convulsions, but he had the commute to imagine.

He arrived early the next day, still September 22. Charlie walked quickly by Strickland's room and glanced in. The man, or someone, was still in the bed. In the hall he checked the chart, using the mobile Cerner, staying away from the nursing station and the chitty chat. It was 7:05, only minutes into his shift, but he couldn't wait. He wheeled the cart back to the nurses' station for the shift change.

Charlie usually had no patience for these details, but he did today. The day nurses colored in the details of the numbers Charlie had seen on Strickland's Cerner screen.

Mr. Strickland's blood sugar had been routinely tested that morning. The lab had found zero glucose in the sample, and assumed there had been an error. A man couldn't survive on zero blood sugar. They did not imagine that Strickland had already been hypoglycemic for over three hours. As the morning wore on, Strickland's sugar-starved brain began eating itself.

Strickland's daughter arrived midday, this time with her older, teenage son. Charlie had seen the boy before and generally tried to avoid him during visiting hours. Apparently, it was he who first noticed something wrong with his grandfather.

The boy had seen a slight twitch in Strickland's arm. That's how it started. At first, it was hardly perceptible. But as the day wore on and Mr. Strickland's glucose reserves wore out, the twitch gained and globalized, until Mr. Strickland was in full seizure. Even the most hardened of veteran day nurses said it was truly horrifying—the man thrashing in his bed, the alarms screaming, the family yelling for some-body please to do something. Strickland was now grinding and frothing like he'd bit a live wire as his brain's temporal lobe pulsed in spasm. The nurses had pumped Mr. Strick-land with glucose all day, but the man kept crashing. The son pointed at the expensive medical equipment demanding, "What the hell are these machines for?"[1]

Charlie pulled up the Cerner computer and went through Strickland's numbers again, reliving the code and the pat-terns, the echoes of his voice. Then Charlie went back to the Pyxis machine, to think on someone else. Mr. Strick-land would survive, at least in body. He'd remain at Somer-set. It took two weeks before Charles Cullen finally finished Mr. Strickland with a midnight dose of dig.[2] But dig didn't appear anywhere on Strickland's chart, and it wasn't in Charlie's Pyxis requests either. Nor did any canceled dig orders appear on his Pyxis. Charlie was good.

Each patient presented a variety of symptoms that could be treated, or exacerbated, by any number of drugs on the ward. Later, he would recall only a handful. Like Melvin Simcoe, from back in May, a corporate manager with four grown children, to whom Charlie gave sodium nitroprusside until his blood was thinned to uselessness. And Christopher Hardgrove, a drug user who had arrived on the CCU already largely brain-dead. And Philip Gregor, whom he had poi-soned and coded but did not quite kill. And Frances Agoada, whose blood sugar spiked dangerously after Charlie deliv-ered an overdose of insulin, and Krishnakant Upadhyay, whose heart he had stopped, as he had Mr. Strickland's, with massive doses of dig.

Really, the variations were nearly endless, especially on the CCU. There was no reason to stop. And so Charlie didn't. After sixteen years, it was still that simple.

PART
II

29

Every case starts with a call. Dispatch sends a marked car, and the uniforms look over the bodies, sort accidents from suicides and what they call "natural deaths." When it's none of those, when they can't say for sure what happened, they call Homicide.

Each body is a death, but not every death is a crime scene. Generally, the very young are accidents, the very old are natural deaths, and almost everyone else gets shot—at least, that was how it panned out in Newark. Suicides don't always look like suicides. For the bodies that come off one of the housing towers, the question becomes: did he jump or was he pushed? Statistically, the depressed don't leap, they fall. You take out the tape and check the charts. If it's a shooting death and the gun's still there, that's a possible suicide, too, no matter how many bullet holes. Bodies on the corner are almost always murder, bodies on the tracks are a mess, and bodies in the river are mysteries. You hear stories of cops poking floaters back out into the Passaic toward another jurisdiction.

The detective on call takes whatever comes during his twenty-four-hour shift. He might get lucky and catch none, but one night, when he still worked Newark, Tim Braun caught four. In those days, he seemed to attract bodies. If he was in the box, he got them. That's the way it works in most precincts: It's up to the detective to figure the priority of the cases, but every new murder shuffles the deck. The top case is the "redball," the one everyone wants off his desk, the one that needs to just go away. In Newark, if the news cameras were on the scene before Tim, it was definitely a redball. If a child or some mayor's shithead son was involved: redball. But that could change. *Redball* is a temporary designation, a hot hand that can go cold quick, and every new murder reshuffles it. Every new body changes the priorities. Every call resets the clock.

———

The first bodies Tim Braun ever saw were when he was working as a security guard at Saint Barnabas Medical Center, his hometown megahospital in Livingston, New Jersey. Tim was still a teenager, vigorous and bulletproof, and the elderly bodies weren't real people to him—they were just anonymous husks, weight that "Big Tim" carried whenever a cute nurse asked. The first body that mattered came later. Tim was a new cop on patrol, a uniform responding to a call; a fisherman led him through the reeds near the river. The guy in the mud was dressed in ordinary clothes. He had pockets and shoes. He was normal but for the red line across his neck and the spine flashing white like a broken smile. He was a victim, what they called a vic. It can sound crass to someone outside law enforcement, but the language of the death business is intentionally impersonal. See too much, feel too personal a connection, and the job becomes impossible. But Tim hadn't learned that yet. That fall Tim took the tests to transfer to Newark, heading toward a career in Homicide.

Newark in the 1990s was the center of the murder universe, "the most dangerous city in America," according to *Time* magazine, and one of the most corrupt, according to everybody else. If you worked in the Essex County Prosecutor's Office you were a detective, and being a detective was a lifestyle, loaded guns and good suits and cop bars that never closed. Tim imagined himself finally chasing bad guys, the way he imagined it as a little kid, the way his dad had done, as a lieutenant in Newark. At first, Tim was always at work, or at least never at home, and partying around the clock. The adrenaline was highly addictive. Detectives were like rock stars with guns. The badge gave you license, and some of the guys abused it. For quiet nights, Tim kept a cold case of Miller and an extra box of bullets in the car, and usually ran through both before the sun came up. His marriage began to suffer, or so he heard later—at the time, he didn't worry about that, or much else. Shifts ran around the clock. Booze helped push everything else to the side, until finally that overwhelmed him, too.[1] Three months after stepping into Essex he asked for a three-month leave. He spent his thirtieth birthday in "a jitter joint," traded the beer for a judo black belt, and came back clean and ready to take on Newark as a homicide detective.

The Essex County Prosecutor's Office had just ten detectives to cover some four hundred calls a year. Braun was fighting a guerilla war in which every civilian was a potential enemy. It was fun at first, but like most detectives, Tim found it almost impossible not to blur the line between that violent world and his personal life. Newark was a brutal place. In Livingston, Braun got written up every time he swore at a civilian; in Newark he discovered that people were grateful to get away without a beatdown, and that the occasional complaints that did make it to the station house were regarded as noise, quickly swept away by the overwhelming flow of cases. Tim learned on the job, put in his years, and racked up medals. He learned that it didn't matter whether the body turned up on the river or on the tracks or on the corner, because 99 times out of 100 whatever happened started with drugs and ended with a gun. He learned that when he paid a call to inform a mother about her son's death as soon as Mama's tears dried, she asked about the free money. Tim didn't understand how they all seemed to know that the state paid victims' families or why, afterward, those families seemed to stop caring. Ninety-nine times out of 100, the family never called the number on his business card, never asked him, *Did you get the bad guy?* He didn't think about how the Newark projects taught these mothers to expect violent death or prison for their children, he just thought: *They don't care, but I'm supposed to? That's fucked up.* And every day was just more dead kids, with always more to come. After a while, it wasn't always clear who the bad guys were anymore.

One case in particular marked the beginning of the end for Tim. It started as an unusual case, a crime on the street but not a street crime, and probably a redball only because the victim was white and middle class, with a nephew in the State Police. Ethel Duryea was a respected fifty-year-old nurse who got gunned down on the sidewalk of an affluent Newark suburb. A jogger found her body in the snow, her purse lying untouched next to her. There were no witnesses, no leads, no suspects, and no clues other than the bullet itself. Tim got the call but it was a stone-cold whodunnit. It took a year before Tim was able to connect the bullet to the gun that fired it, another six months before he connected the gun to a multi-million-dollar insurance scam. Somebody in the emergency rooms of local hospitals was selling privileged patient information to local slip-and-fall lawyers. And some of those lawyers had some political juice in Newark. It was starting to look like Nurse Duryea's murder was a hit on a whistleblower. Tim was told by his superiors to leave it alone. When he ignored the warnings, he was temporarily rotated out of Homicide, put on what Tim called "the rubber gun squad," working the courthouse.

Gradually he got the picture; the cold case was going to stay cold, or Tim could forget his pension. But something about Duryea's case had clicked for him, the way his first murder did. Tim had gotten close to the victim's family and was personally invested in catching her killer. He had spent all of his energy ignoring the world he inhabited, and had never learned what all the families in the projects already seemed to know, that not every bad guy got caught. He had thought his job was helping put Ethel Duryea's ghost to rest. His real job, as he now realized, was only to service the machinery of power. He could sweep the streets, bust street kids, but he could never mess with the machine itself. The redball had gone cold, and neither the family nor the press would know that he'd found the gun that had killed Ethel Duryea.[2] But Tim knew. And while it seemed too crazy to admit, he was certain that the ghost of Ethel Duryea knew, too. She was still out there, a blur at the edge of his field of vision. She wasn't a vic—she was a woman in a bloody nurse's uniform, sitting on his conscience. Soon enough it showed up the side of his arm, too, in the form of a rash the size of a cigarette burn. Each day it grew, until the shingles covered a whole side of his body. For ten years since he'd stopped drinking, Tim had never taken a single sick day. Now he started dipping in. He spent time with his wife Laurie and his young son Connor, thinking and praying. Then he got the hell out of Newark.

Thirty minutes down the Garden State Parkway the blacktop got blacker, the roads smoother. Exit 140A to US 22, Somerville, New Jersey, Somerset County. There were no gang colors on the corner, just neat little houses with American flags and porches instead of ghetto towers, and a gleaming new county prosecutor's office across from a historic town square. Somerset was the richest county per capita in New Jersey—the fourth wealthiest in the country. It was the sort of place where a guy could tap the brakes and slow down as he crossed the finish line to his pension.

The Somerset County Homicide job offered better pay for less work and less danger. He had an office with a door that closed and a padded desk chair that tilted all the way back. He kept the cold case taped up in a cardboard box in his closet. He told himself that Nurse Duryea's ghost would understand. At the age of forty-two, Tim thought he was slowing down, headed toward stop.

30

The call came in on October 3, 2003,[1] a Friday, from Somerset County prosecutor Wayne Forrest. Braun cradled the receiver and figured his options. His view was, the vic was probably a political hack, someone rich or connected, so the local power needed to make the cops dance. A guy dies in the hospital, they call the cops. That was the sort of thing that got Somerville excited. Connections were everything. It wasn't fast-food murder like Newark, but it was the job, at least until Tim's pension kicked in.

As the detective sergeant, Braun's job was to assign and supervise all of the cases that came into Major Crimes. He looked over to the whiteboard, the color-coded dry-erase indicating the on-call rotation, and saw that it was young Danny Baldwin, the new guy, in the box. Easy. Danny Baldwin was hard to miss—not only because he was a former linebacker with a clean-shaven head and a yardstick of muscled collarbone leveled beneath his chin, but also because he was the only black detective in the Somerset prosecutor's office. His six-and-a-half-foot, 250-pound frame twitched with raw energy and ambition, jittering, leg-jiggling electricity. Tim had first met him back in Newark, where Danny had earned a sterling reputation in their elite Auto Theft Task

Force and been one of the few African-American detectives in Essex Homicide. He was ten years younger than Tim, but the senior detective recognized himself in the new detective. Danny was good police, which is to say he made cases and not just files, and when he had heard Danny was looking for a change, Tim had lobbied hard to bring him over to Somerset County.

Danny had been at Somerset for only six months, and aside from a few bank robberies, his time there had been relatively quiet. He'd made good use of his time in other counties, working undercover with some of his old sources for the FBI in a South Carolina murder-for-hire case, and helping solve a high-profile homicide over in neighboring Morris County for Prosecutor Michael Rubinaccio, but he hadn't yet fielded a single homicide case in Somerville. Tim had worked plenty with him back in Newark; he knew he could count on Danny to get this thing off his desk. Braun reached Baldwin at home, relaying what Prosecutor Forrest had told him. "This guy, died in the hospital, go figure, right?" Tim said. "Go to the autopsy, make some overtime. Bang 'em hard while you're at it."

Danny and his wife, Kimberly, had a wedding to attend, but he couldn't turn down the job. His new coworkers in Somerset were already on him for being a big-time Newark transfer winning glory in other counties and wearing good suits instead of the Somerset uniform of Dockers and a jacket, ties that matched the shirt. No matter what his commitments, Danny wasn't going to put his first Somerset homicide call on someone else.

Saturday morning, Danny Baldwin drove out to the Medical Examiner's Office. He observed the autopsy and drove back to his desk at the Somerset County Prosecutor's Office to type up the I-1-00 form, jacketed the paperwork, and called Tim from the car. The deceased, he said, one McKinley Crews, was an older black man with nothing visibly wrong with him.

"It was kinda a waste of time," Danny explained. That wasn't just his take—the state coroner, Dr. Nobby C. Mambo, was of the same opinion: *a natural death.* But the prosecutor had called, and there was pressure. They ran the lab tests, which came back clean.

"Yeah, and who was the guy?" Pressure from the brass like that, VIP for sure. "He look like anybody?"

Danny told him no. He didn't get that sense. He was an older fellow, black, looked sick. Looked dead, in fact, an opinion confirmed by Dr. Mambo. So Braun called the prosecutor, still not quite believing that this was the new job and wondering if there was still enough of the weekend left to head down to his cabin and watch the leaves die.

The next call came down from Prosecutor Forrest four days later. Tim and Danny Baldwin were to report down the street, to Somerset Medical Center, the biggest employer in town with the building to match. A century's worth of donations and steady profits had paid for an unending process of renovations and additions, the most recent being a colossal, new corporate-gifted lobby featuring a player piano that played calming classical stuff from a little black box. Tim and Danny were still eye-rolling when the elevator door closed. It wasn't until they got into the conference room and saw all the heavy hitters gathered there that they started to realize this was no ordinary call. The way Tim figured it was, *Wow, this dead guy must be one hell of a VIP.*

It was a lawyer who stood up first,[2] introducing himself as Paul Nittoly, counsel for Somerset Medical Center. Nittoly was a big white man with a hundred-dollar haircut and a cornflower-blue tie, the kind of guy you see on billboards. He thanked the detectives for coming and explained, in a roundabout way, that the Medical Center wasn't reporting a homicide, not exactly.

Over the previous five months, the lawyer continued, Somerset had experienced five "unexplainable patient incidents" in their Critical Care Unit. Last Friday, there was a sixth incident on the CCU. At this point, he said, the hospital had notified the Prosecutor's Office.[3] Somerset Medical Center's senior vice president, Dr. William Cors, read the names: on May 28, Mr. Joseph Lehman; on June 4, Ms. Frances Kane; on June 16, Ms. Jin Kyung Han; on June 28, Reverend Florian Gall; on August 27, Ms. Francis Agoada. The last on the list was McKinley Crews, who had died only four days previous; it was only after his death that Somerset had called the prosecutor, and Danny had visited the morgue.

Dr. Cors seemed to pick his words carefully, avoiding cause and effect. All six patients had "unexplainable, abnormal laboratory findings" and "life-threatening symptoms," and five of those patients were now dead. Whether those incidents were connected, Cors couldn't or wouldn't say, but the hospital had been conducting its own internal investigation for five months. This investigation, Cors said, had not identified the source of the occurrences. Cors then proceeded to summarize all six patients' medical histories, in brief but technical detail.

Tim had some names on the page—the names of the dead and some medical stuff, spellings scratched out and replaced by all caps—INSULIN and GLUCOSE, which he'd heard of, and a new one, DIGOXIN, a heart drug. The rest was a blur of medical jargon, cc's, mg's, and milliliters. No crime scene, no weapon, no fingerprints or witnesses, no bullet, no gun. Did they even have a crime? Tim underlined the question mark till he split the paper in his notebook.

One seat over, Danny Baldwin seemed to be squeezing the life out of his pen.

———————

The detectives couldn't get out of the room fast enough. Outside, the October sun glared off the tinted windows of Braun's Green Crown Vic. Tim popped the locks and pushed into the driver's side, feeling the relief of cool leather.

Tim knew that Somerset Medical Center pulled serious weight in the community. It was a money center, one of the county's biggest employers and a heavy influence in local politics with at least two former state senators on the board, one of whom was not only the father-in-law to the Somerset County chief of detectives but also good pals with Wayne Forrest. Trouble there lit a fire under the prosecutor's ass, which lit a fire under his. Tim waited till Danny had his door closed before he started grousing. "What the fuck was that?" Tim said. "Tell you what, give me a good, old-fashioned shooting instead of this fucking Greek." Tim couldn't raise his hand in the middle of all the doctor talk, tell the suits, "Um, me and Danny? We do street murders." But he sure wanted to.

Tim started the car and eased out of the turnaround while Danny sprawled in the passenger side with the stack of medical charts. Apparently, if there was a crime, it wasn't in these pages—the medical people had already studied them. Danny was chewing his cheek and bouncing his hams. He was the lead detective here. It would be his job to make sense of the pieces that Somerset gave him, and try to make a case out of them.

But what were the pieces here? Numbers. Lab values. Technical results neither Tim nor Danny understood.

Apparently even the professional laboratory people couldn't explain them. The vics were only potential vics; they might be natural deaths. For now, they were bodies without visible wounds. This wasn't even definitely a crime. They had "incidents," medical ones, which medical people had already investigated for five months, finding nothing. It seemed obvious to Tim that some bigwig in Somerset corporate had an agenda. That was the way it was with a redball, same here as in Newark. It was far worse than being handed a cold case. This one maybe wasn't a case at all.

Danny looked up from his notebook, seeing Bridge Street on his right now and then behind him, wondering why Tim was blowing by the turn to the prosecutor's office. "Basically, they think somebody's poisoning patients, on purpose or whatever. Right?"

"And they've been investigating five months already?" Tim said.

"So, why call now?"

"Exactly. They got juice to call us anytime. Why not call us five months ago?"

Danny scanned his notes. " 'Unexplained incidents,' what they called it," he said. Four with insulin, two with the heart drug. Danny flipped a page, fingered the word. "Digoxin."

"Digoxin, digoxin," Tim said, getting his mouth around it. He pulled the wheel right, circling 360 degrees to merge onto Route 206. "What the fuck is digoxin?"

"You mind I ask, you're going where?"

"Here," Tim said, pulling into the mall parking lot and easing into the fire lane. "Medical dictionary." He opened the door, then stopped. "Okay," he said. "So, let me ask you this. You catch the call Friday. Three days later, we're brought into this happy horseshit."

"So, what happened between Friday and today?"

"Yeah."

"Yeah, well, maybe the lawyers had a weekend to think on it," Danny said. "Maybe, they got scared, is what happened."

"Yeah," Tim said. He thought on that. "You know what?" he said finally. "I bet those assholes know exactly who did it."

31

Redball or not, the investigation couldn't start until Somerset Medical Center delivered the paperwork. The lawyer Nittoly had promised to send the detectives everything from their internal investigation, and as soon as possible. It was late afternoon when the package arrived. Danny considered the contents for a few minutes before walking the package next door to Tim's office.

The envelope contained only the photocopied pages of a single faxed memo. The detectives had known better than to expect a finished investigative report, but they expected more than scraps. Including the cover letter, the memo was five pages long; one of the pages appeared to be missing.

"Check the date," Danny said.

The memo was dated July 25, 2003—over two months ago.

"What's this?" Tim said. "I thought the in-house investigation just ended."

The memo had been sent by Raymond Fleming, a hospital-retained lawyer at a West Orange law firm,[1] and titled "Re: Reverend Florian Gall v Somerset Medical Center," with an attached file number.

Danny didn't know the lawyer, but he took special note of

the title, especially the "v" in the middle. He knew it was a lawyer's nature to make everything look like a fight, but still, it seemed funny to him, like patient and hospital were on opposite sides here.

According to the cover page, the recipient of the memo was Mary Lund. They'd shaken hands with her earlier that day in the SMC conference room. Lund and Danny had exchanged cards; from here on, she was assigned as Danny's liaison at the hospital, the friendly face for whatever the lead detective on this case might need to do his job. Tim remembered her as a middle-aged corporate-type lady with the unforgettable job title of Somerset Medical Center's "risk manager." Apparently, the risk manager had been Ray Fleming's point of contact, too.

> *Dear Ms. Lund;*
> *Enclosed herewith is a copy of my file memorandum which I prepared after our meeting with Charles Cullen.*
> *Thank you for your cooperation.*
> > *Very Truly Yours,*
> > *Raymond J. Fleming*

"Charles Cullen?" Tim said. "They mention him in the meeting?"

"Next page," Danny said. "Memo says he's a nurse. Worked the Critical Care ward with one of the vics. The Reverend. "

Danny flipped to the last page. "Says, 'We agreed that there was nothing so overtly suspicious at this point in time either from the records or Mr. Cullen's demeanor itself that would necessitate a call to the authorities.'"

"Who's 'we'?"

"Mary Lund and the lawyer," Danny explained. "Fleming. Apparently they interviewed this Cullen together."

"July 14," Tim said. "Ten days later they write a memo about it."

"Maybe it took 'em ten days to finish," Danny said. "Bill by the hour, shit happens."

"Then two months later, they send it to us," Tim said. He flicked the paper. "So, where's the rest? The other memos, the rest of the nurses?"

Danny didn't know. But he had a meeting that afternoon with someone who should.

———

In theory, Mary Lund could be the key to this investigation. Lund was a former nurse who had worked her way up the corporate ladder to become the gatekeeper to the hospital world, a woman who could help translate the medical mysteries of the hospital into something the detectives could understand. The only question was whether she'd cooperate. Danny needed more than her polite professional assistance; he needed Mary Lund to actually like him.

Danny parked out front of the hospital, smoothed his tie against the wind, and nodded respectfully at the rent-a-cop by the elevator. Down the hallway of Marriot carpet and bad art he found a secretary with color photos of a panting shih tzu plastered to her computer monitor. Danny read "Trudy" off the name plate, introduced himself, going for serious but not scary, and not quite pulling it off.

As Danny would later remember it,[2] Mary Lund was heavyset, middle-aged, white, no frills—perfectly suited to the title of risk manager. Her suit skirt was corporate sensible, neutral toned and neutered cut. She didn't seem like the type for chitchat, so Danny started right in with the investigative memo the Somerset Medical Center lawyer had sent over. He pulled the fax from his breast pocket, skipping to the parts he'd highlighted.

"So, following the, uh, passing of the Reverend Gall, you and this attorney Fleming conducted an interview with a nurse named Charles Cullen?"

"Yes," Mary said. "We interviewed all the nurses who worked on the unit."

"Okay, okay," Danny said. "And what did you—"

"None of these interviews turned up anything unusual or incriminating," Mary said.

"I see that," Danny said. "So, with this nurse, Cullen—was there anything which made you interview him, anything suspicious or—"

"No no," Mary said. "We interviewed all the nurses on the unit."

"And are there any other memos we might have—anything which might be useful?"

"I wouldn't know about that," Mary said. "That would be a question for our house legal counsel, Paul Nittoly."

"All right, all right," Danny said. "We'll talk to him as well, I'm sure. And this nurse, um, Cullen—"

"Yes."

"You spoke to him."

"Well, as I said—we went through, conducted an interview with Mr. Cullen, like all the others," Mary said.

"This was in regards to one of the patient incidents—the Reverend?"

"Reverend Gall. Yes."

"And this nurse, Charles Cullen—he was the reverend's nurse?"

"Well, yes and no," Mary said. "They rotate."

"I'm sorry . . . ?"

"Rotate patients," Mary said. "The nurses get different room assignments each night they come in. Over the course of his care here at Somerset Medical Center, Reverend Gall was attended by many different CCU nurses."

"And Nurse Cullen was Gall's nurse?"

"No," Mary said. "Charles Cullen wasn't Reverend Gall's nurse on the night he expired."

"Okay, okay," Danny said. "So—who was?"

"I don't have that information handy," Lund said. "I'd have to get back to you with that."

"Yes, please. And that nurse, Gall's nurse, do you have a memo about that interview, or—"

"I'm afraid I don't have anything like that," Mary Lund said. "I'll have to look into it and get back to you."

"All right," Danny said. "I'd appreciate that." He wasn't getting anywhere, but knew better than to let his frustration show. "Another question, about this, um, 'pixies,' or…" Danny held up the memo, the word circled with a question mark.

"Pyxis, uh-huh," Mary said.

"Those are the medicine requests?"

"The Pyxis computer keeps track of each drug withdrawal," Mary said. "It also bills the patient and alerts the pharmacy when to restock."

"And you checked these records?"

"Yes," Mary said.

"And, says here there was nothing unusual, is that right?"

"Nothing out of the ordinary," Mary said.

"If I could, I'd like to get a photocopy of those records," Danny said. "Look at the periods surrounding the, uh, unusual occurrences with the patients—"

"Well, that's not possible, I'm afraid," Mary said. "Unfortunately, Pyxis only stores records for thirty days."

"So…"

"Yeah," Mary said. "I know."

"Okay," Danny said. "So this nurse wasn't the focus of your investigation then."

"No no no," Mary said. "We interviewed all the nurses on the unit. But there is one person you might want to look into."

———————

Danny gave Tim the rundown over lunch at the Thai place across from the courthouse. Tim watched the waitress come and go with the menus before he started in. "So, Lund," he said. "She setting us up or what?"

"She gave us a name," Danny said. "Name of Allatt, Edward."

"That the male nurse?"

"Another guy. He worked on the same floor as the vics sometimes, and had access. She thought we'd want to look at him."

"What's he do?" Tim said.

"He's one of those guys who comes and takes your blood..." Danny flicked down to his notes.

"Yeah, phlebotomist," Tim said, surprising himself.

"Oh, you know that one, right?"

"Hey, I was a hospital rent-a-cop," Tim said. "High school."

"Yeah, well, Lund said they like this phlebotomist guy."

"He a suspect?" Tim said. "I thought they didn't have anyone."

"Mary Lund told me, 'Allatt is one you'll want to look at.' What she said."

"She say why?"

"Guess this guy has a beef with the hospital. Local guy, some issue with the expansion plans, maybe union stuff."

"He a suspect?" Tim said.

"Just said he was suspicious, and had a beef," Danny said. He read from the notebook. "Her words: 'Allatt might be the one responsible for these unusual occurrences.'"

"Hey, okay, good," Tim said, writing it down. "They don't have anyone, then they give us somebody. I'll take it. Anything else?"

"Not yet," Danny said. "I asked her about the thing they sent, the nurse from the memo."

"Yeah, the leaflet they sent?"

"The investigation," Danny said. "All four pages of it." Danny flipped again, fingered the page. "The male nurse they talked to. Charles Cullen."

"What'd she say?"

"She told me about Allatt."

"What about Cullen?"

"Nothing," Danny said. "I guess he wasn't the focus of the investigation." Danny told Tim about the rest of the conversation, about the Pyxis machine, and how it only stored records for the previous thirty days. "Going back, that's what, September 7 or 8, right? So we can only look at the drug orders for Mr. Crews."

The only problem was, Crews's coroner's report had come back normal; according to Mambo, he had died of natural causes.[3]

"Okay, well, that sucks," Tim said. "How about the other nurses? We got anything for them?"

"The lawyer might," Danny said. "Lund didn't."

"She didn't have any of their interviews? They did interviews, I thought."

"She didn't have shit," Danny said.

Tim held his breath, let it go. "So what you're telling me," he said finally. "We got nothing."

"Well, no," Danny said. "We got Allatt."

32

It was Danny's case but as supervisor, Tim had co-lead, and he was particular about doing the standard-operating-procedure stuff himself. First he ran Edward Allatt's name through the state's motor vehicle system, checking for a registration and license. He found the guy and his car but no red flags, so he transcribed the address and personal info in his notebook before plugging the name into the National Crime Information Center database. *Edward Allatt* came back clean, no hits. Dead end. Tim tried again using alternate spellings and nicknames. Nothing. So the guy had a car and he had never been in jail. Next, Tim logged into the New Jersey Department of Justice's PROMIS/Gavel database, which followed the progress of criminal cases through the New Jersey court system. Tim had gotten some big hits like this—even if they'd never done time, bad guys tended to be mixed up with the court system one way or another, whether as witnesses or victims or acquitted of charges. But *Allatt*, *Alatt*, *Allat* came up clean. The phlebotomist was a dead end. Tim sat for a moment. A redball sat burning on his desk and he had nothing to chase. They'd set up an interview with this Allatt guy tonight, catch him at home, see him tomorrow. Meanwhile, Braun figured, what the hell. He flipped to a clean page in his notebook and typed "Charles Cullen" into the database.

Charles Cullen was in the Motor Vehicles database as the registrar of a baby blue Ford Escort station wagon and the possessor of a valid driver's license. NCIC came up with two hits for Cullen: once for criminal trespass in Palmer, Pennsylvania, another for drunk driving in South Carolina, both charges over ten years old. Cullen owned no firearms, had no registered pets, and hadn't been involved with so much as a speeding ticket for a decade.

There were still some loose threads to pull before he closed the book. Tim stood up from the terminal, walked back to his desk, and dialed 411 for the Palmer, Pennsylvania, police.

Tim identified himself as a Homicide detective from Somerset, New Jersey, and asked for the records bureau. The female voice on the other end laughed and told him, "Nope, we don't have one, just me!" Tim thought, *Oh great, Barney Fife,* and explained he needed background on a guy Palmer picked up in '93 and would she be so kind as to pull the case jacket.

"Just a sec," the lady said. Tim could hear the phone conk on the desk, the drum roll of big metal file cabinets opening and closing. A couple minutes, then she was back on the line, saying, "Uh-huh, it's here, a case jacket with a yellow Post-it."

She had one Charles Cullen. Date of birth February 22, 1960. Arrested in Palmer in March 1993 for trespassing and harassment, charges dropped. Braun had already started into his thank-yous when she said, "And oh, and there's a note." Something handwritten and underlined and—now what's this word?

————————

Danny followed up with a call to the Pennsylvania State Police, nodding at Tim while the state trooper, Robert Egan, tried the word a couple ways.

Digoxin.

This time, it was a word Braun recognized.

Digoxin had been found in the blood work of a patient who'd died of a suspected overdose at Easton Hospital six years ago. Apparently, this Charles Cullen had been working as a nurse at Easton at the time of the incident, and a couple years later there was an investigation, and the Pennsylvania State Police had pulled his file. That was it. The investigation had long since been abandoned, and the State Police had nothing else on Cullen, but Danny was so excited he wanted to run right through the wall. Instead, he just bounced his leg and thanked the trooper, keeping his voice cool until he got off the phone. Digoxin. What were the chances? Braun honestly had no idea what to say. Either this was one of the biggest coincidences in the history of homicide, or somebody was seriously fucking with them. But just who, and for what purpose, he didn't yet know.

33

Danny Baldwin's list had half a dozen places of employment for Charles Cullen, and that number was growing. All were medical centers located in New Jersey and northern Pennsylvania, and some dates overlapped—Danny had tried to work it up chronologically, but the info just wasn't there.[1] He and Tim sat in Tim's office, flipping through what was available, trying to make some order. As far as Danny could tell, Cullen's career started back in 1987 with Saint Barnabas Medical Center in Livingston, New Jersey.

"Saint Barnabas?" Tim said. "You've got to be shitting me." This guy's first nursing job just so happened to be at the same place Tim Braun had his first security job. Braun laughed it off, another coincidence in this case. "I'll take this one," Tim said, and grabbed his coat. Danny didn't mind. He had a case to run.

The drive from Somerville took him between the hills to a suburban main drag that had outgrown the houses lining it—front doors opened onto traffic, porches piled with dead toys. The money was all up on the hilltops, fake manor houses with yard signs advertising burglar alarms. The Saint Barnabas complex was built upon a rise, halfway between high and low. It was here, just past the old swim club, where Tim used to park for his shift. He felt a tingling numbness of recognition as he pulled into the lot. It had been decades since he had been here.

Tim had first worked at Saint Barnabas nights and week-ends during high school in the late '70s, commuting from his parent's home in a '63 Bel Air he called the Beer Wagon. After graduation he put what he'd saved into a brand new '78 Mustang, four-speed, midnight blue—a good car, but he beat the shit out of that, too, enjoying the present too much to think about much else. Tim enrolled that fall semester at Wesley College, and had started on a football career there, even being named Defensive Player of the Week after their game against Penn State, and receiving a personal congratu-lation from legendary coach Joe Paterno. But Wesley didn't stick. Tim enrolled in the academy and was wearing a real badge within a year. In between, he had the job at the hos-pital.

At Saint Barnabas, Tim was entry-level, but the rent-a-cop blues and iron-on badge conveyed instant authority, just like nurses' scrubs or a doctor's white coat. Tim was amazed to discover what a guy in a uniform could get away with.

The Saint Barnabas Tim had known was buried beneath nearly half a billion dollars of construction done in the past six years alone, floated on bonds risk-rated AAA, as safe as betting on death and taxes. He pulled the Crown Vic past the smudged guard booth where he had collected parking dollars and marveled at the unfamiliar building.

Units, annexes, and offices had been added. The facil-ity offered both an obesity treatment center and a twenty-four-hour McDonald's. The trip down memory lane was making Tim feel a little old, and maybe a little dizzy. He stopped to take stock at the new gazebo, a little oompah-pah

Disneyworld thing where off-duty nurses could smoke during break. It was the sort of cheerful place you might stop in for coffee if you didn't know better. And why not? Tim's son had been born at Saint Barnabas. And at some point beyond retirement. Tim would probably end up here too, tied to machines, watched by strangers in disposable green uniforms. Everyone ends up here, sooner or later.

The smokestack he remembered was still standing tall but no longer spewed smoke. And he could no longer locate exactly where the helipad had been. At that time Coast Guard divers flew to Saint Barnabas, with the largest hyperbaric chamber in the world and the state's only burn unit—Tim had felt proud every time, a kid saluting the military airmen. You could hear the Sea King before you saw it, a tractor trailer with wings. Behind the piped-in Muzak of the lobby's built-in ceiling speakers, Tim swore he could still hear those big blades churning, bringing burn victims by the load.

34

The idea was to take a look at Charles Cullen's old personnel files, hope to find something, anything, about the guy. It was a fishing expedition, blind information gathering, but that's how investigations work. He didn't figure there was much chance of a hospital spilling its guts to a homicide detective, not when their former employee was the suspect; call up the HR department, and next thing you know you'd be transferred to a lawyer. Anything a hospital didn't want Tim to see, that was exactly what he was looking for.

Tim had called in a favor, or tried to, looking for a back door. He'd asked a former cop who'd retired to Saint Barnabas security to pull files, whatever the medical center had on Charles Cullen, briefing the guy about the investigation in the process. Cop to cop was usually better than a subpoena, though Tim wasn't sure if the rule still applied when one of the cops was now making solid six figures for the corporation. The front desk had a manila envelope waiting with his name on it. Tim waited until he was back behind his desk with a coffee to flip through the twenty-two-page file, finding copies of Cullen's CPR license, W-4, and vaccination records. The rest consisted of fragments of medical charts with names blacked out, and handwritten reports on mimeographed Unusual Occurrence Forms. He read a few, squinting at the handwriting before picking up the stack and walking it down to Danny's office.

He flopped the file on Danny's desk. "You see these?"

Danny flipped through. "Huh."

"Yeah, huh," Tim said.

Danny got to the last page and started again at the beginning. "Write-ups, looks like."

"Well, yeah," Tim said. "Pieces of them, anyway. Who the hell does their filing?"

The file seemed oddly incomplete, fragmentary even—but then, it was something of a surprise that they had any records at all, over a decade later. The takeaway was that something had clearly gone down with Charles Cullen at Saint Barnabas Medical Center. But the file was short on the sort of details that make sense, or a criminal case.

It didn't look like much, even if they could read the handwriting and decipher the medical shorthand. The paperwork made no mention of the internal investigations[1] that had framed Cullen's final year at Saint Barnabas.[2] But within the photocopied scrawl were a half-dozen reports for when Charlie hadn't properly signed out a drug, withheld prescribed medication, hung an unprescribed IV, repeatedly shut down a critical patient's respiratory vents or written orders for unprescribed insulin.[3] Though they couldn't see it, and Saint Barnabas surely hadn't realized it, Charles Cullen had, in effect, been caught in the act, at the hospital where his killing career had started. But Cullen's write-ups were not sufficient to be reported as nurse-practice issues to the State Nursing Board or the Department of Health and Senior Services. Cullen had simply been cleaned from their system. A few years later the hospital underwent renovations, and the paperwork for the investigation, the evidence bags with tainted IVs, a couple file drawers' worth of notes—all that got cleaned out, too. Even the metal filing cabinet was removed. The only indication that a criminal investigation had ever existed was now a rust outline on linoleum.

———————

Danny Baldwin drove back out to Livingston the next morning. The HR department directed him upstairs to the office of Ms. Algretta Hatcher, the nurse recruiter for Medical Center Health Care Services, the wholly owned staffing agency for Saint Barnabas.[4] Hatcher didn't know Charles Cullen personally, but she could illuminate some of the nursing-practice issues. Several were serious; in a handwritten note dated March 14, 1991, one supervisor wrote about a "deep concern re: Charles' attitude toward making this dual medication error." She felt that Cullen was "not at all concerned re: the error, or the welfare of the patient."

Danny asked Hatcher to define "dual medication error"— did that mean giving a patient twice the amount of a drug as was prescribed?[5] Ms. Hatcher didn't know, and there was no further mention of it in the file. Danny had a skeleton, but no meat. Ms. Hatcher didn't know where the rest of the file had gone, but she guessed it had been destroyed. Danny didn't think Hatcher was lying; the paperwork was fifteen years old. But why save some pieces and not others?

According to the state records, Cullen had moved from Saint Barnabas to a job at Warren Hospital in Phillipsburg, New Jersey. Tim called the Warren HR secretary and left a message. The callback came later that afternoon from a senior Warren administrator. Warren Hospital could not locate Mr. Cullen's records. Tim promised them a subpoena and slammed the phone. An hour later, a Warren lawyer called back with the information that Charles Cullen's personnel file had been destroyed. Meanwhile, one office down, Danny was on the phone with Hunterdon Hospital, getting their HR and another dead end. Minutes later, Hunterdon confirmed it by fax.

"Hunterdon says they store the files with an archiving company," Danny said. "And the archiving company can't find Cullen's personnel file."

"No kidding," Tim said. He tossed his pen on his desk and leaned back in his chair. "So they destroyed it?"

"They can't find it, is what they say," Danny said. "Cullen's file is just lost."

"Lost," Tim said. "I know the feeling. What kind of happy horseshit is this?"

They had one more hospital on their New Jersey list: Morristown Memorial. Tim called, asking for background on a former employee; this time, he didn't mention anything about a homicide investigation, and Morristown didn't say they'd lost or destroyed Cullen's personnel file. He'd take the trip north to pick up the paperwork, then he and Danny would swing over to talk to the Somerset Medical Center lawyers.

————————

Somerset Medical Center's internal investigation was being handled by Paul Nittoly, one of the lawyers they'd met at the briefing. Nittoly's firm had been brought in by the Somerset Medical Center administration on September 19, nearly a month after the insulin incident with Patient 5, Francis Agoada, and nearly a week before Somerset reported that incident to the Department of Health.[6] Tim didn't know Nittoly, except that before hanging his shingle with the Drinker Biddle and Reath law firm, the guy had been an assistant prosecutor in Essex County. The Newark PO pedigree told him Nittoly was probably smart and a scrapper, familiar with what homicide detectives needed to make a case. The former AP had the potential to be their ace in the hole.

Nittoly met the detectives at his secretary's desk: mid-fifties, broad-featured, graying in that distinguished way money guys do, the good dark suit with an Easter-egg tie. Danny clocked the clothes down to the wingtips as Nittoly led them back to an office outfitted with the usual leather-bound tomes and introduced them to his private investigator, a hulking guy named Rocco E. Fushetto. Then Nittoly settled in behind a desk while Rocco stood to the side, arms tight across his chest.

Nittoly's notes, interviews, recordings, and contact master list for the CCU staff would represent a jump start on the investigation and keep the detectives from wasting their time covering old ground. Tim figured they'd have a heart-to-heart on the details of Somerset's five-month investigation, free of the medical mumbo jumbo. He figured he'd be lugging back whole file boxes of paper.

But as Tim Braun would later remember it,[7] Nittoly seemed determined to keep the meeting brief. He said that he and his private investigator had investigated the occurrences but had not identified the person responsible. They hadn't generated any final reports, Nittoly told them, and they had failed to reach any definite conclusions. As soon as they realized they had a police matter, they contacted the Prosecutor's Office.

"How about your interviews with the nurses, then?" Tim said. "Anything at all would be helpful."

"We didn't generate any type of report," Nittoly said.

"Do you have the tapes, or—"

Nittoly shook his head. "These were informal sessions," he said. "We didn't record anything."

"Okay, just anything," Tim said. "A legal pad, rough notes on the investigation, or—"

"We didn't take any notes," Nittoly said.

Tim blinked. "No notes." He and Danny exchanged a look.

"We didn't really write anything down," Nittoly said.

"How about names and contact info?" Danny said. "For the staff. You know, so we don't trample the same ground."

Nittoly looked over at Rocco. "Sorry. We've already given you everything we have. You got the package?"

"Yeah," Tim said. The four pages. They got it.

"About that memo," Danny said. "There's a nurse mentioned, a nurse Charles Cullen. You speak to him?"

"He was one of the nurses we interviewed on the unit," Nittoly said.

"Anything special, or—"

"Nothing comes to mind," Nittoly said. "I remember he was kind of a strange guy."

"An odd duck," Rocco said.

"Okay, okay," Tim said. "An odd duck."

"Yes."

"But you didn't write anything down when you talked to this nurse?"

"No," Nittoly said. "Sorry."

Tim was trying to keep it cool but his mind kept screaming the same question: *What kind of a lawyer doesn't write stuff down?* Tim thought about asking him. Then he thought about punching him. Then he thought about the parking lot. Nittoly started to turn the questions around, asked if the detectives had any leads yet, anything off background, but

Tim and Danny weren't playing. Five minutes later, they were done.

Tim waited until they were back on the highway before smacked the steering wheel. "Okay," he said. "Wanna tell me, what the fuck was that happy horseshit?"

"It's bullshit, what it is," Danny said. *Everything* ends up on paper in an investigation. Detectives knew that, lawyers—especially former prosecutors—knew that, too. There were printouts, records, memos, date books. You make lists, you make notes in interviews—at the very least, you've got names and phone numbers on a piece of paper, so you know who to talk to. A five-month investigation, six suspicious deaths, and a unit's worth of nurses, and the guy came out without so much as a doodle on a legal pad?

"And these are lawyers," Tim said. He was driving hard, flashing cars out of the fast lane. "What else are they good for, except making paper? How did they even do the billing?"

"Maybe they just don't wanna look stupid," Danny said. "Show a couple detectives how bad they fucked this thing up."

Tim could imagine it—Rocco, the private investigator, looking through those medical charts, probably making as little sense of it as they did. It was a nice picture, but it didn't change the facts.

They'd given them nothing but a memo and a name: Charles Cullen. An "odd duck," who wasn't a suspect. A guy with red flags in his past. Danny sat, watching the highway, wondering why they'd given them that, if they really didn't have anything else on the guy.

35

Danny took the morning, driving west to Pennsylvania to the Pennsylvania State Police barracks. He was briefed for several hours by Corporal Gerald Walsh and State Troopers Egan[1] and Bruchak, soaking up all he could about their investigation into Charles Cullen and the incidents at St. Luke's Medical Center. He was back on 78 East in time to meet Tim and talk it out over late lunch. They chose the diner this time, taking a booth in back where Danny could lay it out. The investigation in Pennsylvania was barely a year old, and it had been a whopper. They had bodies, physical evidence, dozens of cooperative witnesses, and a strong suspect—everything a homicide detective could want in a case, except a happy ending.

According to the Pennsylvania State Police file, it wasn't the St. Luke's administration that had called the cops, it was a St. Luke's nurse named Pat Medellin. She had seen some unusual deaths on her unit at St. Luke's, and she had also seen Charles Cullen marched out for diverting dangerous meds. Medellin felt certain that Cullen was responsible for the unusual deaths on the unit, and pressured the hospital administration to do something;[2] the St. Luke's hospital administration told Medellin that Cullen had not harmed any patients. Their investigation into the matter was closed.

Pat Medellin wasn't satisfied with that answer. On August 29, 2002,[3] Medellin stepped out and told her story to an acquaintance who worked as a cop with the Easton, Pennsylvania, Police Department.[4] It snowballed up the command from there: the cop told his captain, the captain pushed it to the coroner, the coroner carried it to the office of Lehigh County district attorney James B. Martin.[5] One by one, the Pennsylvania state troopers called the St. Luke's staffers to the carpet.[6] Their stories of death on the night shift were damningly consistent.

Many mirrored that of Nurse Lynn Tester,[7] who noticed that "people on the mend" had been dying, suddenly and strangely, and soon after Nurse Cullen changed their IVs.[8] Nurse Robin Saulsberry observed Charles Cullen sneaking from her patient's room shortly before her patient unexpectedly coded and died; Saulsberry later shivered when she recalled how Cullen had watched the unit's EKG monitor, too transfixed to even look away when he spoke. Saulsberry, who held a PhD in chemistry, strongly believed the patient had been given Pronestyl—the drug Cullen was discovered to have dumped from the med closet shelves.

She was certain more patients were coding and dying since Cullen had begun on the CCU. Nurse Tester calculated that while Cullen worked only 26 percent of the hours, he was somehow on hand for 58 percent of the deaths.[9] Another nurse[10] recalled that when Cullen worked the CCU, they'd average twenty to twenty-two Code Blues a month, but after Charlie left, they didn't have a code for six weeks.[11] Charged by the state, coroners Zachary Lysek and Scott Grim had gone to work on a caseload of medical charts. Privately, Lysek worried how many deaths Cullen might ultimately be responsible for; for all he knew, it might be fifty. Then again, it might be none. He had his suspicions, but speculation was useless, even dangerous, in such a situation. Certainty could only come from the science. To that end, the DA had hired an outside medical pathologist, Dr. Isidore Mihalakis—the same doctor involved in the investigation into Helen Dean's suspicious death at Warren Hospital years before. Dr. Mihalakis spent months reviewing the charts of seventeen patients that St. Luke's had selected, but found nothing prosecutable in the paperwork. Meanwhile, Charlie Cullen had moved on, with neutral references, to Somerset Medical Center.

Cullen's personnel file at St. Luke's presented a simple and unremarkable story of a nurse who resigned after being repeatedly reprimanded. "Charles resigned" was the way it was phrased in the Employee Change of Status Record. "Would not consider for rehire—medication issue." The words *vecronium bromide* or *vec* never appear, nor do the names of any of the other powerful drugs that Cullen had stashed and used. It was easy to understand that St. Luke's administrators did not have the sort of concrete evidence required to conclusively determine that their nurse had definitely and intentionally administered an overdose to a specific patient. At the same time Danny Baldwin and Tim Braun couldn't help but notice that whether by design or accident, St. Luke's Hospital had consistently dealt with the Cullen problem in a manner that created the fewest possible legal ramifications for themselves and the slightest possible paper trail for others.

———

Tim Braun and Danny Baldwin had worked hundreds of cases and seen as many variables on the means and motives of murder. None provided the slightest context for this. DA Martin's investigation was a shocking document, but it was the final page that surprised the detectives the most. Only five months before Braun and Baldwin started their investigation,[12] the Lehigh County DA had closed his. Eight months of work had been, from a prosecutorial standpoint, a waste of time and paper.[13]

Why would DA Martin drop the case against Cullen? The most obvious answer was that he didn't believe he could win it. Could he even prove he had a victim, much less that Cullen was to blame? Braun tried to imagine the next eight months: traveling the same road with fewer resources, no witnesses or evidence—and, somehow, reaching a different destination.

Danny had no choice but to start back in on the medical reports. Danny spread the files across a table in the conference room. Each of the six potential victims had a file, mostly scribbles and printouts tracing their progress, prescriptions, and decline. The medical Greek was starting to make some sense, thanks in part to hours spent flipping through a *Physician's Desk Reference* and the patience of Danny's OB/GYN wife, Dr. Kimberly Baldwin. But even clarified into laymen's terms, the charts and lab reports were little use. The hospital had already told them as much: the dig had somehow gotten into the patients, and it was apparently in their labs. But it wasn't in their charts. The smoking gun was nowhere on these pages. That was the whole point.

The dig might not be the smoking gun, but they were fairly sure it was Cullen's murder weapon. It was useful to think of the dig in a syringe, loaded and pointed at someone. Picturing the weapon like a gun made this medical murder stuff less abstract.

Like any other weapon, the dig had to come from somewhere. The most obvious source was the medical cash register machine—the Pyxis drug dispenser on the CCU floor. The record of that withdrawal should have been recorded in the Pyxis records. But here, the detectives had another dead end; Mary Lund had already told them Gall's death was over thirty days old, so those records didn't exist anymore.

"But somebody saw them," Danny said.

"What do you mean?"

"The Pyxis records. When Gall died, they knew he was a digoxin OD, right? They must have looked at his Pyxis. For when they called in the lawyer, talked to Cullen."

"This is from the pages we got, what Fleming faxed Mary Lund."

"Right," Danny said. "The interview." Danny squared the paper to Tim and fingered the sentence:

" 'Mr. Cullen was aware that requesting medication from the pharmacy would show up on the Pixis [*sic*] computer including cancellations.' "

"Yeah, what the fuck is that about?"

"Dunno," Danny said. "But they're looking at the Pyxis." That interview with Cullen was July 14. It was within Lund's thirty-day Pyxis window.

"So the lawyer and Lund had access to his Pyxis report," Tim said. "They'd seen his drug pulls from the night Gall died?"

"That's how I read it," Danny said. That would make sense. They would have been looking for the smoking gun, too—maybe Cullen ordering huge amounts of dig, or for suspicious patterns in his activity. And for whatever reason, they were focused on his canceled orders, too. So where were those Pyxis pages now?

"Their investigation was ongoing until the day they called us," Tim said. "You'd think they'd have a file."

"Yeah, well, " Danny said. They'd been down that road. "Maybe they just looked them up on the computer, never made a printout."

"Yeah, maybe," Tim said. It sounded like bullshit to him, but so many things did in this case. As far as they were told, Cullen wasn't a suspect, the paperwork never existed, and, apparently, the Pyxis showed nothing interesting anyway. He read the words again, out loud. " 'There was nothing so overtly suspicious...that would necessitate a call to the authorities.' "

"Meaning, there was no reason to call the cops." Danny said. "It's like they were thinking about it five months ago, asking and answering the question."

Tim was finding this investigation uncomfortably familiar. Homicides and hospitals and suspects they couldn't figure a way to touch—the connections between this redball and the Duryea case would catch him in the shower or the car, conjuring the cold-case file box stuffed in his closet, and a feeling he didn't want to name. The Duryea case had stung him, sent him scurrying toward the refuges of apathy and retirement, but it was hard to be indifferent when the clock was ticking. Increasingly, Tim was convinced it continued to tick every night that Cullen returned to work. It was ticking now.

———

That afternoon, Danny Baldwin paid a visit to Mary Lund. He told her that their nurse Charles Cullen had a criminal record and a checkered work history, which included several hospitals that had fired him for nursing-practice issues, and that Charles Cullen was, at this point, a strong person of interest to the Somerset County Prosecutor's Office. Danny needed the hospital's mortality rate on Cullen's wards, and he needed Cullen's work schedule for that year, too. He knew a request like that would tell the hospital who they were looking at, but they had no choice. There was no access to the hospital except through the front door.

Lund assured Danny that the hospital would take measures to closely monitor Cullen while on shift. But Danny knew watching this guy wasn't going to be enough. If their investigation was going to catch Cullen, they'd need to come up with something no previous investigation ever had.

———————

Charlie had figured out months before that he was going to have to abandon some of the ways in which he usually got his drugs. He knew it even before the meeting with Fleming on July 14. He didn't need a corporate lawyer to spell it out for him.

He had been a nurse for fifteen years. He had seen the Pyxis arrive and he'd seen it change. Now digoxin would be treated with the same security protocols previously reserved for narcotics like OxyContin or morphine. They'd already taken those precautions with insulin. His actions were subtle, his effects public. That affirmed him. That pleased him.

One of those effects was the investigation. Charlie had been through several, and they were each, in a way, affirming. The process rolled out as a slow-motion game of hide-and-seek. Charlie found that the lawyers told you where they were going to look. And then, eventually—*Boo!*—they looked there. End of game.

He was aware that Reverend Gall's death had thrown up red flags. Obviously the man was important, a reverend, and the consequences would outlive him. Somewhere, surely, a whole congregation was swaying like wheat before the wind. They'd been noticing his canceled drug orders on the Pyxis as well. So Charlie decided: no more canceled dig orders for him. In fact, no more dig orders. He would never order dig at Somerset again, even if he had a patient for whom it was required. Another way to show them. To ride one-handed.

He'd played this game before. He adapted quickly. In fact, only the day before his chat with the lawyer Charlie had used dobutamine and it worked fine.[14]

Charlie had discovered long ago that when you change the contents of the IV bag, you change the man—simply cause and effect, with Charlie starring as the cause. There was no reason for him to stop.

36

Their grunt work had yielded red flags in a half dozen counties, a strong person of interest in Charles Cullen, and a growing mountain of paperwork. In squad meeting that day, Tim filled in the larger Somerset County Prosecutor's Office team on Danny's investigation, one that had already flooded beyond the tidy bounds of Somerset Medical Center and was expanding rapidly across hospitals and state lines. And yet they had no hard evidence, and no case. In order to make one, they'd have to sort through every piece of information they could gather in every jurisdiction, and hope to piece together a pattern. Tim told his prosecutor that the fastest way to do that was to form a task force.

Tim outlined his thinking for Prosecutor Wayne Forrest, starting with the limitations of the Somerset County Prosecutor's Office. The SCPO had never before taken on an investigation of this scope, and they weren't outfitted for it. This redball was a type of investigation nobody in the office had any experience with; added to their usual nine-to-five police work, it threatened to overwhelm their tiny office and jeopardize the case. A task force would allow Tim and the SCPO to piggyback on other counties' manpower and resources, including a hot new piece of FBI software called Rapid Start, which consolidated a sprawling pool of data into one searchable database. Tim heard Prosecutor Michael Rubinaccio's office had it over in neighboring Morris County, as well as a girl who was whiz-bang with it. For gathering and connecting dots, a bigger team and better software seemed infinitely more efficient than flipping through notebooks in a conference room. But it also meant opening up their investigation to join forces with detectives from other counties, in other prosecutors' jurisdictions. It meant giving up solo possession of the redball.

Forrest wasn't interested. In fact, to Tim he seemed angry at the suggestion. Tim followed Forrest to his office after the meeting broke up, but the fifteen minutes spent making this point behind his boss's closed office door got him nowhere. This was their case, Danny was the lead, it was Forrest's call. They weren't sharing it, period.

That afternoon, Somerset County detectives Douglas Brownlie, Nick Magos, Stuart Buckman, and Edward Percell all filed into the twenty-four-hour diner behind Danny and Tim, six armed guys in crew cuts and ties eyeing the rotating pie case. They took the usual table in the back. This was as close as they were going to get to a task force.

Brownlie and Magos could keep chasing down details at the hospitals. They could start the paper on the subpoenas, working with Assistant Prosecutor Tim Van Hise on pulling personnel files and old investigations and whatever else they could find. Buckman and Percell would help with still more loose ends, pulling the bulk of Cullen's family-court file over at Warren County, chasing nursing records from two states, doing legwork canvassing Cullen's coworkers. Meanwhile, Tim and Danny would stay focused on the case at Somerset.

The problem was, whatever happened to the Somerset Medical Center patients was apparently locked up in the mysteries of medicine, and Tim and Danny didn't have a clue about that stuff. Somerset Medical Center was full of experts, but their five-month internal investigation had yielded exactly four pieces of paper and no answers. They knew that the patients had been poisoned, with drugs; but Mary Lund couldn't offer any drug records from the Pyxis, Paul Nittoly couldn't offer any interviews or background, and nobody seemed to have any physical evidence. They were running out of places to even investigate.

As for the victims—right now, they still didn't even have one, not technically. The ODs at Somerset weren't confirmed homicides; they were "incidents" and "unexplained medical occurrences," only potentially related to a bunch of screwy numbers on some lab reports that any defense lawyer who'd ever won a drunk driving case could easily dispute. All they had was Charles Cullen. The evidence that Charles Cullen was involved with incidents at other hospitals was circumstantial at best. They had no evidence against him at Somerset. All their background research pulled up were approaches that had failed. They needed another source, and some paperwork that mattered.

———

During their initial briefing from the Somerset Medical Center administrators, Dr. Cors had told them that in addition to calling in the police, they'd also notified the appropriate state medical departments. Danny put in a call to the New Jersey Department of Health and Senior Services, what everyone else called the New Jersey Department of Health, or DOH.[1] His calls bounced between DOH Investigator Edward Harbet, Investigator Kathey Demarkey, and Assistant Director Alma Clark, but didn't yield anything beyond confirmation that the DOH investigation had uncovered some issues at Somerset. Danny thought it logical to join forces and share information with the state agency. But the DOH rep couldn't provide any further information without a subpoena, which would take time.[2] Meanwhile, the DOH investigation had been turned over to something called the Center for Medicare/Medicaid and Social Service. That sounded to Danny like some sort of licensing issue rather than anything homicide related.

There had to be a way to go over the heads of the DOH. Danny dug back through his original notebook, flipped to page one. "Okay, so, Cors said Somerset had alerted the DOH about these incidents. Blah blah—here. He says they also called the State Nursing Board."

"We've got a call already in," Tim said. "Same issues as the DOH."

"And he also said, 'The New Jersey Department of Poison Control was also involved in this matter.' "

"Okay," Tim said. "They reported the same shit there. When was that?"

"Don't know," Danny said. He was sick of burning days leaving messages, nobody calling back. "Why don't we go find out?"

———

The New Jersey Department of Poison Control was only a few months away from moving out of Newark. Until then, the center's old offices were locked deep within a monolithic institutional building with endless corridors and the haunted smell of a damp library. The main entrance was chained off; broken furniture and rolls of gum-stained carpets littered the halls. Poison Control seemed to be the last tenants left in the building.

Exactly what Tim and Danny expected to find here, they

couldn't say. All they knew was that Somerset Medical Center had contacted the poison experts in relation to the ODs. Tim imagined a laboratory full of bubbling beakers. He hoped that the guys in white coats would be as useful as ballistic experts were in normal homicide cases—maybe they could even trace the poison, if Tim could get a sample.

They found Dr. Marcus up a flight of stairs and at the end of a linoleum hall. There was no lab, none of the Frankenstein stuff the detectives were expecting, only an open door and an office piled with books and papers, the usual desktop golf novelties doctors always seem to get, plus a collection of poison-related knickknacks, stuffed rattlesnakes, and some sort of tribal art. Tim had seen places that looked better after police had turned over a house during a search warrant.

Steven Marcus, Poison Control's white-haired sixty-something director, had a reputation in the toxicology field for both his extensive experience and direct manner, and was considered either a troublemaker or a straight shooter, depending on which side of the argument you were on. Marcus spotted the two hulking men in mustaches and suits lurking by his door, and marked them instantly as detectives. Tim introduced them as being from Somerset County. Marcus began shuffling the piles around his desk into a white squall of paper, finally revealing a short stack of cassette tapes and a portable recorder. "You're late!" he said. "I was expecting you five months ago."

———————

Danny hit Rewind, hit Play, settled back on his perch on Tim's office radiator to listen to the scribble of tape head hitting dial tone.

Surreptitious calls were the best. Better than wires. Without visual clues, blind to the subtle semaphore of gesture and expression, phone callers were forced into articulate communication. You want people to tell the truth, Danny found, it was best not to give them a chance to lie—break down the door, serve the search warrant in the shower, catch them cold. Tapes and wires were even easier, and often more revealing.

The Marcus tapes presented a very different picture of Somerset Medical Center's unexplained incidents and internal investigation than the one presented to Tim and Danny. SMC administrators had never mentioned their interaction with Poison Control, or the results of their calculations. Or the fact that they'd been instructed by NJPC to call the police nearly four months ago. And they certainly hadn't mentioned that it had all been on tape.

God forgive them, Danny thought, for anything that happened in between, because he sure wouldn't.

37

Danny watched the spinning cogs of the tape, hearing the familiar female voice[1] of Mary Lund introducing herself over the phone to NJPC pharmacist Bruce Ruck. He heard Marcus get loud with Dr. Cors and Lund, telling them he was alerting the DOH. Telling them the evidence suggested that someone was poisoning their patients, telling them they had a police matter.

"So it was Marcus, not Somerset, who first got in touch with the DOH," Danny said. "Somerset said they weren't going to go to anybody until they'd done their own investigation." Danny had to assume that was the reason nobody at SMC ever mentioned the conversations.

"You know, those are the guys we should be going after." Tim stabbed the tape recorder with his pen. "Those assholes right there."

At the squad meeting that afternoon, Tim had an important new directive for the detectives working the Somerset Medical Center case. From now on, whenever dealing with Somerset, or any of the hospitals they contacted, the information flow was to be strictly a one-way street. "We take information, but we don't give them shit," Tim said. "Play dumb if you have to, whatever it takes, but do not share what we have, or where we're going—period." Tim had no idea what Somerset knew or didn't know, only that he couldn't trust them. After all the runarounds, Tim figured that telling the suits what he was looking for was the surest way never to find it.

"What kills me, this guy is working, right now," Tim told Danny afterward. Sixteen years and nine different hospitals, but always the same pattern.

"If that's going to change, we're going to have to start leaning harder on the hospitals."

"That," said Danny, "and start pulling bodies out of the ground."

———————

The case needed a definite homicide victim. First Danny made the trip to the Norfolk Street office of Dr. Mambo, the regional medical examiner. They handed the ME copies of the medical paperwork Somerset had forwarded from their six unexplained incidents. Mambo consulted with Dr. Jackson from the State Toxicology Lab. Of the six, they both liked Gall best. His outrageously high dig levels were the most likely to constitute a smoking gun. But the SCPO couldn't build a case on paperwork alone.

They'd need to check Gall's fluids themselves. Luckily, Gall was what homicide detectives call a "fresh kill."[2] His body was the closest thing they would ever have to a crime scene.

Danny called down to Tim Van Hise, to help him nail the legal language for the sworn affidavit, then walked the paperwork to the Superior Court judge's chambers so the Hon. Roger Mahon might put his name on it. Danny asked His Honor if he would also be willing to put the whole thing—both order and affidavit—under seal. If this were going to work, he needed to keep it as quiet as possible.

38

Danny had been required to deliver hundreds of notifications to murder victims throughout his career, and he'd hated every one. The first time Danny told a mother that her son had been killed over a pair of sneakers he cried more than she did. Nobody wanted to hear that their loved one was dead, that was bad enough. The word *murder* only amplified the hurt. It was one piece of the job he never looked forward to, but over the years he'd gotten used to it, gotten good at it even. His visit to Lucille Gall was something new.

Danny had to be careful—he didn't want to just walk in and blurt it out all at once. Or to give her the case from the perspective of a homicide detective. Mrs. Gall was a nurse, so she would understand the lingo, but it was still important to lay it out slowly, allowing her the opportunity to absorb the background before he hit her with the specific bad news, and the request. Danny ran through the scenario, reminding himself, *Break it into small pieces. Tell it straight and steady, without hedging or flinching. And, no matter what, make sure the woman is sitting down.*

The address in Danny's notebook was for an older development within a manicured suburb, older residents, not renters but owners, Halloween decorations whittled down to a single long-stemmed deli pumpkin, uncarved, no muss. Danny parked the unmarked car on the street, avoiding the driveway, glad to have arrived in daylight. He had this part planned. First, he climbed out of the car and stopped, taking a moment to smooth his tie, gathering himself in full view of every window on the street. Then he pulled the badge from his inside pocket and held it, shield out, in his right hand, and placed the business card between the fingers of his left as he slowly walked toward the Gall home. He always went through this routine, especially when he was responding by himself. Being African-American, it didn't matter that he'd just stepped out of a new cop car in a $500 suit. One unit he worked, the homeowner saw him and called the police on the police.

Danny could feel the eyes on him through the window. The woman who answered the door was white, thin, and what the young detective[1] read vaguely as "older," with short blonde hair.

They stepped inside a neat living room filled with dusted wooden furniture and Old World touches, a look Danny thought of as "Catholic." He took a moment, remembering to breathe, to go slow, and to tell it straight. He started at the beginning, once Lucille was sitting down.

Lucille's initial reaction was shock. Her jaw physically dropped, as if the idea was expanding so rapidly that her mouth unhinged like a snake eating a rabbit. She was devastated. Then she got angry.

Accepting her brother's death had been difficult, particularly after investing so much energy and prayer in keeping him alive. Her reverend brother had asked her to keep a constant vigil during his hospital stay, and she had, staying dutifully at his bedside sometimes twelve hours a day.

When Reverend Gall was first hospitalized, Lucille had made peace with the possibility of her brother's imminent death, and placed him on Do Not Resuscitate status. If medicine could not help him and God did not, at least she could spare him the indignity of lingering. But her brother did get better. By the end of his first week at Somerset, Gall had stabilized enough that Lucille rescinded his DNR order. Once again, she had reason to hope. She had still more hope as she left his bedside at 9 p.m. on the evening of June 27. But then just before dawn on June 28, Gall had suddenly crashed. And so after the tears, Lucille was required to make a new peace, reminding herself that this was God's plan, God's hand, and not hers to question. That was what her brother would have preached in Sunday Mass—God calls, you answer. But now that peace was shattered, and Lucille Gall was livid.

Hospital lab tests had found elevated levels of the drug digoxin in her brother's blood. Danny started to explain what that meant, but Lucille stopped him—she knew dig; she was an RN and a former hospital risk manager and had worked with dig for decades. She understood exactly what Danny was saying. It wasn't God Who had called.

"Someone killed him," Lucille said.

Danny had numbers for her. Lucille immediately recognized that those dig levels demanded an autopsy.[2] But Somerset had not autopsied Reverend Gall. They had recorded his passing as "a natural death." Lucille's rage was logical and inquisitive, and moved forward along the same path Danny and Tim had walked for weeks. She had been there day after day, 9 a.m. to 9 p.m. She was known to the staff, both as a family member and a fellow professional. At the very least, she should have been notified as a professional courtesy. Lucille would have understood exactly what the high dig levels meant. And she would have demanded an autopsy. Was that why they didn't tell her?

Danny decided that, in terms of winning Lucille Gall as an ally to the investigation, pissed off wasn't such a bad place for her to be.

"Your reverend brother spent his life in the service of God, helping others," Danny said. "And he can still help people, even now."

Lucille was watching him now.

"We need his help," Danny told her. "We need *your* help."

Danny said that with Lucille's signed permission, they could stop her brother's murderer from killing anyone else. But Danny was wrong.

39

October 21, 2003

Ed Zizik was six years into his retirement as an electrical engineer for Automatic Switch in Edison, and he still hadn't grasped the allure of idle time. His volunteer job at Somerset Medical Center gave his days structure and meaning, and his wife of half a century appreciated that it got him out of the house.

Zizik was a cheery and familiar man, always nattily dressed for his job at the gift shop register or manning the information desk, and he'd become a popular character at Somerset. When the ambulance arrived at the Zizik house on October 16, there was no question which hospital he'd go to.

Charlie only had two patients that night, and he shot up both with 8 mgs of Xanax. Mr. Zizik received his at 8:30 and was calm throughout the night. Charlie tended the lines, studied the telemetry, and, sometime after midnight, set about his ritual task of stripping the unconscious Mr. Zizik for a sponge bath before starting with the Keri lotion. Together, he and Amy made quick work of it. It was a good shift, if uneventful.

The next day Charlie was assigned to different patients,

for whom he logged only one drug request. He returned home at daybreak to find Cathy in her bathrobe, angrily clearing her kids' breakfast dishes. Their time in the apartment together was filled with argument, walking now familiar battle lines, Cathy wanting Charlie to move out, Charlie not refusing, but not packing either. Work was his only true home.

Charlie was already in the nurses' station when Amy Loughren arrived, but he barely acknowledged her. She had seen this version of her friend, his mood screwed down, his mouth like a paper cut, and she knew not to take it personally. Amy tended to her patients, occasionally spotting Charlie with the Cerner cart and stationed in the doorjamb of his patient's room like a dog jealously guarding a bone. He was bent to the Cerner all night, typing, scanning, a Rachmaninoff on the keyboard. He would leave his post only to approach the nurses' station to pull drugs from the Pyxis, and he did that only when the station was empty. He was back and forth all shift; that night, Charlie withdrew perhaps forty times more drugs than any other nurse on the unit. Rather than bunching his orders, Charlie made a separate entry for each. These drug orders would make little sense to a knowledgeable nurse.

The administration had been watching his Pyxis entries all summer—but were they watching now? Charlie assumed they were. He felt his Pyxis orders were an open letter, addressed chiefly to himself, but available to anyone who cared to look.

Part of the game lay in Charlie's habit of using the Pyxis machine to order staples more easily accessed from the supply closet. He was the only nurse who would take the time to enter his passcode and the patient's name to request hydrogen peroxide or aspirin or ointment. He did it just to see the big drawer swing open. That night, he ordered all of those things, each requiring a separate and laborious entry, each opening one or another drug drawer. He ordered heparin, then thought about it—were they watching heparin? The lawyer had talked to him about canceling dig. He hit Cancel for the heparin. It was a new trick, one of many.

Twenty seconds after the heparin, he ordered more ointment. Another twenty seconds and he ordered the ointment again. Then he ordered Tylenol, acetaminophen. Then potassium chloride. Furosemide. Two more Tylenol. A few seconds later, two more Tylenol.

He drove home, parking, sleeping, not sleeping, Three Stooges, History Channel, another fight with Cathy, and then back in the little Ford, still thinking, still curious, and ordering, right away, Tylenol. It was a new night, but still the same night in his head. The whiteboard listed different patients, but he had the same patients in mind. He made as many trips as possible. He ordered nitroglycerine, then, eight minutes later, more nitroglycerine. Then nitroprusside, but just two units—and two units of nitroprusside didn't even constitute a full dose—every nurse knew that.

Metoprolol, ondansetron, Xanax, potassium chloride, magnesium sulfate, metoprolol, metoprolol and nitroprusside again, one dose. The sun came and went and Charlie on shift with it, back on the unit, doing the same. The next night, the same. The next night also.

Charlie's Pyxis records for the night of October 20 said he pulled furosemide, furosemide, insulin, Tylenol, hydrogen peroxide, propofol, propofol, heparin, heparin, ointment, haloperidol, magnesium sulfate, ointment, heparin, insulin, norepinephrine, dobutamine, heparin, dobutamine. The charts said Mr. Zizik's heart stopped on October 21st at approximately 2:30 a.m. from an overdose of digoxin. But dig appeared nowhere on Mr. Zizik's chart. Nor was it in Charlie's Pyxis.

40

On October 27, Danny drove up to Newark with the first assistant prosecutor, Robert Lang, and Assistant Prosecutor Tim Van Hise. The meet was at Saint Michael's Hospital—Danny's call. He needed an outside medical authority to read the charts on Somerset's six suspicious lab values, and he wanted someone other than Somerset to do it.

The group from the Somerset County Prosecutor's Office was met in the lobby by Paul Nittoly and his private detective, Rocco. Danny gave a cool hello and made introductions. He didn't say anything more until he got his results.

Dr. Leon Smith was Saint Michael's chief of medicine. He had reviewed the charts of all six patients Somerset had presented to the detectives, and didn't find them quite as "unexplained" as Somerset had. Dr. Smith presented the group with a very different interpretation of the charts than the one Dr. Cors and Nittoly had first handed to the detectives back on October 7.

Dr. Smith had focused on the four most abnormal and suspicious patient lab values;[1] these were, as it happened, the only four that had occurred more than thirty days before the detectives were called, and whose Pyxis records were thus apparently unavailable.[2] Dr. Smith could not offer any medical explanations for what had happened to the four patients. It was his professional medical opinion that all four appeared to have been given an overdose by an outside source.

Paul Nittoly turned to Danny for a reaction, but Danny had already cut from his group and was out the door, running through the rain to his car.

———

Tim drove past the courthouse, classic rock on his radio, windshield wipers beating against a cold October rain. On either side of the road the houses with yards worth raking had leaves gathered into those happy-colored recycling bags for the chipper, some orange and decorated with jack-o'-lantern faces so you could keep them as a display. Front yards sported fake cemeteries, machine-made cobweb spun over talking tombstones from the CVS. Twenty minutes later, he turned off the interstate, stuck doing twenty miles an hour behind an Accord with a joke rubber leg bobbing from the trunk as he crossed Woodbridge Township to Perth Amboy, where Florida Grove Road turned off toward the Holy Trinity Cemetery.

Danny was waiting for him under an oversized umbrella, watching a backhoe manned by workers in yellow rubber suits. The guys were on time. Tim had called the Gustav Novak Funeral Home the day before, gotten the number of the outfit they usually used in the Trinity Cemetery, and told them to be there at noon. He'd warned them, "This time, you've gotta take someone out instead of putting them in," expecting a reaction, but finding that, pretty much, it was all the same to the grave diggers.

The guy on the backhoe was pretty good, working the hydraulic joysticks on the big machine without crushing anything with the bucket. A few digs and dumps and he was done. Another worker crawled into the hole, taking a hand-hold on the grave stone and lowering himself down before pulling in the shovel. Tim and Danny watched the guy gopher out a few shovelfuls before the spade hit concrete, the hard, hollow sound reflexively triggering the thought of pirate-movie treasure. An hour later the digger had the vault exposed at the bottom of a neat, rectangular hole, the dimensions having been figured just right to allow the guy to work a chain around the vault sides. All the newer graves had one; concrete didn't break down or crush like a coffin might under the pounds of dirt piled up, the reason older cemeteries were often too uneven to mow. The men set up another tripod, this one maybe ten feet tall, and centered on the casket. Then they fitted it with a block and tackle and hand-cranked the whole vault, a thing which must have weighed seven hundred pounds easy, up out of the ground like a septic-system version of King Tut's tomb. The wood still looked new, the brass still polished as the coffin was loaded into the back of a Chevy Suburban and driven back to the turnpike and the regional medical examiner's office.

Danny met the casket at Mambo's office, accompanied by one of the young detective sergeants in the unit, Brian Hoey. As it happened, Gall had been Hoey's pastor. Hoey was there to testify, before God and the regional ME, that the body was his priest, or had been. Danny handed Brian a camera and some extra film while the Medical Examiner popped the casket lock and recorded the contents.

1. One black Bible.
2. One pair of gray glasses.
3. One white pillow with ribbons and flowers.
4. One pair of black shoes.

5. One religious robe, tan.
6. One pair of black pants.
7. One white religious robe.
8. One pair of black dress socks.
9. One tan religious scarf.
10. One black belt.
11. One black shirt.
12. Three color photographs.
13. One white neck-collar.
14. One DNA card.
15. One set of fingerprints.

Mambo was fastidious and professional. He wasted little movement as he changed gloves and moved back to the recorder, describing the body as he found it: The exhumed and embalmed remains of a 69-inch, 155-pound, well-nourished and slightly thin white male, appearance consistent with the stated age of sixty-eight.

The man's scalp was bald, and his forehead was unremarkable. The conjunctivae of the eyeballs and eyelids were pale, the irises were light gray, the pupils equal, round, and of intermediate size. His face was undamaged by the excavation. A light green mold covered Gall's lower nose and most of the cheeks. Nothing was coming out of the body's ears.

Mambo removed the religious garments, finding a tracheostomy opening filled with gel. Three roughly sutured incisions on the right upper chest were covered in thick glops of white granular gel—the result of the embalming, as were the white plastic trocar buttons dotting his abdomen. Moving down the chest he found more mold, greenish-gray to black. No mold on the arms, plenty on the fingers, thick furry colonies between the webbing, black, then green, ending at the knees like furry short pants. The molds on the shins were yellowish, the feet were covered in mold as thick as slippers. The name tag on the toe was marked Somerville Medical Center. Mambo wrote it down, and prepared to go inside.

Following the Y-shaped thoracoabdominal incision, Mambo worked along the trachea into the lungs—dark red, firm, and filled with a granular embalming gel. The reverend's heart weighed out at 660 grams and showed signs of wear and repair. Mambo then set to work collecting samples for the toxicologist. He scooped gel from the right neck, gauze from a bedsore on the sacrum, and mold from the body, placing each sample carefully in a small labeled tube. He clipped samples from the nails of each hand and removed the whole nail from the left big toe, siphoned up fluid from the abdomen and spleen, clipped body hair and small sections of the lungs and kidneys, the liver and small bowel, both testes, a rib, the diaphragm, the spleen, brain, spine, and heart. Mambo bagged the contents of the reverend's stomach, pulled a syringe of viscous fluid from Gall's eye, and, dust to dust, filled a small tube with soil from the grave itself.[3] Mambo's night was over. But over in Somerset, the night shift was just getting started.

41

The night before Halloween, Charlie was heading for work at the hour most everyone else headed home. He steered through the working-class suburb along with other cars like his own, late-model compacts with hummingbird engines and bumper-sticker personalities, tailgating one then another as they merged into the stream, Honor Student, Earth Mother, Marine, together but separate, each alone along the river of tar. He had been this alone all his life, never understood, always judged by the bumper sticker and hood ornament of first meetings until he had found another way to get what he needed from the wasteland. The drive was deadening, just car wash and dead Chinese takeout, dead auto parts store, dead tan center. Signage had been stripped to individual letters and eyebolts, frames hanging naked as gibbets. Price Choice, Child Care, Nail One. Stonewashed men in cigarette-brand hats crossed the empty tar expanses from Quik-Mart to Quik-Mart, men without professions or uniforms, men unlike Charlie. In the empty lots, quick weedy growth, fibrous sappers woody as fingernails.

With the highway, the pace quickened, sudden and clean. I-78 comes with the exit, a chute of traffic fast in four lanes and forty minutes through real farms, gentle hills, and flaming forest, surprisingly rural as Charlie crossed the line back to New Jersey, tootling through suburban streets, more upscale than his Bethlehem neighbors, split-level Mod Colonials with attached garages, faux shutters affixed neatly to picture windows, front doors with American eagle knockers, expensive seasonal facades of decorative cornstalks and gourds of surprising size and rustic array. The quality of the surroundings, a town you'd call "nice," seemed a positive reflection upon him personally. Charlie crossed the Somerville town line into the signifiers of status that marked his professional station, the prestige houses and prestige cars, un-rusted Nissans and Subarus—and suddenly the police car, *wow-wow*ing him with its siren.

The officer was nice enough, but Charlie was miffed. The officer told Charlie he was impounding the car. Charlie felt he was persecuted—but he always thought that when he was pulled over. This time, however, he was right. He *was* being persecuted.

Charlie argued. The impound was supposedly for parking tickets, still unpaid from when Charlie lived in Phillipsburg. But, Charlie complained, he didn't have any outstanding tickets, none that he knew of—in fact, the Phillipsburg house had a driveway. What tickets could he possibly have? It was unfair, and he was ready to throw a tantrum. Except, surprisingly, the officer actually listened to him. He called him "sir" and seemed to mean it. He promised to have the whole thing cleared by that afternoon.

In the meantime, Charlie would be driven to work in the police car, a late-model Ford still shining with paint and wax. He slid into the warm cave of hard leather seats and official purpose and found himself, despite everything, enjoying the experience. And when a few hours later, Charlie received a call telling him that he was entirely correct, a mistake apparently, just as Charlie had said, just so, and as recompense the officer would deliver the car right to the hospital—well, it was just the sort of story he could tell Amy, when they next worked together. It was a perfect illustration of how his misunderstood correctness manifested in the circumstances of his crazy life.

The shift itself was unremarkable, boring even. Charlie occupied himself with his patients and their charts, their soaping, grooming, and lubrication, allowing his mind to wander back to the story, imagining how Amy would think of him then, and how she'd laugh. His night was nearly over when he got the message to come to the office.

"Terminated" was the word they used. In Charlie's experience, they never said "fired."

42

Amy was home raking leaves on her day off when her friend Donna called and broke the news about Charlie. Her first reaction was to cry, but then she got angry. Then, sometime during her four-hour commute to the Somerset Medical night shift, Amy fell apart again, and she had to sit in the parking garage and fix her face in the rearview mirror.

Charlie had been fired. *Her* Charlie. The nursing station suddenly seemed so dull. Over the long nights she'd heard so many stories from his life, how he'd always been a target for bullying and bad luck, how he'd been pushed from hospital to hospital because of his depression. She had tried to shelter him, standing up to the residents when they lambasted him for using the wrong drug. Once, she'd even taken the fall for him, claiming that she'd been the one who'd administered it. But she had failed him. Charlie was in the wind again, cast out from another job, and on the same week he had learned that his girlfriend, Cathy, was pregnant. He was such a sensitive soul, Amy could only imagine the hell Charlie was going through now, and so the tears came again, right there on the ward. Amy asked one of the other nurses to cover for her while she huddled at the corner phone of the nurse's station, reaching Charlie at home.

"Sweety, honey—hey, what's going on?"

Charlie's speech was halting. "I don't know, if you know, this whole issue," he said. "Of why I got terminated." Charlie explained that he been sat down just before the end of his shift by someone from Somerset HR. They'd fired him for "inaccuracies on his application," referring to the dates of his previous employment at St. Luke's Hospital. "They were approximate, you know," Charlie said. After sixteen years of nursing, he couldn't be expected to remember every little date.

Amy didn't understand. He'd been at Somerset for nearly a year already. Somerset had embraced him, they'd even turned Charlie Cullen into something of a local celebrity— a photograph of Charlie, along with a short personal statement, was prominently featured in a nurse recruitment flyer the hospital had mailed out to thousands of potential employees. *Charles appreciates the technology—and more!* His featured quote was about how easy it was to chart patients through Cerner. He'd acted coy when it came out, but Amy could see that he was clearly proud of his star turn and enjoyed the feedback. He'd even styled his hair for it. Why would HR scrutinize his application now? Why did they even think to look at it?

Charlie didn't know. Maybe, he said, it might have something to do with the increased attention at the hospital after the death of Reverend Gall.

"It was an investigation, so they were certifying everything," he said. "Looking for any little thing." He was a scapegoat. "Also," he added, "it might have been because of the part—the reason I left St. Luke's." Charlie said that he hadn't really told Somerset, or Amy, the whole story. "There was an investigation at St. Luke's. Maybe someone at St. Luke's saw my picture in the brochure."

Amy didn't understand. Why would it matter that St. Luke's had seen it—what did that have to do with anything?

Charlie could imagine the reasons. He told Amy he'd resigned from St. Luke's under a cloud. The administration had persecuted him there, too. It had taken six months to clear up, but in the meantime it had cost him other jobs. Charlie had previously reapplied for a position at Easton Hospital. Easton wouldn't hire him. Charlie suspected they'd been warned off by someone at St. Luke's; in fact, attorney Paul Laughlin had contacted a staff member of Easton's ICU.[1] Charlie told Amy what he was experiencing in Somerset was more of the same, and exactly what had happened a year ago, at Sacred Heart Hospital. "There, they said that I wasn't getting along with my coworkers and, well..."

Amy had to laugh at that one. "Oh, let's see, what'd you do—did you just not talk?"

Charlie grinned into the phone but didn't interrupt her.

"Don't worry, sweetie," Amy said. "You'll get another job. *Everybody* needs help right now. You'll be working again before you know it."

"Yeah," Charlie said. "I know."

43

Tim remembered how, shortly after he'd first started at Somerset, the county had been rattled by a small earthquake. It was a minor event, hardly worth remembering, except for the way it lit up the police switchboard. The SPCO had a good laugh about that, calling cops to report an act of God, but they understood it, too; even in an imagined crisis, people always turned to the uniforms. Sometimes it was a cop or a fireman, sometimes a doctor or a priest, but the uniform was an assurance that the world wasn't falling apart, that a safety net existed. Then along came Charlie, a guy who'd been putting holes in hometown safety nets for sixteen years. The world might not have known about it, but the SPCO did, and it had even the seasoned detectives spooked. Every member of the team had a family, and at one time or another, every one of them had relied upon at least one of the hospitals Cullen had worked at. Most cops, most people, held genuine respect for the experts who plumbed the mysteries of the human body. Working the Cullen case had reminded them that beneath the white coats and scrubs, they were just people. And that was scary. Homicide cops knew people, and what they were capable of.

But as frustrating as it was to admit, Tim couldn't stop

Cullen, despite everything the detectives had learned about him. The investigation had brought to light a troubled work history, resulting in at least three previous investigations and possibly a fourth, and an equally troubled personal life that included perhaps a dozen suicide attempts and at least one arrest. The SPCO detectives had zero doubt that their suspect was a killer, but that didn't mean they could convince a jury to put him away for good. None of the facts they'd assembled definitively connected Nurse Cullen with a crime at Somerset Medical Center. Arresting Cullen now would succeed only in tipping him off to the fact he was being watched. All Charlie would have to do was pick up a phone to get back on the street. Tim would bet that the next call he received would be from a lawyer.

At this point, Danny's only option was to stay focused, try to somehow build his case, and hope Cullen didn't try to run, or kill anyone else, in the meantime. But every day, their killer was out there, in the world, walking into post offices and shopping malls and who knew where, or at what risk. Trying to contain that risk had been the inspiration for the phony traffic stop the night before Cullen was fired.

Tim and Danny had come up with the idea together and done it legally, Danny and Assistant Prosecutor Tim Van Hise going through a judge for the order. While Charlie Cullen waited on his bogus parking ticket problem, the detectives unscrewed the door panel of his impounded Ford and installed a radio tracking unit. From now on, Cullen's movements would now be followed at a safe distance by an unmarked car, with a detective from the Major Crimes Unit and another from the Narcotics Squad trading shifts around the clock.

To do more than watch from a distance—to actually stop Cullen—the SCPO needed to definitively prove that he had killed, or attempted to kill, at least one person. They had two

Somerset victims already lined up as potentials—Reverend Gall and Mrs. Han, for murder and attempted murder, respectively, and a medical consensus that deadly levels of various drugs had been fed into their systems. They had the victims, the weapon, and a suspect. But they couldn't tie them together.

Tim couldn't simply trace a drug back to a syringe and find its owner, the way he could with a bullet to a gun. The only records of access to the drugs would have been in the Pyxis machine. But, as Mary Lund had told them, Pyxis stored the drug data for only thirty days. Reverend Gall had been dead nearly four times that long. The relevant records were gone, and the case against Cullen was stuck.[1] At least, according to what the hospital had told the detectives.

Tim thought about that for a few seconds, then decided, what the hell. He swiveled over to the keyboard and typed "Pyxis" into the browser, finding the company that manufactured the system, a Midwestern outfit called Cardinal Health. Tim dialed the toll-free number, was connected with a sales rep, and introduced himself as a detective sergeant with Homicide and Major Crimes, Somerset, New Jersey. That got the guy's attention.

"Look," he told the guy. "I'm hoping you can help us here." Tim explained that he was trying to figure out a method of recovering data from one of their medical machines, the way you do when you spill coffee on your laptop. "It's some older information," Tim explained. "Half a year. Is there any way to recover anything that far back—maybe do some sort of data-recovery thing?"

The rep didn't seem to understand the question. There was no thirty-day window. The Pyxis system stored every piece of data entered into it from the moment it left the factory floor. Cullen's entire paper trail had been sitting on the hard drive this entire time.

"Just pull it up," he said. "Is there something wrong with your machine?"

——————

This time there was no friendly banter with Mary Lund's secretary, no knock, no smile, no please. Danny was too angry for that.[2]

Mary sat at her desk, eyes big, visibly frightened of the giant towering over her. Danny told Lund what he needed and when he needed it.

He told her that if she didn't want the FBI ripping her little office apart and an obstruction-of-justice charge on her bail ticket, she'd better pick up the phone, right fucking now, and get him the paper and not any of this just-four-pages-and-one-missing bullshit, either.

Mary picked up the phone.

——————

Danny typed up the incident in the black-and-white of police-report-ese:

This detective responded to the Somerset Medical Center and met with Director Mary Lund, to discuss the necessity of obtaining Cullen's PYXIS activity in its entirety.... During this meeting we also discussed various alternatives that may allow us to obtain this information.

Note: throughout the course of this investigation detectives were informed that the PYXIS system only stored data for (30) thirty days.

At the conclusion of this meeting, Ms. Lund made several telephone calls inquiring about possible ways of retrieving this data.

As a result, the requested information was subsequently obtained and turned over to this detective
along with work assignment sheets for every patient in
the Critical Care Units during Cullen's tenure at this
Facility.

The Pyxis reports printed out like a spreadsheet. Danny
saw each of Cullen's trips to the drug computer as a time-
stamped line of information, showing the units and type of
drug ordered, and the patient to whom it was billed.

But the orders on the evening before Reverend Gall's
overdose the Pyxis indicated that Cullen had not withdrawn
any digoxin during his shift, and that evening looked very
much like the evenings before and after. This was supposed
to be the jackpot. But if there was a smoking gun there,
Danny couldn't see it.

44

On November 4, 2003, the detectives started scheduling interviews with the Somerset Medical CCU nurses, hoping to find a source of information unfiltered by corporate lawyers. The Somerset Medical Center administration lawyers requested that all interviews be conducted within the hospital, in the presence of Risk Manager Mary Lund. The assistant prosecutor had agreed to the conditions. Both Danny and Tim were furious, Tim going so far as to tell the AP, the prosecutor, and the police chief, too, that the whole interview process was now officially a "crock of shit." In private, the chief, the detective captain, and the other detectives agreed with Tim[1]—but they didn't say it in the meeting, in front of their boss—which, of course, was exactly his point.

Orchestrating that waste of time was Danny's problem. Danny delegated detectives Russell Colucci and Edward Percell to conduct the interviews.

The daily reports provided an encyclopedia of information about nursing procedures and scheduling and physical layout—all essential groundwork, none of it game changing. Not all of the nurses had worked with Charles Cullen. Those that did used many of the same words to describe him—"quiet," a "loner," a little "bizarre" in his personal behavior, but professionally "excellent." Most showed at least a mild affection for their quiet, quirky coworker, and they were particularly appreciative of his willingness to pick up shifts.[2] Reviewing the interviews later, Tim and Danny couldn't help but come to the conclusion that aside from the murders, Charles Cullen might have been a pretty good nurse.

But what the interviews didn't reveal was anything of the slightest use to a homicide investigation. The descriptions they gave were brief and sterile. Danny couldn't be sure if the nurses didn't know anything, or if they were just being quiet in front of Mary Lund. Each time his detectives asked a question, it seemed like the nurse would reflexively glance over at Lund before speaking. Finally toward the end of November, Danny decided to change tactics. From now on, he'd be doing the interviews himself, and alone. So far, all the detectives had done was ask the nurses to provide information, with an administrator sitting right there. The detectives had been told not to share any of their suspicions with the Somerset Medical Center staff. The nurses were confused by the process, and had little incentive to open up. They didn't even know exactly what the investigation was about. For all they knew, they were the ones in trouble with the law.

Colucci and Percell had been told to run it that way—Tim and Danny couldn't risk a leak to Cullen or the newspapers, or even to the Somerset Medical administration. But Danny knew that if they were going to get anywhere, he would have to bend the rules, and take the leap of trusting somebody. Colucci and Percell weren't in the position to make that call, but Danny was. And so, only three days after storming into Mary Lund's office to demand the Pyxis information, Danny and Mary were spending five to ten hours a day crammed together in a little room off the Somerset Medical ICU,[3] both of them hating every minute of it.

———————

By necessity, the two had reestablished a friendly, if false, work rapport. But Danny noticed that something fundamental had changed in Mary Lund. It was as if the woman was suffering a slow-motion nervous breakdown. Lund was getting it from both sides, the bottleneck between the hospital and the murder investigation. She was the risk manager in a situation of unprecedented consequence in lives and jobs and dollars.

Mary had been losing weight steadily since the investigation started, and it didn't seem to Danny like the intentional kind—Danny had known women, when they lost a pound or two, to go out and buy something new to show it off. Mary Lund had lost maybe twenty pounds but she was trying to hide it, shrinking inside her pantsuit, nervous as a hare. The presence of Danny Baldwin in the room wasn't helping her nerves, either.

———————

Amy had been telling her girlfriends for weeks that she was definitely not down with the whole investigation thing.

Waves of paranoia swept the unit. Each nurse secretly feared the police interviews had something to do with her personally, and that it could affect her future. The nurses whispered together in the hallways, forming alliances, choosing sides. Each shift amplified and distorted the rumors from the shift before. Most of the rumors were about Charlie. Two weeks into it, the rumors were about Amy, too.

Everyone knew she was "Charlie's friend." They remembered the stink Amy had made about signing for insulin.

Apparently, there was a death involved, and both insulin and Charlie were mixed up in it. Some of the nurses now avoided Amy, as if suspicion was contagious. Her friends were worried for her. To tell the truth, Amy was scared for herself.

She always played the tough girl, but inside, she was terrified—totally out-of-her-mind scared. What had she done? Amy's heart condition required that she take daily antianxiety medication. Had she taken too much Atavan one night and made a mistake? Were there narcotics missing, was the insulin issue to blame? It could be anything. Amy called to ensure her RN license hadn't expired. It hadn't. So what was it, then? Amy wondered whether she needed a lawyer. Every time the detectives made an appointment Amy would call in sick. After two weeks she could avoid it no longer. Her manager sent her to the room.

Inside, she found Mary Lund and a police detective, a big black guy in a suit and tie. He asked her to have a seat. He called her "Ms. Loughren." There was a water pitcher and Dixie cups. Amy felt like a criminal. Her heart was going to explode if she held it in, so she let it all out.

45

Danny had already been conducting interviews for a week,[1] and right away, this nurse seemed different. She was clearly afraid for her job, just like the others, but the difference was, Amy came out and admitted it. And she didn't glance over at Lund when she did.

Amy Loughren had graduated from nursing school in 1988, making her maybe a few years older than Danny. She was a white woman with bleachy streaks of blonde hair, blue doe-eyes, and high, prominent cheekbones—tall and attractive, but not a fragile sort of beauty, more rugged and practical and, despite her conspicuous curves, clearly comfortable with the guys. There was something easy about her personality that turned the formality of interview into a conversation with flow.

She started right in, telling Danny that she had heard rumors that this investigation had something to do with her friend Charles Cullen, and both the rumors and the investigation "pissed her off, royally."

Clearly, this girl wasn't holding anything back. Danny sat back in his chair, letting her vent, knowing right away, *she's the one*.

———————

Amy didn't remember finishing her shift or the long drive home. At some point she realized she was sitting in her driveway, trying to make sense of her day as her breath turned to frost on the windshield. She'd been so defensive at first, so fierce. Protective of her Charlie. She'd told the detective exactly what she thought of his investigation, and she didn't care that Mary Lund was there to hear it. But the detective hadn't reacted as she'd expected. He listened, seemed calm, maybe even happy. That didn't make sense, with him getting yelled at like that—Amy thought she even caught a smile. And then, rather than ask her questions, the detective started to give Amy answers. Things about what had been happening on the unit, information about Charlie. Some of it sounded familiar. A lot of it surprised her. Amy glanced over to see how Mary Lund was reacting, but Mary was gone.[2] Amy had been so keyed up, she hadn't even heard the woman leave.

"Look, Ms. Loughren," the detective said. "I don't know *why*, but I trust you. Okay?" He slid a piece of paper across the table. Amy could see it was a Pyxis printout. It was Charlie's, from the night Reverend Gall had died.

By the time Mary Lund walked back into the room, the Pyxis page was off the desk, and the angry, defiant Amy was gone. In her place was a silent woman whose eyes held a glaze of tears and shock. Mary had looked across the table from the nurse to the detective, but Danny was no longer speaking, either. He was using every muscle in his face trying not to smile.

Amy had seen Charlie's Pyxis and knew it right away. It was obvious, at least to her. She had always fought to defend Charlie against the bullies of the world, the unfair accusations. The paper Danny showed her told her not to. For the first time, it was possible to imagine that Charlie had done something strange and terrible during those shifts. She could believe that now. But what she couldn't do, what she still couldn't imagine possible, was reconciling that paper with her idea of her friend.

When she got home, Amy dumped her coat and her purse and fished the big bottle of Cabernet from on top of the fridge. She sat with a glass at the kitchen table. How was she supposed to deal with this? There wasn't a self-help book for this one. She'd seen the drug orders. She knew what happened to Gall. Nurses didn't do this. A nurse had done this. Her friend had done this. Maybe.

Maybe it was selfish, but that was what hit her first. She trusted Charlie—or had, like she'd trusted few others, and even fewer men. That was what her tough-girl persona was all about, armor against the world. After a lifetime spent wrestling with issues of trust, those struggles had come to define her. She made no secret of her torturous childhood. Her sexual abuser had practically been a member of her family. They trusted him. But Amy knew people, and what they were capable of. Growing up, a little girl hiding in closets and hampers and behind basement doors, she had prayed over and over to the universe, begging for the superpower of invisibility. Instead, he had found her, again and again. In the end, she decided, the only one she could really trust was herself. She carried her piggy bank to the local mental health clinic and asked the stunned secretary, "How many sessions will this buy me?"[3]

It had taken years of therapy to stop the guilt. Her decision to survive, and then thrive, had been a conscious one. She didn't want to be damaged, squeezed, and trapped in the wreckage of her childhood. She had decided she was too tough for that, and she acted the part. She had decided, with the therapist's help, to engage in the world. And that was impossible without some capacity to trust her relationships with other people. That was part of her decision to go into Critical Care nursing. The patients there needed everything. Their dependency dwarfed her own, and she rewarded that trust with care. That's what nursing was about: a good paycheck, yeah, but also a relationship which healed both parties. Or so she had thought. If the Pyxis was right, Amy had failed her side of the bargain. She hadn't kept her patients safe. Now she didn't feel safe, either.

46

Tim and Danny had started in the predawn darkness of November 24, still smelling of their shave and shower, the front seat of the Crown Vic outfitted with Styrofoam Dunkin' Donuts to-gos and a clean stack of newspapers. They drove north out of Jersey, into the back roads and farms and vegetable stands of what Tim called "deep bumblefuck" New York, getting deeper with every turn into the mountains. The plan was to close the deal in person—away from the hospital, and before the girl changed her mind. At the time, they hadn't realized that Amy was a long-distance commuter, hours away.

Danny told Tim about the girl, a fourteen-year nurse, midthirties, kids, blonde and pretty and tough. She was known on the unit as a friend of Charlie's, maybe his best friend. Giving Amy the details of the investigation had been a gamble, she might pass them on to her pal Charlie. Danny still wasn't sure exactly why he took it. Partly it was his gut, telling him that there was something wrong with the pattern of canceled orders he'd seen on that Pyxis page, telling him to trust this girl when they could trust nobody else. Mary Lund leaving the room had given him a chance to test it.

"Why'd Lund leave the room?"

"No idea," Danny said. "Maybe she needed to use the bathroom. Anyway, she's gone, I slide this nurse the Pyxis printouts and she's like—*bam!* It knocked her over."

"She say why?"

"Yeah, well—first she was just like—stunned," Danny said. "Then she's just like, 'Oh-My-God, Holy Shit,' like that, over and over. Sorta slowed down talking, like a witness, you know?"

"Wow," Tim said. "So she thinks Cullen's dirty."

"I think she's trying to figure it," Danny said. "She kinda disappeared, I mean—it was like the information was too much, it blew her circuits."

"She say anything else about the Pyxis, what she saw?"

"Mostly it was the 'holy shit,'" Danny said. "She also said something, said, 'Charlie and I, we wrapped a lotta bodies together.'"

Danny explained how he thought maybe she was going to cry. He didn't know when Lund was going to walk back in, and he didn't want to tip her off, so they changed the subject.

"This nurse had talked to Charlie after he was fired, called him. Somebody had seen his picture, he said, probably somebody from St. Luke's. Said they must have called Somerset."

"What picture are we talking about?"

"Thing they sent out in the mail," Danny said. He dug under the newspapers to his folder. "Check it out. Our guy on the hospital recruiting pamphlet."

Tim glanced from the road. It was a recruitment flyer, something the hospital gave to potential nursing employees, Charlie Cullen smiling like a school portrait. "You're shitting me," Tim said.

"Look like a killer to you?" Danny said.

"Yeah, well," Tim said. "Who does?"

———

The detectives arrived at the Loughren address a little after 10 a.m., finding a white Colonial in the woods, the girl standing cross-armed in the window. She watched the two men emerging stiffly from what she assumed was an unmarked police car, the black detective and now a white detective, both big guys with suits and mustaches like matching salt-and-pepper-shaker homicide cops, carrying a box of donuts and a tray of takeout coffee to her front door.

Amy brought them into her living room. The men settled in, a little too big around the coffee table. Amy tucked her feet under her on the couch as Tim took the lead, laying out the Somerset Medical case, in detail now, and not using the official language to do it. Danny glanced at his partner; he'd given her some inside information to bait the hook, but the plan was to take it slow from there. Now Tim was just telling Amy everything. Tim gave Danny a shrug: what the hell. He'd started it. They had to trust somebody if they were going to make this case.

———

The Pyxis sheet Danny had shown Amy at the hospital was only one of a stack. The detectives watched the girl picking through the pages, getting agitated. It wasn't any one specific drug order, she said. It was all the orders combined.

"First of all, if you printed out all my Pyxis orders, they'd be, like, a tenth of this," Amy said. "Less, probably. Nobody orders like this."

"So what does that tell you?"

"Nothing specifically," Amy said. "But it's weird." Charlie had been making a separate request for each drug he ordered. "It would be like ordering a dozen eggs, one egg at a time," she said. And many of the entries were only seconds apart—even when Cullen had been ordering the same drug, for the same patient. Amy could think of no logical reason to do that.

"How about the dig?" Danny said. "We're interested in that."

Amy flipped through the stack from the beginning, starting with Charlie's drug pulls from early in the year. "See that?" she said, running a fingernail down the columns. "And that, and that?"

The detectives leaned in. "That's the dig, yeah," Danny said. He'd flagged that before. "Is it unusual?"

"Uh, *yeah*," Amy said. "Charlie was ordering dig like—I don't know, ten times a month."

"Is that a lot?"

"That's maybe more than I've ordered the whole time I've worked at Somerset."

"Okay," Tim said. "Wow."

"And this was in the ICU," Amy said. "Dig is really not that common a drug there."

"Amy," Danny said. "We want to ask something from you. We're trusting you with this. Nobody else, none of the other nurses, know anything about this. The hospital doesn't know this."

"We're not currently sharing our information, um, *freely* with the hospital," Tim said.

"We don't want them taking a defensive posture to the information, legally," Danny said.

"What Danny's saying is, Somerset's been covering their asses from day one," Tim said. Danny glared at him. Tim ignored it.

"They didn't tell us we could get this Pyxis. They didn't tell us about—well, let's just say, we're not totally sure we're on the same side of this thing."

"They didn't tell you about Pyxis?" Amy said. "But you—"

"We knew about it. We just had, uh, a problem getting the records for a while."

"How about Cerner?"

Tim looked over at Danny. "I'm not sure what—who's Cerner?"

Amy couldn't believe it. They didn't have the Cerner data? Neither Tim nor Danny had heard of it. Lund had never mentioned it; nobody at the hospital had. Amy had to wonder, *What the heck have they been investigating with?*

Amy explained that if you wanted to learn about patients, Cerner was the tool. It was a computer system that kept patient records, the way Pyxis did with drug orders. Pull the Cerner data and they'd have a running time-line record of every patient's progress on the CCU and a time-stamped record of every time Charlie had ever looked at a chart. They didn't know that?

"See, that right there," Danny said, writing it down. "That's why we're trusting you. But if we're going to be able to do this, you're going to need to keep the relationship, um, separate from the hospital."

"Don't tell them shit," Tim said, "would be the idea."

"Okay," Amy said, "I won't say anything."

"Good," Danny said. "I know we're putting you in a difficult situation—"

"I won't say anything, really," Amy said. "Swear."

"Look, Amy, here's—let me say this," Tim said. "We wouldn't be taking a risk showing you all this, if we didn't think it's important."

"It's clear to us—and I think it's clear to you, too—that Charles Cullen was doing something wrong at the hospital," Danny added.

"We think he killed a patient. Maybe more than one. And we think he may have been killing patients for a long time."

"Oh God," Amy said.

"And, see Amy, here's the thing. If we don't stop him, he's going to kill patients again, somewhere else."

"My God," Amy said. "I screwed up! I told him I'd help him get a job—I'm his reference . . ."

"It's okay," Tim said. "That means you've got a reason to talk to him. Because, here's the thing."

"We need your help," Danny said.

"You can help us stop Cullen. We want you to work with us."

"Keep up with Charlie, see how he's doing."

"Be our eyes and ears."

"Wait—what?" Amy said. She pushed back from the table. "You tell me he's killing people, but you want me to stay friends with the guy?"

"I know, I know, I know," Tim said. "But, yeah."

"Not friends," Danny said. "You don't have to be friends. Just—keep in touch."

"Like, undercover."

"You can't tell anybody at work, Amy."

"Not even your friends."

"Nobody."

"Yeah, I . . ." Amy wasn't saying no, but she started shaking her head that way.

"I know, it's a lot to process."

"Yeah, no," Amy said. "I'll—need to think about it—"

"Think about it."

"I will, I—" *Rrring!* The telephone shocked her. Amy reflexively put a hand over her heart in protection.

"Please," Tim said, "if you want to get that, or—"

"Yeah, hold on, hold on," Amy said. "It might be my

daughter, from school." She leaned to check the caller ID.
"Oh, God." She triggered Talk on the cordless, glanced
hard at the detectives, waving them closer. Tim and Danny
leaned in.

"Hi Mar-ryy," Amy said, sounding singsong casual. It
was Mary Lund.[1] Tim looked at Danny. They were busted.

Amy held the receiver away from her ear so they all could
hear. Mary Lund said hello, and that she was just following up after the police interview last night. Mary wanted to
know: how did Amy think it went?

"Fine," Amy said. "It was fine."

"Fine," Mary repeated. She sounded too quick, nervous.
Amy popped her eyes at the detective, shaking her head in
slow motion and silently mouthing *Whatthefuck*…

"Well, I'm sure you're glad it's over," Mary said. "If the
police ask for anything else, or if you plan on making any
kind of statement, maybe you'd better just go ahead and
make sure that you have the hospital attorney with you. For
your own protection."

"Um, really?" Amy said. "I don't think that's necessary,
Mary. Is it? I mean, I'm not the target of their investigation
or anything."

"Amy, that's not a good idea," Mary said. "If the police
try to contact you again, you should tell them to speak
directly with one of our attorneys. We have a—"

"I appreciate your call, Mary, but really, I feel fine. This
really isn't about me, they said I'm not a suspect."

"Amy," Mary said, "I strongly suggest that you have a
Somerset Medical Center lawyer with you if you speak to
the police again. Their investigation has…stepped up a
notch."

Amy finished the call and dropped the phone. What the
hell was going on? It was like someone had changed the

channel in the middle of her life and switched to some detective story.

"See, that's what we're talking about," Danny said.

"They're covering their asses," Tim said. "We're trying to catch a killer."

Amy reached over for a cigarette and threw herself back into the groaning wicker. How weird was that? It was too much to process, but at least Lund's call had made one thing clear:[2] the hospital was concerned for themselves. Amy would have to look after herself. Right now, having two big homicide cops in her living room made her feel like the safest girl on earth.

"Okay," Amy said, snubbing her cigarette. "Turn on your tape recorder, boys, and tell me what you want to know."

47

Amy had to rethink Charlie Cullen's eccentricities and quirks in this new light. Why was he so secretive with his patients? Why was he early to work? Why did he only sometimes wear glasses, and why was he always typing away on the Cerner computer? It seemed paranoid associating his every personality trait with sinister intent, naïve to not at least consider the possibility.

With so many questions to explore, it felt good to talk freely to the detectives. She wasn't afraid, she wasn't careful. Amy learned in her teenage penny-paid therapy not to be crippled by the truth. When she'd come to her family and told them the truth about her molester, they'd acted as if Amy was the problem. It had taken years of therapy to see it otherwise.

She talked for an hour, lighting and smoking and stubbing her butts in the little glass ashtray, her painted nails waving the smoke away toward the screened porch windows. This was her guilty pleasure, heavy on the guilt; she recognized how stupid she was, smoking and partying despite her heart condition. Sometimes she could feel it stop beating until her pacemaker kicked in. Somehow death didn't scare her like it was supposed to.

But to risk her job as an undercover agent, lie to Charlie, lie to her employer, to everybody? Could she? There was real risk in that. The detectives could be wrong, or they could be tricking her. They were strangers. Charlie was her friend. Shouldn't she take his side, no matter what?

Amy leaned back to the sofa and folded her arms. Maybe getting more involved was a bad idea. "What, exactly, are you asking me for here?" she said. "Like, what would I do?"

"Small things, small things," Tim said. "Nothing dangerous."

"Phone calls, mostly," Danny said. "Make some calls for us."

"Maybe, down the road, wear a wire."

"You mean I'd have to see him?" Amy said. "In person?"

"Maybe, just—just forget about that right now," Tim said. "Did Cullen ever talk about euthanasia, or anything like that or—"

"Huh? No. No. I don't think so. No, I—"

"Okay, okay," Tim said. "Well, what we're asking is for you to help us."

"Really," Danny said. "It's that simple."

Amy said she'd have to think about it. "I'll call you tonight," she told them. "There's someone I need to talk to before I can definitely say yes."

———

The old house was frighteningly quiet with the detectives gone. Amy[1] sat thinking in her kitchen, listening to the fridge tick until the school bus arrived. She heard the porch boards croak, the screen slap metal, her daughter running up the stairs with her oversized book bag, then stamping back down. Alex walked into the kitchen for a juice box and found her mother at the table, trying too hard not to look serious.

Alex could see that something was wrong. She figured it

was something with the school play. Her mom was directing it this year, a story about aliens landing in a boring small town and making it fun. *Invasion from Planet Zorgon.* Alex thought it was a pretty good play because kids who didn't want speaking parts could just play the townspeople of Humdrum Falls. All you had to do for that was look surprised, which was mostly just pointing with your mouth open.

But, Amy told Alex, this was way weirder than anything on Zorgon. Someone she knew in the hospital, another nurse, might have killed a patient. It might have been on purpose. And maybe he'd done it more than once. Okay, so her daughter was eleven years old, she knew what a serial killer was, of course she did. Policemen had come to the house. They wanted her mom's help to catch the bad nurse. Alex sat across from her mom, never taking her eyes off her but never releasing the juice box straw either.

Amy wanted Alex to know that this decision might change their lives. The detectives were asking her to buddy up to a man they accused of murder. People might talk. It might even be dangerous—Amy didn't think so, but she couldn't be totally certain. Amy was sensitive to how something at this age could change you forever. Her daughter was closer by the day to becoming a teenager. *Wow,* Amy thought, *talk about social suicide.*

"So, it's a family decision," she told Alex. "We need to figure out, as a family, are we going to be able to, you know—can you handle this?"

"Is that going to happen? That stuff?"

"I don't know, honey. That's the thing—I don't know."

"But it might happen."

"Yes."

Alex wound the straw around her finger like a ring. "Is there a best-case?"

"Well, if it works, the man goes to jail."

"Forever, right?"

"I don't know what's going to happen," Amy said. "If there isn't enough evidence to put him in jail, or if he gets out—I don't know if we'll be in danger."

Amy watched her daughter taking this in. A serial killer, her mom as an undercover spy, the potential delay of Planet Zorgon. Amy knew how weird this must all be to Alex. It was that weird for her, too.

"So, Mom, this guy is really killing people?"

"He might be, honey. Yes."

"Well," Alex said. "Then you have to find out, right?"

48

Danny settled into a sweatshirt and jeans before spreading out on his living room floor with his growing stack of paperwork, including the new information he'd requested from Lund. One stack of paper contained the mortality records from the Somerset Medical Center CCU for the time Charles Cullen worked there. The other stack listed Cullen's shifts during that time. Danny cross-indexed the two, looking for a pattern.

He'd tried indexing patient deaths against Cullen's birthday, those of his children and ex-wives and girlfriends, his parents and known siblings. Then Danny tried wedding anniversaries, divorce anniversaries, feast days, and holidays—anything that might correlate with the deaths, some rule of murder. The more items he added, the more ideas came to mind. Soon he was comparing the names of the deceased with Cullen's family's names, then comparing initials, then using the initials to spell words... Danny put the pad down and rubbed his eyes. It was four o'clock in the morning. What was the point? You throw enough variables into the mix, you can find a pattern in anything. The whole world was a code to the paranoid, but that didn't give it meaning.

It was nearly dawn by the time Danny finally crawled into bed. He lay there for a few hours, awake behind his eyelids, still scrambling the numbers and letters to find a reason, as if reasons were what mattered.

———————

Tim didn't have the same responsibility for marshaling all the mind-numbing drugs and dates and details that Danny did as lead detective, but his head was still busy, doing the math on murder, the odds on catching their guy. They'd been grinding away for months already, but they were still feeling their way in the dark. Adding it up, Charles Cullen had been doing exactly this for sixteen years at ten different hospitals. The guy was a veteran in a field of homicide in which the detectives were just rookies.

Tim Braun had read up on the Internet about the medical murderer type—the two lady nurses who did it as a sexual thing, the orderly who killed patients to decrease his workload, the Kevorkian types, mercy killers, psychopaths, who knew what else. The FBI had specialists in Quantico who dealt with nothing else, agents and shrinks and guys who were both. Maybe the FBI had a whole file on guys like Cullen, a recipe box they could look at, with tips on how to catch one. Tim knew an FBI guy, maybe he could put them in touch with the Quantico experts. He didn't know if it would help, but could it hurt? The promise let him get some sleep at least.

But when he brought the FBI idea up at the morning meeting, Prosecutor Forrest shot it down—they weren't going to bring in anyone. Tim understood the ambition—you didn't succeed as prosecutor by giving away your cases—but that didn't mean he agreed with it. This close to retirement, Tim had the luxury of taking orders as suggestions, anyway.

Charlie had been out of work for a month already, his girl-friend was pregnant but wanted him to move out of her house, and he was in no mood to answer the phone. But then the voice on the machine was Amy's, sympathetic Amy. She knew how he was, knew he was too spent to pick up, and knew to call back anyway. This time he picked up with a knowing "Hi."

"Hi, honey," Amy said.

"Hi," Charlie said.

"How are you?"

"Oh, good," he sighed. "All right. Um, you know how it is . . . I applied for unemployment but they denied that."

"Why? Why would they deny it?"

"Well," Charlie said, "they're saying, ah—because I put—I'm gonna appeal it but—"

"Yeah," Amy said, "but if you're terminated, can't you get—I mean, that doesn't make any sense."

"Yeah," Charlie said. "Well, I wasn't employed for that long."

"Well," Amy said, "I'll write you a reference, you know that. But what—you know, I, yeah, I was calling too because they've been asking weird questions. At the hospital."

"Mmm," Charlie said.

"And it's like they've been, kind of calling people in for, like, internal stuff? And, um, you know, somebody had asked me about you."

"Okay," Charlie said. Waiting to hear where this was going.

"And, you know. I kind of—I kind of wanted to give you the heads-up about that." Amy waited, hearing only breath on the other side of the phone, so she continued, "And they asked me, they were just asking me shit about certain patients and I can't, you know, I can't remember any of 'em, I can't remember any of their names or... you know. And I was... I didn't know. I didn't know if they had been questioning you..."

"Right," Charlie said. "Well, they..."

"'Cause I'm kind of... honestly, Charles, I'm a little bit nervous, that's all," Amy said. "Asking me just like stupid shit like, certain medications, and, you know, asking me about dig..."

"Well," Charlie said, "there's the one patient I recall, a Reverend something."

"Right."

"They had asked me about that patient, too. Ah, but again, I... I didn't know anything about the patient. I had heard, ah, you know, ah, ah, Joan talk about it the following day or two—"

Amy cut him off. "I mean, is this something I should worry about or—"

"I—I don't, I don't think so," Charlie said. "I mean, I think they're probably talking to other people. I mean— I know the insulin thing, it's ongoing, so... I don't know what's happening with that."

"They've really been talking," Amy said. "And I know they've asked about you. I wanted you to be aware of that, because—I know that they've questioned other people and your name has come up. And, I, and, ah, you know— and I was mad. That's when they put—when they pulled me in."

"Right," Charlie said.

"But you know me, I'm freaking nervous! I'm a worrywart. And I don't have you around to make me feel better."

"Yeah. Well, um, I don't know if I'm the focus of their

investigation," Charlie said. " I mean...like I said, I'm ter-minated."

Amy laughed, "Yeah, you're already gone, dumbass!"

Listening in on a headset from the next room in the pros-ecutor's office, Danny had to admit, the girl was really a natural on the wire.

49

Tim was concerned that Lund might suspect Amy was talking, and try and shut her down, so he and Danny devised a strategy for protecting their source. That December, Danny told Colucci and Percell to continue their interviews at Somerset, to keep getting any information they could. And to ask each CCU staffer pointed and incriminating questions about nurse Amy Loughren.

The questions would shift the focus away from Charlie Cullen, and help preserve the anonymity of their confidential informant. But it would also make life that much more difficult for Amy. As far as her coworkers could tell, she was now the target of a murder investigation.

Amy learned about it almost right away, not from the detectives directly but by a phone call from her friend Annie, the health care aide's thick Jamaican identifying her from the first *'ello . . .*

"Ay-mee," Annie said. "I just wanted to let you know. They're asking all kinds of questions about you, over and over, they're—"

"Who is, sweetie?"

"The detectives. The investigators, they're here. They're asking everybody."

"I know they are."

"Every single person, over and over and over, 'Amy Amy, what about Amy?'"

"I know," Amy told Annie. "Don't worry. Everything is going to be okay." Not that she was quite sure of that yet herself.

The detectives registered Amy as a "Consensual Confidential Informant approved for audio intercepts, both telephonic and body," and provided Amy with a room in the prosecutor's office. But after her first taped phone calls, Amy found it more comfortable to talk from her living room couch. In between work and sleep she sat up with a stack of printouts, turning pages, making notes. The pages told a story. It was far more frightening than she'd ever imagined.

Tim and Danny had asked her to concentrate on Reverend Gall—they had their case there. Amy saw the lab reports from the State Medical Examiner indicating that Gall's cause of death was overdose by digoxin. The Pyxis showed that Charlie had withdrawn digoxin the day before the reverend coded and died. That might have been a coincidence, if it had been the only thing wrong. But there was a larger pattern. It would take Amy weeks of poring through the papers to fully appreciate it.

The Pyxis hadn't been entirely revealing to Tim and Danny—Danny had seen some patterns, but the Latin names were mostly just a list of unpronounceable words. The detectives had looked for the drug names they knew and the dates they'd been given. The rest was just noise. But Amy knew the drugs, and she knew ICU nursing. And from a nursing perspective, Charlie's drug requests made no sense.

On page after page, night after night, Charlie Cullen was ordering drugs his patients couldn't possibly need. He was withdrawing rarely used drugs in absurd quantities and with alarming frequency. And, according to the paperwork, Charlie was doing something that made even less sense. Over and over, Charlie was ordering drugs, then canceling the orders. The night Gall died, for instance, Charlie had ordered then canceled digoxin. As far as Pyxis was concerned, Charlie had never withdrawn the drug. And yet Gall had received it, and died.

One cancellation in itself wasn't a big deal. Every nurse makes the occasional mistake. But mistakes didn't look like this. Charlie was making the same errors on a nightly basis, sometimes even hourly. It seemed like a system—as if he was making errors on purpose.

Meanwhile, Amy was increasingly making mistakes of her own. She was exhausted from the double duty of moonlighting as a CI after working shifts on the CCU, and near the end of her Sunday night shift, she realized that she'd punched the wrong drug order into the Pyxis. *Great,* she thought. With the detectives spreading suspicions about her in the hospital, even innocent mistakes might get her fired. Amy hit Cancel on the order, just as the drug drawer popped open.

Amy looked at the screen—it was canceled there. The record would show that she had not taken the drug out. She did it a few more times to be sure. Then she called Tim. She came in the next day, fanning the paperwork across the desk to show them how it worked.

———

Amy went back through the paperwork, showing Tim and Danny where Charlie had called up a drug and canceled it, over and over. In theory, the Pyxis drug drawer had opened for each of those cancellations. Cullen could have taken the meds without acknowledging it in the records. Amy showed how Charlie had called up and canceled dig at least twenty-seven separate times between when he started at Somerset and June 27—eight times in the month of February alone. None of the other nurses in the unit had ordered even a fifth of those numbers.

It was a good theory, impressive, if circumstantial. Could Tim and Danny prove Cullen was stealing drugs through canceled orders?[1] They couldn't prove he'd done it in the past. They could set up a camera on the Pyxis, try and catch him at it—but according to the Pyxis records, there was no point. After the twenty-seventh—four days after Gall's death—Charlie's dig requests stopped entirely, including his dig cancellations. But the inexplicable lab results had not stopped.

Maybe Cullen had some other way he was getting drugs. Or maybe her friend wasn't the one responsible for the strange incidents at Somerset. Either possibility was hard to live with. Amy was either failing to solve this mystery, or she was setting up her best friend, turning his mistakes into evidence of murder.

"So, what does that mean?" Danny said. "That he stopped doing it? Or just that he's doing it in another way?"

Amy regathered the papers and stuffed them back in her bag for the long drive home. "I don't know," she said. In fact, she wasn't sure of any of it anymore. "I'll let you know if I figure it out."

50

Amy took a bath and slipped into her oldest and softest pajamas. She laid out by the fire, pretending to relax with a book. When that didn't work she put down the wineglass and picked up the phone. Charlie answered on the second ring.

"Hi, Charl!" Amy said. She couldn't believe it—she was genuinely glad to hear his voice. "How's it going?"

"Okay...," Charlie said.

"Okay?"

"Okay. Not, you know, I mean—it's just getting me more and more worried," Charlie said. "Because you know, again, like I said, it's been a couple of weeks of it. And you know everything is sort of a...I feel like everything is closing in on this." His girlfriend, Cathy, had told him not to worry, that everything happened for a reason, that God took care of things. But sometimes, Charlie knew, you had to take care of things yourself.

But Amy wasn't like Cathy. "You know," he said. "You get me."

"Has she been that supportive, though?" Amy asked. "I mean, she's really saying, 'Don't worry'? I mean, she was being so horrible before."

"I think she realizes that, you know, I'm not in a really good space," Charlie says. "But then, we did get into a major argument a couple of days afterward. You know, and that had to do with—a guy from where she works wrote her actually like, a romantic letter. And—"

Charlie had already told her about his girlfriend's "friend." "Is this the guy that bought her like lunch or something?" Amy said.

"They had dinner," Charlie said. "And, ah, she went upstairs for dinner up at, you know, on his floor and stuff. And he, he wrote some weird letters that were, you know, complaining about the night he worked there, when she wasn't there. And then he wrote—I mean, 'You know you have to restore my soul, you have to—' "

"*What*?" Amy shrieked.

"You know, 'you have to,' you know, 'lighten my heart'— all this weird stuff," Charlie said.

"Oh my God," Amy says. "Didn't you want to puke?"

"Well, she, like, kept it with her other personal papers and stuff," Charlie said. Charlie had come across the note while he was packing her a lunch. He'd confronted Cathy, but Cathy was indignant that he'd been snooping. She'd told him it was a joke. Then Charlie found another letter in her purse. Their fights were just pinwheeling now.

"We got through that, it's been okay since, as far as I know," Charlie said. "I actually went over to his house to ask him about it and—"

"You went over to his house!?" Charlie was a trip. He was stalking his pregnant girlfriend's boyfriend.

"Yeah," Charlie said. He sounded to be enjoying the story. "Well, see—the weird thing about it is—and this is part of the whole weird thing, um, he—"

"Wait—you know him?"

"No," Charlie said. "But, um, he actually lives in the house where she used to live, which is another weird coincidence. The exact same house on the street—not the block, the exact same house that she used to live in."

"Okay, Charles. That's fucked up."

"Well," Charlie said. "You know. She's saying it's some weird coincidence."

"No, that's not a coincidence," Amy said. "You know that."

"Well, that's the way I thought about it," Charlie said. "But she's still saying it. I mean, I don't know how, this is just, just weird stuff. But since my life is a series of weird stuff lately, I'm getting used to it."

"Um-hmm," Amy said.

"Because," he reminded her, "you know, I've gone through some minor depressions, and, ah—"

"*Minor?*"

"Well ...," Charlie drawled, stretching the moment.

"Come on, Char."

"I've, you know, well, been feeling—suicidal. But I've worked through that—so far. But—"

"Honey!" Amy said. "Are you really?"

"I'm scared right now," he said. "I don't see how it's gonna work out. And especially if they still think that I had something to do with the patient deaths. 'Cause I, you know—I have two children already, and have one more on the way ..."

"Which is all the more reason to keep it together," Amy said. "How about seeing somebody, how about getting an antidepressant?"

Charlie sighed. That wasn't a conversation that interested him. "You know, I mean—I thought about it," he said. "But, you know—I don't know why all of this is happening right now. I'm hoping it will all work out. But I'm, um, very scared of my own future. You know, I guess—it's just the holidays coming up too, because I haven't told my ex-wife yet." Charlie was behind on his child support. The only bright spot of the week had come when Child Services called and offered him a reprieve. Charlie had no idea that it had been orchestrated by homicide detectives: They didn't want Charlie looking too hard for work and finding it in another hospital.

"You know, but they're saying, 'Okay, you're trying, so we're not gonna issue you a warrant for nonpayment.' Which is nice of them, so far. But I haven't had a lot of self-confidence lately," Charlie explained. "You know, if I had more confidence in myself, maybe, I would be more joyful about the whole relationship, about what's going on, but…" Charlie drifted back into his problems with Cathy again, the new man he saw waiting wolfishly in the wings. What did she see in him? "I mean, I met him, he didn't strike me as anything, you know, really spectacular."

"Well," Amy said. "He's not smart like my Charlie."

"Yeah," Charlie said. Amy always knew what to say.

———

That night, Amy had a dream. Charlie was back at work. She watched him load the needle, inject it into an IV, and as the plunger pressed home Amy felt a surge of adrenaline. It was *her* pressing that syringe. *She* was the killer. And she was enjoying it.

But then Amy was the patient. She lay in the hospital bed. Charlie was there. He stood at the end of the hallway, where she had so often seen him, the portable Cerner cart in front like a pulpit. Charlie was talking, but Amy couldn't understand, and she couldn't answer. In a panic, she realized that she couldn't move at all. It was the injection. She'd been paralyzed. She was still paralyzed when she woke up. She checked her heart, feeling it flutter under her palm like a live bird. She didn't need to look up the nightmare in her dog-eared dream books. This was a no-brainer to interpret. She felt unsafe, powerless, she knew that. But there was something else in there, too. It wasn't until she'd finished breakfast and had the house to herself that she was able to puzzle out the rest.

What had bothered her was where Charlie had been standing—his usual position at the end of the L-shaped hallway. It was an isolated spot, closest to the doors to the elevator, farthest from the nursing station. She'd never much thought about it before. Now she wondered why.

Amy lay back on the couch and closed her eyes. She'd used this method hundreds of times before, a sort of self-hypnosis that she'd learned for confronting the painful episodes from her childhood. She'd breathe and disappear. It wasn't remembering so much as reliving.

She could place herself on shift, back with Charlie. She saw Charlie in the corner of the CCU. He was cute, in his shy, drippy way, hiding behind the computer. Every day after report, he'd wheel the portable Cerner computer away down the hall. He reminded her of a sad little mailman in his cardigan, towing his cart away. She had always assumed he wanted to work in quiet. She hadn't considered that he wanted to be by the doors to the hall. But that was where the drugs came in.

Standing by the doors, Charlie was the first and often the only person to see the runner from the pharmacy. Charlie always caught the runner; he was helpful like that. He always relieved the runner of his delivery tote of drugs. At the time, it had seemed like Charlie was the nice guy, saving the runner a trip, stocking the unit, doing his busy work. Now she saw something else.

My God, Amy realized. *Charlie didn't have to touch the Pyxis system at all.*

51

Amy pored through the paperwork that night till her eyes cracked. She brought the paperwork to bed with her, fell asleep with it, and read it in the morning before heading out for the long commute south, to use the Pyxis herself, another long weekend of overnight shifts.

Amy tried not to think of herself as being a traitor, but every day, it was more difficult. She had broken rank and felt unbearably at risk of being fired by the very institution she was working to improve, and utterly alone in the stress of that. She was still a nurse, but only the detectives understood her full identity. Tim and Danny were almost always working late now; Amy would swing in after her shift, share a coffee while handing off another stack of paperwork. Seeing the detectives working made Amy feel a little less alone, a little more brave.

It had been Amy who first told the detectives about the Cerner patient records. The SCPO investigators would want those records, unmolested and in full. Detective Douglas Brownlie had started the paperwork for the subpoena. Meanwhile, Amy had another way.

She felt something like the guy in that Johnny Cash song, the one where the auto worker brings a new car part home in his lunch box every day for twenty years and ends up with a full Cadillac. Except Amy didn't have twenty years to pull all of Charlie's Cerner records without anyone noticing. Instead, she brought a bigger purse to work.

Apparently, none of her coworkers had noticed how lengthy her Cerner printouts had grown; the privacy of the night shift afforded such liberties. Amy read through them quickly on the screen during her shift, then thumbed the pages, more slowly, alone in the car. She told herself it wasn't suspicious—a nurse, in a nurse's scrub uniform, parked by the roadside reading medical charts, but she knew it was suspicious, of course it was. These days, she seemed suspicious even to herself. She was trying to track Charlie down, figure out his methods of murder, if in fact he was a murderer. But in the process, she was acting like Charlie, too.

The slide between the Friday shift and the Saturday shift was easy: out by 11:00, home by 1:30 or 2:00, and a whole Saturday with the kids before heading back for the overnight. But by Sunday she was always exhausted, this Sunday more exhausting than most. Amy sat at the nurses' station for report, feeling like an imposter. She didn't trust herself tonight. She was nursing in a crime scene, but too tired either to nurse or investigate. Working with the prosecution had made Amy skittish. She was scared for everyone now, including her patients and herself. The stress soon crystallized into a splitting headache.

Amy walked to the Pxyis machine to order up a Tylenol, then just as quickly stopped herself. Everything was so loaded now, even the most usual things. Even pulling out a frigging Tylenol in a hospital.

Nurses called it self-dispensing. You wouldn't really call it a secret, but it wasn't exactly in the brochure. When a nurse needed an aspirin or a Tylenol for herself, she would often pull the med out of the Pyxis machine. It was a little thing, like a waitress eating a French fry off a plate. Amy fretted over her karmic bank balance daily, but had never been bothered by this. So why the huge guilty rush? Now she was angry with herself—it was just a Tylenol, for chrissake, so her head didn't fall off while she worked her ass off on the overnight. Amy decided, Screw it, she'd work with her teeth gritted.

Amy pressed Cancel on her Pyxis acetaminophen order. Of course, the drawer popped open anyway, and she instantly thought of Charlie as she bent to shut it, and another guilty wave twisted up her breathing. And then she stopped, and looked. There was the Tylenol, in its little cassette. The dig was in the same drawer, practically neighbors.

It would be that easy. As she went back through his Pyxis requests, it all began to make sense to her. The information had been in the computer the whole time. He wasn't always ordering dig; he didn't have to. He could order Tylenol. The dig was in the same drawer.

After her shift, Amy returned to the beginning of the Pyxis stack. The detectives were trying to convict Cullen for the murder of Florian Gall, focused on him and the dig. The problem was, the dig orders didn't match up with the dig deaths. But the Tylenol orders did. Maybe there was no way to prove he'd ordered one thing and taken another, but no nurse would look at his pattern of Tylenol orders and not find it bizarre. Amy couldn't help wondering if she was the first at Somerset to notice them.

The Tylenol orders weren't the only odd pattern. Studying the Pyxis again, Amy found other curious combinations of drugs that Charlie had consistently ordered. Nitroprusside. Norepinephrine. Nitroglycerine. Pavulon. The list went on and on, sometimes half a dozen in a night. Amy knew these drugs to be more commonly used in a cardiac unit. Charlie was working in Intensive Care. His orders emptied the drawers. Then, time and time again, Charlie ordered a restock from the pharmacy. His position in the hall with the Cerner meant he'd be the first to take the delivery. At the time, he was seen as being helpful. Now Amy wasn't so sure. The refill orders were unusual, and showed up on his Pyxis. The Somerset Medical Center attorney, Fleming, had asked Charlie about that, as he'd asked about his frequent cancellations. But had anybody asked Cullen what he was doing with all that heart medication?

Before bed, Amy picked up the phone to tell Tim. He and Danny were trying to trace a single gun; she thought the Pyxis was pointing to an entire arsenal. She still didn't know what he was doing with it all.

Amy went back to the bathroom, making a basin with her cupped hands and lifting the frigid well water to her face, but her heart palpitations were not irrational. She'd been looking for answers to who her friend really was. The answers had been there, on the pages of Charlie's Pyxis data, and the distinct pattern of drug combinations he'd ordered.

They were combinations which, from a physiological perspective, complemented each other, fitting toward a purpose the way individual notes contributed to a chord or an apparent disharmony of multiple boozes combined into a cocktail. It all made a terrible sense now. Amy needed to sleep, but she was afraid to dream.

52

Amy laid out her new discoveries across the table for Tim and Danny the following afternoon. Charlie had been bartending, she told them, titrating a pharmacopeal mélange, from both drugs he'd pulled from the Pyxis machine's cabinet and drugs he hadn't.[1] Each drug in the cocktail had a specific biochemical effect. Together, they were a biochemical symphony. In combination, it didn't require nearly so much of any one drug to push a vulnerable patient over the edge. One drug pushed while the other pulled.

Only the patient's reaction mattered. The gap of time between the serving of the cocktail and the patient's reaction was suspenseful. There might be a crash or a code or a Lazarus-like recovery. The cocktail was the riddle and the lab reports were the answer.

She had imagination enough to make sense of the patterns, but she couldn't begin to imagine the monster that amused itself with them. All she was certain of was that it wasn't the same gentle soul who was her friend Charlie. The emotional disconnect bothered her as much as the murders themselves.

Amy considered herself to be a perceptive person—a spiritual traveler, a listener with well-tuned antennae for the frequency of vibes. Growing up as she did, she had always assumed that if she was near another monster she would feel it. And yet, standing next to Charlie, she had never felt anything like evil. Maybe she'd gotten him wrong, or maybe her antennae were broken. Or maybe, Amy thought, she was half blind, and could see only the good in people.

———————

Charlie's Cerner pages comprised all of the charting he had done at Somerset. Each page told her she had assumed wrong. Charlie was not, actually, the world's greatest nurse, the greatest chart keeper Amy had ever seen. He had hardly typed a line.

It was, in fact, the *worst* charting Amy had ever seen. There were blotches of words here and there, blurts, spasms of hurried and misspelled observations. It couldn't have taken him more than a minute to do that work. Whatever he was doing on the computer, it wasn't input. That meant Charlie had been outputting something.

Amy had to wait until her next shift to print out the rest of the records. This time, she couldn't wait until she got home. That morning she called ahead, then brought her paperwork to the second floor of the prosecutor's office to share her discovery with the detectives.

The Cerner automatically kept track of everything a nurse did within the system, and provided a time and date stamp of every page a nurse had browsed. Charlie was browsing all night. He wasn't just reading, he was—*hunting*.

The word dragged a fingernail up her arm.

———————

In her dream that night, Charlie was standing by the Pyxis, laying out the IV bags. Helpful. He did this alone.

There were patients on the ward, listed on the white-board. Strenko, Simco, Strickland, each with a number. The room numbers were a kind of lottery; the nurses worked different numbers every day. Some nurses thought certain numbers were lucky and played them in the lottery. Some of the numbers reflected on themselves, front and back, like 212. Some were birthdays if you were born in February.

Now Charlie's at the Cerner. On the screen is a patient, not his. Now another patient, another.

The nurses are in the rooms, tending the cells. Charlie is in his. He draws the shades and closes the door and pulls the horseshoe curtain around the patient. Why so secret? Is Charlie in the room? Which room? He has three patients in three rooms. All three blinds are closed. It could be any of the three. It's like three-card monte. Where's Charlie? But he's not in the rooms. Charlie is at the nurse's station, pulling drugs. Why so many? He's alone at the Pyxis, but he's not using the Pyxis. Why so often? Another nurse needs to pull a drug and Charlie offers to do it for her. Why so helpful?

On top of the Pyxis, Amy can see the IV bags, clear little udders in a row. Each has a sticker with numbers and letters, ten-point type, you'd need your glasses to see. Is he wearing his glasses? He is not. Charlie is vain. He's handsome. He can't see.

You'd have to slow down, stop, study the bags to figure which goes to which patient. Does he? He has the cocktail in his hands and he sticks one. Does he know the name or the number? Does he know where it goes?

He's back behind the Cerner computer cart now, a new patient up on the screen. Then another. Then another. Why so many, Charlie? What are you looking for, hon?

Charlie, what are you looking for?

Charlie doesn't know. That's why he's looking.

It's a lottery.
Amy's awake.

————————

Crossed with the Pyxis reports, Cullen's Cerner records were the most incriminating piece of evidence the SCPO had against him thus far. But in order for the detectives to understand it, Amy needed to provide a quick primer.

Cerner had been introduced to the medical profession only a few years before as a compact and efficient way to input notes on patients, to look up their allergies, code status,[2] lab values, etc. But nurses were only supposed to do that for the patients they were caring for on shift.

What nurses never did, at least not any nurses Amy had ever known, was use Cerner to look up the status of other nurses' patients. But that, it seemed, was exactly what Charlie Cullen had been doing.

Amy started with Charlie's June forays into the chart of patient Florian Gall. The hospital records showed that Gall had gone into cardiac arrest at 9:32 a.m. on the morning of June 28 and died approximately forty-five minutes later.

Gall was not Cullen's assigned patient on the night he died. Yet the Cerner records showed Charles Cullen snooping into Gall's medical chart at 6:28 a.m., then again at 6:29 a.m. on June 28. He was checking in, only minutes apart, looking for something only a half hour after the dig spike had registered in Gall's lab work, and three hours before the dig levels in Gall's system would stop his heart.

"And that's just Gall," Amy said. The Cerner records contained lines and lines of Charlie Cullen's log-ins at the computer, thousands of them, sometimes hundreds a night.

"He was studying them," Danny said. "Why the fuck was he studying them?"

Amy thought she knew. The nurses had IV bags lined up for them. But what if Charlie had made a drug cocktail, and injected it into one or more of the IV bags sitting by the Pyxis? He wouldn't need to bring them to the patient's rooms, he wouldn't need to be present at all. The other nurses—even Amy—would do that work for him. Charlie could simply retreat to his corner and use the Cerner to scan the lab reports and the patient's progress. Cerner would tell him where his loaded IVs landed. He wouldn't need to be present for the death to feel the impact; you could just scan back on the Cerner anytime and follow the action. It could be that same night or the next day, it didn't matter; the event was always available on the screen to be relived again and again. Was that what he was doing? Amy felt her heart beginning to sicken. She had delivered his drug cocktails. And her friend Charlie had been following the action across the ward, like the box scores on a sports page.

53

The Gall toxicology report came in at 10:38 Saturday morning. Most of the paperwork was dedicated to what they *didn't* find: some ninety-six different drugs, from acetaminophen to zolpidem. What the tests did find was digoxin, and plenty of it: 23.4 mcg/l in the vitreous fluid, 32.0 mcg/kg in the spleen, 40.8 mcg/kg in the heart, and 104 mcg/kg in the kidney. Now Mambo could amend his report. Cause of Death: *Digoxin Toxicity.* Manner of Death: *Homicide.* They had both a murder victim and the murder weapon. But they still didn't have any sure way to convict the murderer.

The SCPO team was meeting twice a day now. The Pyxis reports and Cerner printouts were the single largest piece of evidence they had tying Cullen to the drugs that had killed Gall. But the Pyxis news merely demonstrated that it was possible for Charles Cullen to have gotten the drugs he needed to kill. Prosecutor Forrest knew that was a far cry from proof of murder.

Charles Cullen could easily claim the Tylenol orders were valid and real.[1] Amy's read of the Pyxis suggested Cullen had been playing a code game with patients across the ward, a supposition that was perhaps too complex to ever prove. Nor could they prove that Cullen's numerous Pyxis cancellations were anything other than mistakes, or that his Cerner stalking across the ward was anything other than a creepy but harmless obsession. And with Cullen out of work, it was obviously too late to catch him red-handed without risking another murder. There was only one sure way to put Cullen away: he'd have to confess his crimes, or at least one of them, to someone he trusted. If the Reverend Gall wasn't going to end up a cold case like Ethel Duryea, Tim would need to ask Amy for another favor.

The detectives set Amy up with a phone in one of the old offices of the Narcotics Division, where outgoing calls came up on caller ID as private number. She caught Charlie at home at just before 11, giving him her sunniest "Hi, honey!"

As their conversation turned to the case, she said, "I think the thing that bothers me so much, Char, is that I really felt like you were one of the reasons that I was there. It's just not the same without you. And you know, I mean, it sucks. It *sucks* without you there."

Charlie was certain now that he had been fired because of his photo in the nursing advertisements. Somebody had seen it, they'd reported him, checked the dates on his application. Charlie liked this version of events; it was a reminder of his lasting effect on the world, his picture and its consequences. He was a victim, but a famous one. They'd mailed him out, his face, smiling, handsome, *Charles*. It appeared in two magazines, as well.

"You're a star, Charlie!" Amy said. She told him she missed him terribly. Couldn't he come back to her—back across the state line, to Somerville? "I want—I want to see you, okay?"

"Okay," Charlie said.

"I mean, I don't know," Amy said, her voice charged and flirty. "I, I honestly don't know how Cathy would feel about that, but—"

"She tells me that, you know, she would have no problem with me seeing someone else, and I shouldn't have any problems with her seeing anybody," Charlie said.

"Right," Amy said quickly, pulling back. She'd felt safe playing on the edge, using charms she knew would appeal to him as a man but assuming he wouldn't cross the line of platonic friendship. He never had before. But, seeing other people? "Well, maybe, you know even—maybe you, me and Donna, we can get together," she said. Not a date, just a reunion with nurses from the unit.

"All right," Charlie said. He didn't sound quite as interested now. "So, yeah, ah…yeah. We can try and arrange something."

"Do you have my phone number?"

"Ah, yeah, I still have it," Charlie said. "You know, somewhere…"

"I know you won't call," Amy teased. She needed to reengage him without engaging his sex drive. "I know you're a dumbass, you're not gonna call, you're not gonna get in touch with me, and you know this sucks. It just sucks."

Charlie picked up on her pity, and pushed for more. "I just like, right now, I feel like totally worthless, is what I feel right now."

"Well you're not, okay? You're not."

"Because, I hate to say it, but you know, to me, my job is an important part of my, of my sense of identity. Who I am."

"I know, Charlie."

Charlie started to explain again about why he'd been fired, rambling unintelligibly on the subject for several minutes about the dates, why he'd gotten them wrong, the way they'd gotten *him* wrong...

"How about Zoloft?" Amy suggested. "How about some Prozac?"

Charlie stopped. "Well, I don't know."

"You know what, they have the new one," Amy said. "Zoo-Pro, you know?"

"One of each."

"Yeah, *seriously*, though, I mean—"

"Right." Charlie wasn't interested in that kind of help.

"This is a, a real shitty time for you."

"I just got so depressed. I just didn't care at all."

"Charlie," Amy said. "How can I help?"

He already had his résumé out there, on a couple job-search websites, Amy had heard they were good for hospital work, but with the holidays coming, and the prospect of child support again, he was having trouble staying positive. "I feel like I have like a month or so before I really start freaking out."

"And that's why you're gonna need me as a support, you dumbass!"

"Yeah."

"You *know* you've got to keep in touch," Amy said. "And I will definitely keep in touch. And actually, I'm being— I'm being kind of rude, 'cause I'm using one of my friend's phones, because my phone died, so I should probably get off 'cause it's long distance."

"Yeah, I guess so," Charlie said.

"So I will e-mail you and you will definitely call me. Promise?"

"I will."

"No, promise!"

"I—I promise."

———

Tim waited till he heard both clicks before time-stamping the tape. Amy had been pitch-perfect on the phone, drawing him in, making plans for future contact, and providing critical information the detectives could get nowhere else. The problem was the information itself. Charlie Cullen was actively looking for work.

Tim honestly didn't know what he was expected to do next. He had wanted to get the experts at the FBI involved, but Forrest had forbidden him from contacting Quantico. The SCPO would have to grind out this case alone; meanwhile, every day they worked was a day Cullen was out in the world, free to kill again. It might be days before he was back in an ICU. The reports from the surveillance team backed it up. Cullen was out there, interviewing, and who knew what else. The slow, case-building approach was taking too long. The only thing left was the direct approach.

54

The detectives watched Charlie Cullen out in front of the house, pulling out trash cans.

"This is going to work or it's not," Tim said.

"Can't argue with that," Danny said. "How you want to do this?"

"Let's kill the little prick with kindness," Tim said. "And if he resists, let's just kill him." He buttoned the automatic window and whistled.

Charlie looked up to see a car smoking in the December air. An official kind of car, big and new, New Jersey plates. The driver had his window down, his arm out like trying to catch a waiter. "Hey Charlie," the guy yelled. "Come here."

Charlie stopped, not sure what to do with the trash. He had the two barrels, trying to drag both to the curb at once, which wasn't working except by dragging them backward.

The detectives stepped out of the car.

"You know who we are?" Braun asked. Smiling at him. Friendly.

Charlie stopped and blinked at the ground. Two of them, both with mustaches, the white guy in a leather jacket and a black guy in a suit. Charlie thought he saw another guy, waiting inside.[1] "You're policemen."

"That's right, Charlie, we're policemen," Braun said. "Actually, we're detectives, Charlie. And do you know why we're here?"

"I assume it's something related to the Somerset Medical Center," Charlie said.

"And you assume that because..."

"Well, from the New Jersey license plates."

"Well, let me tell you, that's very perceptive, because you're right."

"Am I under arrest?"

"You're the target of our investigation, Charlie. We're investigating the deaths at Somerset, and we need to ask you some questions."

"Yeah, I was—they questioned me at the hospital, twice," Charlie said. "About the unusual incidents. They did that recently, asking me about the incidents there."

"Great. Okay. Now we want to talk to you, too."

Tim opened the backseat, patting the frame as if he were calling a dog, hoping Charlie followed directions. "Come on. We'll go for a ride. We can talk back at our office."

"Um, I don't—I don't have my coat," Charlie said.

Charlie's head was turned toward the ground but his eyes were glancing up now, stealing looks at the street, at the men, at the back of the car.

"You won't need the coat," Tim said. "It's warm in here." He patted the backseat again. "Let's go." Not telling him he had to, not saying it was a choice, either.

It was different from the other police cars Charlie had been in: roomier, more comfortable, and with no divider between the front and back seats. The detectives were all chitchatty during the drive, keeping it loose. They talked about work, sports, even the weather. Tim knew the pizza place near the intersection where Charlie grew up in West Orange, he remembered the mascot of Charlie's high school team. They drove Cullen across the state line, and showed him, unofficially, the interrogation room of the Somerset County police station. And when Charlie seemed loose enough, they let it rip.

Back in Newark Tim used to have guys handcuffed to an eyebolt on his desk. He'd look up from typing their statement and there's the guy, asleep in the chair. In for murder, going away for twenty years, snoring away. It took Tim a while to realize that for some guys, the stressful part was getting away with it, day by day. Getting caught was a relief. Getting caught meant at least there was nothing left to worry about, at least for some guys. But not, Tim realized, for guys like Charlie.

———

It was 2 a.m. when Braun's unmarked Crown Vic pulled back in front of Cullen's house. They had nothing. Cullen slid out across the backseat and headed silently toward his door. Braun rolled down his window.

"Yo, Charlie," he said. "Look at me."

Charlie squinted against the high beams.

"Next time you see me," Braun said, "you're wearing handcuffs."

Then Tim Braun stuck an arm out the window, a fist balled at the end of his leather jacket. He knew it was ridiculous, but there it was, he couldn't help it. He was so frustrated. His fist out a window was as close as he could get to a threat.

Tim was expecting a smartass answer, a *fuck you* or whatever. That was what Tim would have done, a guy stuck his arm out and said that. Charlie just nodded and turned and walked slowly back to his house. Like it didn't touch him. He didn't need to say *fuck you*. He was a free man and they didn't have enough on him to arrest him. To Tim, that was *fuck you* enough.

55

While Braun, Baldwin, and Capt. Andy Hissim had worked on Charles Cullen in Somerset, another team had approached his home in Bethlehem. SCPO detectives Lou DeMeo, Andrew Lippitt, Edward Percell, and Douglas Brownlie, accompanied by SCPO assistant prosecutor Tim Van Hise, Deputy Chief Norman Cullen, and Lt. Stuart Buckman, had been joined by Detective Delmar Wills, a liaison from the Northampton County District Attorney's Office. They served a warrant on Charlie's girlfriend, Catherine Westerfer, at her front door, then spent three hours combing through Cullen's house and car, searching chiefly for controlled substances Charles Cullen might have stolen from the hospital.

The search had come up with one blister pack of pills, one bottle of CVS allergy medication, and one bottle of ibuprofen. Each was emptied and the capsules and tablets counted, photographed, and bagged for storage in the Northampton DA's evidence facility. Analysis of these drugs would turn up nothing stronger than cold medicine.[1]

Braun and Baldwin rode the interstate home from Cullen's house in uncomfortable silence. Danny Baldwin was more than aware that as lead detective on this case, the fallout from what they'd just done would fall on his head first. It was Danny who had gone to Assistant Prosecutor Tim Van Hise, asking the man to trust him as he vouched for probable cause on the search warrant, working with him for hours to get the legal language just so. It had been a risky move, and before Van Hise had headed over with him to the judge's quarters he'd said, "Baldwin, this is your ass on the line—you sure about this?" Danny had said yes, absolutely. Now he wasn't so certain. He knew better than to bother trying to talk it through just yet, not in the car. Frustration radiated from his partner like heat off an animal.

They'd gone at Cullen for six hours, throwing everything they had at him. Charlie had been perfectly willing to go through his personal history. He showed no surprise that the detectives knew about the allegations at Saint Barnabas, St. Luke's, and Warren hospitals. Charlie didn't deny the allegations. He only said he'd never been charged, and the hospitals had cleared him. After that, he didn't see any reason to say anything else. So the detectives tried to overwhelm him with their knowledge of his secret methods for getting digoxin.

They told him they had his Pyxis records. They had seen his requests and cancels for dig on June 15 and 27. In fact, as Danny had first noticed, Cullen was canceling orders all the time on Pyxis. What did Charlie think about that? Could he explain it? He said he couldn't. He didn't have to.

"Maybe I hit the wrong button," Charlie told them. Then later, he offered, "Maybe I wasn't wearing my glasses."

That didn't make sense, and the detectives told him so. If he'd made a mistake, and hit the wrong button, why didn't he follow up by hitting the correct one? Charlie didn't know. They asked him again, and he just shrugged, then stared at the floor. He knew he wasn't under arrest. He was going to walk. Braun wanted to stop the guy, physically if he could, just put him down before he killed again. But there's only so much you can push a guy when he knows he can walk away anytime he wants.

Finally, their pushing hit a dead end. The detectives kept asking him questions, and Cullen kept repeating the same answer over and over, how he "couldn't talk about that." That word, *couldn't*. It wasn't a denial, but it wasn't a confession, either. So the detectives pushed harder.

About six hours of this and Charlie was in tears. The prosecutor had told them finally, shut it down. And now here they were, worse off than when they'd started. On the ride back, that was the first thing Danny actually said out loud. It was blown. And it was picking the guy up without enough evidence for the arrest that had blown it. The guy was spooked now. He knew he was being watched, knew he was being investigated.

"You know the next call we're gonna get," Danny said finally.

Tim figured Cullen would have that lawyer by morning and that would be it, game over. They'd rolled the dice on getting a confession. But their chances of ever getting anything out of Cullen now were about zero.

———

Charlie waited until Cathy was gone for work before calling Amy. He had so many things to tell her, the week had been exciting, big-time crazy. He could hardly wait to tell her. So when he got Amy's machine, Charlie told it instead.

"Thursday—a big, big-big-big commotion!" Charlie said breathlessly. "Taken down for questioning, and Cathy was taken, um, was questioned for a couple hours and—for five hours. Big *big* ordeal, um, and, I guess, the whole thing at, ah, Somerset is probably getting a little bit…bigger. Um, but yeah, uh, well, um, Friday's possible. I didn't even think I was going to get to go home on Thursday," Charlie continued, "but, uh, so far nothing new that…*anyway*," he said. "Uh, I talk too much!"

Charlie hung up before he realized that in his excitement, he'd forgotten to tell Amy the other big news. She'd been right—those new job-search websites really did work. Charlie was going to be a nurse again.

56

Tim left the office, fishtailing out of the parking lot into the slushy tracks of the winter's first major snowstorm. It was all they talked about on the radio and he could imagine it, one hundred counties full of schoolkids cursing their luck that the first big snow would fall on a Friday night. The weather made a good excuse for Tim to cut out early; he had a follow-up phone conference scheduled with the FBI guys, a call Prosecutor Forrest had ordered him not to make. Tim figured maybe he'd get a cup of coffee and pull over, do the call in the car with the heater blowing.

Tim knew Danny would have loved to have been part of these conversations, and he knew better than to include him. Danny was ten years younger, still pushing forward in his career. Pissing off prosecutors was no way to get ahead.

Tim was absolutely certain that his prosecutor was making the wrong call. So instead of arguing, Tim had just ignored the order and did it anyway, reaching out to the FBI behind Forrest's back. The risk seemed worth it. It might help make the case, and it probably wouldn't cost him his job. Probably. That was seven days ago. In the meantime, they'd already taken a run at Cullen and blown it.

It was tempting, talking to the big boys, to smooth over

the rough spots and mistakes—like making Cullen cry, and the bit about threatening the guy in his driveway. But prettying it up for Quantico would be counterproductive. He couldn't expect to get the right help without giving Quantico the straight facts. All the same, this wasn't a conversation Tim was much looking forward to having.

———

Braun had first gotten in touch with the FBI through a contact in the Newark branch. He in turn had put Tim in touch with a state agent, who reached out to the people at Quantico—who, as far as Braun could tell, ate this sort of thing for breakfast. Serial killers weren't a redball for them; it was their job description. The Quantico profilers had seen killer nurses before. But they'd never seen anything quite like what Tim had in Charles Cullen.

On the phone,[1] the FBI agent had explained to Tim that 99 percent of the serialists of the medical-murder type were female. And with women, they said, you tended to get two things. Either *I'm going to be the hero* or *It's a mercy thing—I really hate to see them suffer.* A male medical killer was rare but not unheard of. Their motivations tended to be sexual, or based on power and control. As far as the Quantico profilers could determine, Cullen didn't fit any of the types. He seemed to be "a male actor who was maybe a little feminine." This presented them with an unstudied subspecies of serialist, still in the wild, just beyond the net. The Quantico profilers had sent Tim a sort of questionnaire about his serial killer, designed to help them further categorize Cullen's personality type. The hope was that they could make predictions about what the guy might do next, and give Tim advice on the best way to handle him.

But Tim had already handled him[2]—they'd basically

kidnapped Cullen. He'd screwed up. Now Tim was in the awkward position of having to sit in his idling car, listening to what he should have done.

"Usually," Quantico said, "we give our strategy *before* the guy's interviewed, so…"

"Right," Tim said.

"I mean, time's a little short, we've got a minimum of information, and you've already made a run at him."

"Right," Tim repeated. He hadn't expected it to be *this* uncomfortable. "In the event that we get another crack at him, when it comes time to put the charge on him…that's when we might anticipate putting the nippers on him," Tim said. He explained that they had a new development, a confidential informant. It felt good to have something positive to report.

"And who is she again?"

"She's a coworker of his and—"

"Okay—another nurse?"

"Another nurse," Tim said. "They had developed a friendship—probably the one and only friendship he had developed while working there."

"Says here he's 'a loner,' " Quantico said.

"Yeah, actually that was supported last night by this guy's girlfriend, who is six months pregnant now."

"With *his* kid?" Quantico asked.

"It's believed to be his kid, yeah."

"Okay, let me ask you this, Tim. What hard evidence do you have on this guy that your prosecutor's gonna deem usable?"

Tim didn't answer.

"Or, do you have any?"

"Well," Tim said. "Circumstantial is the evidence that we're compiling."

He waited for Quantico to jump in on that, too. When the agent didn't, he continued. "Uh, hard evidence? Eyewitness evidence? That, we *do not* have."

He waited again. Nothing.

"Much of what we're compiling is circumstantial evidence such as, uh, records. Computer entries, um…" Tim clicked his tongue, thinking. "And…prior history, prior patterns of similar-type behavior from other places of employment. Things of that nature."

"Okay, because these cases are pretty similar, in that they're a bitch to work."

"*Yes*," Tim said. "*Yes*, they are."

"It's almost like the bank tellers who embezzle and get fired—because the bank doesn't want people to know their tellers are stealing. They end up working at every bank in the state. These people just go hospital to hospital."

"Right," Tim said. "Okay."

"You know, most times they don't confess—due to the nature of the crime and the lack of hard evidence. I mean, don't feel bad thinking that you don't have hard evidence on this guy, it's typical for these kind of cases…"

"Wait…uh, you say most *don't* confess?"

"These type of guys—it's rare to begin with, for people in homicide," Quantico said. "And most of these guys don't end up confessing. They *do* know what they're doing, and there *isn't* the hard evidence, so—I'm not saying that to discourage you. I just don't want you to think that, you know, you've not done your job. This is a tough case."

"Well, that's comforting!" Tim said. He forced something like a laugh, *huh huh huh*.

"Yeah," Quantico said. "Well, it's comforting in a sort of a negative way."

"Well, listen," Quantico said, apparently to a second

agent on the line, surprising Tim. Tim hadn't realized this was a conference call. The FBI had a way of making you feel two steps behind. "Would it be premature for Tim to tell us about last night?"

"No, that was the second question," Quantico 2 confirmed. "I was going to ask what kind of evidence you had, first—and then second, I wanted to hear how last night went."

Tim was getting double-teamed now. He was starting to wish he hadn't called. It was like listening to brainy aliens discussing dinner plans.

He took a deep breath and dove back into the evidence, describing Cullen's digoxin cancellations, and how they'd confronted him with it last night. He told them how, each time, Cullen had said it was a mistake, or "I didn't have my glasses on," or "I don't remember that happening."

Quantico 1 cut him off. "Yeah. So basically you guys ran a couple of these things at him and he came up with lame excuses?"

"Yeah," Tim said. "Yes." He explained how after they took him in, they'd spent the first few hours in the car just building rapport. It was later, in the office, that they turned up the heat. "We tried to, you know, not *confront* him, but…"

"Tim?"

"Uh, yeah?"

"Did you stay the good cop through this whole thing?"

Tim thought about that one. "Uh, yeah," he said.

"So, do you think you've got the better rapport, because of the role you played? Or at least—you never challenged the guy too much…"

"No." Tim said. He didn't think he'd challenged the guy as much as Danny. Danny had kind of come in swinging. Then their captain had come in and used some psychology course he'd taken, touching Charlie on the leg, which Tim thought made things kind of awkward.

"How'd you guys leave the door open? At the end."

It was the window I left open, Tim thought, *with me pointing my fist out of it, telling Cullen next time I see him I'm gonna fucking arrest him.* But that was obviously not the right answer.

"Um…we left it, um, you know, 'Give us a call if you think of anything else' …things of that nature."

"So, you didn't say the equivalent of, 'Well, we know you're a guilty little motherfucker, we know we're gonna get you' …"

"Well…heh heh." Tim tried that laugh again, wondering how these Quantico guys always seemed to read his mind. "Yeah, he was, uh—made aware," Tim said. "That was mentioned to him, yes."

The other end of the line was silent for a long time.

"Okay," Quantico 1 said finally. "The prosecutor—without the confession last night, is he still going to move forward on the whole thing?"

"No."

"The confession is the hinge to the whole thing."

"At this early stage, yes."

Their silence lasted long enough that Braun wondered if he'd dropped the call.

This was bad. Tim read the silence as failure. They'd taken a run at Charlie, maybe their only chance to get him to talk, and they'd blown it. Now he was out there, and they had nothing but a confidential informant. Amy's calls with Charlie were filling up tapes, but getting them no closer to a confession. And her last call had gone straight to his machine; Charlie wasn't even calling Amy back anymore. Even the FBI couldn't help. They'd lost him.[3]

"We've got our thinking caps on here," one of the Quanticos said finally.

"Yeah," Tim said. "That's what I'm trying to do here, too."

———

Amy pulled into her driveway, kicked her boots on the mat, and found the kitchen light and the bottle of wine in the fridge rack. Home. The drive had taken nearly twice as long in the snow. She was done with work, done with the unit, done with Charlie Frigging Cullen. At least for tonight.

She peeled out of her hospital scrubs, washed the institutional stink out of her hair, and wrapped it high in a towel. She rediscovered her wine and flopped back on the living room couch when she noticed the answering machine, blinking red with a message. She wasn't particularly eager to find out what it was.

The plan was for Amy to make a personal connection to Charlie, then bring him in to Somerset County. The hope was that he'd say something, anything, to incriminate himself. And at that point they'd lock him up. Amy had made the personal connection all right, pushed for a meeting, flirted with the guy, and for what? Charlie was still out there, thinking about her. He had a car and she was in the book. What was to stop him from coming to her house? He'd done that before to other women, like the one he'd stalked when he was working at Warren Hospital. Charlie had told her that story one night at work, and at the time she'd laughed. It didn't seem so funny now, with her kids asleep upstairs. For all she knew Charlie was out there now, standing in the snow just beyond the black windows, watching. There was no way to see outside without turning off the light—and there was no way she was turning off the light.

Amy flipped the deadbolt on the front door, locked the

back screen, and drew the curtains. Somehow, she still didn't feel safe. She had to know where he was. Amy flopped down by the message machine and fingered the flashing button, facing her fear.

It was Charlie. He didn't say anything about coming to find her, that was good. But he did have other frightening news. He'd found a help-wanted listing from a hospital called Montgomery, seeking experienced nursing staff for their critical care wards. He'd driven out and filed an application. As references Charlie had listed Lehigh Valley, St. Luke's Hospital, and Somerset Medical Center.[4] He included the Somerset Medical phone number and the name of his manager, Val. Charlie ticked the box that indicated that he had been fired from Somerset, writing "I had incorrect dates on application" as the reason for his dismissal. Charlie had presented Montgomery with two state RN and ACLS licenses in good standing, and sixteen years of experience with nearly every type of unit and machine and drug.[5] He wanted full-time work, preferred overnights, would work on weekends and holidays. He was looking for $25 an hour. He was ready to start immediately. And on December 8, Montgomery Hospital penciled nurse Charles Cullen onto the training schedule for that Thursday's night shift, starting at 7 p.m.

The HR guy had emphasized *sharp*. That wasn't a problem, Charlie had told him. He was a good nurse, and always early.

57

Even in the middle of the night, Tim answered the phone, a cop habit, the same as doctors or plumbers. That thing about good news always waiting until morning, it was true, but it was the job description. Nobody called doctors and plumbers with good news, either.

Tim tried to get in a few hours of sleep after Amy's call, but he eventually stopped pretending and found his suit and gun. The office was the place to be right now. He was alone there. He could think.

Tim sat in the dark, counting his certainties. Charlie Cullen was a bad guy. And they'd get him, Tim had to believe that. Sooner or later, they would. But as he'd learned in the Duryea case, later was too late. In Charlie Cullen's case, it had been too late for a long time.

Tim watched the sun come up through the office windows, watched the first kids climb their new sleds up the courthouse hill. Then he closed his door to make a private call.

Tim dialed 411 in Norristown, Pennsylvania, and connected to the Montgomery Hospital switchboard. They passed him up the line through administration until he landed at the desk of Vice President Barbara Hannon.

Tim was calling as a private citizen, but he introduced himself as Sergeant Braun of Somerset County Homicide anyway, knowing the effect it would have. Tim told Hannon that if she wanted to keep her patients alive, she needed to pull their new nursing hire off that night's shift schedule. That got the woman's attention. She promised to do it right away.

Tim couldn't tell her who Cullen was, or even his background. He couldn't say that she had hired a serial killer, not in those words; it wasn't legal. It probably wasn't even legal for him to be making a call like that in the first place. Tim figured, fine; Cullen could sue him later.

———

The morning meeting was a full boat, everybody grousy and tired from the workload and the new winter weather, then even grousier when the report came in that the suspicious deaths at Somerset were about to hit the papers. Somehow, it had leaked. The DOH, Somerset Medical Center, and the prosecutor's office had already received calls from reporters. Tim thought maybe those calls were going both ways. Sometimes it felt like the prosecutor's office had press agents on the payroll.

So, gathering facts under the media radar was finished. Charlie's name wasn't out yet, but it was only a matter of time. And once the media got a name, the lights would go on. Everybody would freeze up with a lawyer, and the rest would play out in court. The circumstantial case they were building over nearly two and a half months wasn't anywhere close to bulletproof, but it was done. The FBI had been right on this one; this case was a bitch to work.

Making any case on circumstantial evidence, you wanted to involve the suspect directly, get him to talk, even ask him to help you understand the case, hoping he'd hang himself in a web of lies. Then later, in jury trial, you display those lies, tearing each one down and destroying all reasonable doubt. That's how circumstantial cases get built, lie by lie. But if the suspect lawyers up, it's over. There wasn't a lawyer alive who would let his client talk in a situation like this. Let alone confess.

Cullen wouldn't talk to detectives, but maybe he'd still talk to a friend. Tim and Danny talked it out, then they called Amy at home and told her they needed one more thing.

It was a move they hadn't intended to make for months, but they no longer had a choice. Amy had to get Cullen talking, and quick. And she had to do it face-to-face.

58

The microphone was just a little pack, like in the movies. The tech helped rig it up, a professional process undermined by Amy making jokes because it had to be placed high, between her breasts. It was the first time the detectives had seen her pacemaker scar.

And that changed the mood. They offered to let her parachute on the whole deal, right now, not wanting her to die from the stress or whatever. Amy assured them it was fine, and, despite her hammering heart, made it believable with practiced calm. The next question was to the tech, asking, Hey, is the pacemaker gonna screw up the mic?

After the tape-up Amy excused herself to the bathroom and locked the door. Quiet. She planted her purse across the sink and studied herself in the mirror. She looked the same. But wasn't there a hint of her secret mission, the secret-agent gizmo?

Amy shot herself a fierce look, the kind she'd flash her daughter to get her to behave. She fixed her hair and then felt silly about it and unfixed it. Then she flicked the light and stepped back out onto the homicide floor, wired for sound.

———

Amy had set the lunch date with Charlie and tried to keep it short. Charlie had wanted off the phone anyway. He said it was probably bugged. That seemed to amp the romance of their rendezvous for Charlie. In fact, it was Amy's phone that was tapped.

Afterward Amy called Tim with the details on the meet, at an Italian restaurant called Carrabba's. Tim was impressed—the girl was choosing food she actually wanted to eat, thinking not just about bringing down her friend as a serial killer but about expensing some homemade sausage, too. Hell, Amy wasn't just the most fun CI he'd ever run, she might even be the best, he thought. If the girl ever wanted to quit nursing, she'd make one heck of a cop.

The detectives had outlined the plan in the squad room earlier that afternoon. The goal was to have Amy draw Cullen over the state line so they could put the nippers on him in New Jersey, to avoid the extradition process. While they were at it, they'd put Amy on a wire, hoping to God she could get Cullen to talk. But when Tim and Danny drove over to scout the location, they found Carrabba's closed. It was an accident, but a good one. Meeting at a closed restaurant, seeming to switch it up on the fly—if Cullen was paranoid, this would make it look unplanned.

Tim and Danny set up in the unmarked Crown Vic, parked idling in a vantage spot. They saw Amy get out of her car, Charlie come in from his blue Escort, the two of them saying hi and complaining about the restaurant being closed. By the time Danny had gotten her tuned in on the box she was back in the car again, Charlie following in his. The detectives rolled with them.

Amy was freaking. She could drive, turn the key, press the gas and use the signal, but she couldn't hear the signal, or anything except the wooly whoosh of blood in her ears. She tried a few sentences out loud—to herself, to the gods, to the detectives—telling them she was on her way to a new location, a place called The Office, trying to be official. And then when that two seconds was over she decided, *Screw it,* and cranked the dial on the stereo, letting a solid sonic wall of FM power metal wash it all away.

Amy saw Charlie's little car still wobbling in her rearview as she signaled right into the Office parking lot, felt a fresh spike of panic over the challenge of parking between yellow lines, and killed the engine to inhale a half second of silence.

Then she bobbed to the rearview, shot herself a *Be Cool* look, and sprung out into the air, calling, *"Hi, sweetie!"*

59

The wireless unit was borrowed from Narcotics. They both knew it was a piece of shit, a tool not much used on the mean streets of Somerset County but hopefully good enough. They heard a car door slam, greet-greet *Hi-Hi* chitter-chatter and double doors into restaurant noises, the rhubarb of laugh and talk, bright sounds of tine and plate. They heard Amy ask for a quiet booth, *Good girl.* Tim and Danny slid reflexively into their leather buckets listening hard.

"Hi hon-ney, how are you?"

Charlie winces at the December sun. "Oh, all right," he says.

"Yeah?"

"Yeah," he says. "Oh-kay."

Amy nods at the bloody nicks below his nose and lip. "Well, you shaved."

Charlie rolls his eyes. "Yeah, I shaved too closely." He touches his chin, feeling dried blood. "I shaved once, then I looked at myself in the mirror, said, Oh my god! With my glasses on."[1]

They push through the double doors into the good-time décor, a beer-o-clock theme with hanging mugs for regulars and tables out behind. Amy now takes another look at Charlie. The too-close double-shave, the new haircut and, okay—he *did* look like he'd dressed for a date.

"Look at you!" Amy says. "With the decked-out shirt."

"I know," Charlie says. Despite the December weather, he was in dated tropical wear—a loose shirt in the same ice-cream white as his pants and shoes. "I'm all white." If not for the repeating jungle leaf print running along one side of the shirt, he might have been in uniform.

Amy tells the hostess they're playing hooky from work, sneaking smiles at Charlie, making it fun as they follow the waitress to the back of the bar. Charlie and Amy slide into opposite sides of a vinyl booth.

"So," Charlie says, jumping right in. "They were talking about me on the radio."

"Wait—*when*?"

"Oh, when I was driving here," Charlie says. He'd been following the news closely for several days. Newark *Star-Ledger* reporter Rick Hepp had an unnamed source confirming that the Somerset County Prosecutor's Office was investigating a string of possible homicides at Somerset Medical Center, with an unnamed local male nurse as the lead suspect. The news leak had exploded from there, gathering scope and juicy specificity by the hour. "I was listening to the classics station, it was a local station, like 99, a local oldies station. Or, it was—"

"And it said…?"

"My name," Charlie says. "'Charles Cullen.' And, you know, and the other one, 101.5, it just mentioned that it was a nurse. I'd read it too, before—the investigation, they'd mentioned it."

"And this is..."

Charlie had been following himself in the papers. "The Newark *Star*.[2] And I read it in the *Morning Call*—it's a local paper—that they'd contacted the nurse's employer, what they thought would be the employer, and—what they thought— that's Montgomery, so..."

"Oh, Montgomery," Amy says. "Is that—"

"How's everybody doing today?" the server, Joel, asks. "Maybe you folks wanna start off with a couple drinks?"

Charlie glances at Amy, unsure. Amy's having a Corona. But Charlie's been sober for weeks now. He promised his daughter he'd stay that way.

"Um, yeah," Charlie says. "Um...Miller? Or Michelob?"

"We have Michelob Ultra."

"Yeah," Charlie says quickly. "Good, good..."

"That's, like, low-carb, dude," Amy says.

"Oh is it?" Charlie says. "Oh, ha-ha. No no no, not that. I'll have a Corona."

Charlie waits until the waiter is gone before he continues. "Yeah, and so my eldest is thirteen," he says. "So I just told her, I took care of that. "

"So you just told her...because you were worried it was going to hit the papers?"

"Well, I didn't talk to her until a couple of days ago," Charlie says. "When they took me up for questioning. Because they told me, you know, next time they see me, they're going to put handcuffs on me and take me in, so I wanted to call her and let her know."

Charlie tells Amy he'd been waking up and going to bed wondering, *Can I sleep through the night, or are they already at the door?* When the call did come, it wasn't the police at all, but a reporter from a newspaper. Charlie is famous. He wants Amy to know this is way bigger than his recruitment flyer. "And, well—it was in the *New York Times*, so—"

"Did you folks have a chance to look over the menu, or..." It's the waiter again.

Charlie drops his head and studies his placemat until the kid disappears and he has Amy's attention again.

"Okay," he says. "So...you want me to start from the beginning?"

Over the wire the noise grew by degrees, with the early after-work crowd becoming louder round by round, plus there was an electrical something interfering with the mic frequency—air traffic control or a pager or the girl's pacemaker; they didn't know, only that it was a strain to listen to.

The men leaned in, ties hanging, as if getting closer to the box was going to help with the headphones. They heard Amy tell Charlie, "All right, let's start from the beginning," which made them lean in even more.

When—when everything happened at Somerset, they only said—"

"That there was an issue with my application," Charlie says. "You know, something like that. I mean I went to the first interview, that was fine, then when I went to the second interview, when they pulled me off the floor—the first one was at upper management, that was for the Reverend..."

"What happened? I—I mean, honestly, I don't even know what happened with him."

"I don't know," Charlie says. " I mean, he seemed fine at the time."

"He seemed—I mean, did you have him?" Amy knows all of this, of course; she knows more than Charlie could imagine. The point is to make him say it. "What did he have?" Amy asks. "What was wrong with him?"

"I think he was liver failure and kidney failure," Charlie says. "We had to dialyze."

"I think I had him," Amy says.

"Yeah, well I had him once. Or twice," Charlie says. "When he was over at the ICU."

"So you had—he was in the ICU and then he moved?"

"Yeah, they moved him, and, then, they...they all talked how about how he passed away, and the dig levels were high...I'm not sure if I heard the...but I remember seeing him but I don't remember, so..."

"Who had him, though, when all that went down?"

"It was me, I think I had him that night," Charlie says. He explains to Amy how they'd shown him his signatures. He says he didn't remember every time he took meds for a code that wasn't normal, but he made mistakes sometimes, and sometimes forgot his glasses—and anyway, you know, really, it's like, who remembers this stuff?

"And management got called in when?"

"Sometime after that," Charlie says.

"So, when Risk Management questioned you, did they actually show you the chart?"

"They showed me the chart," Charlie says. "And they showed me my signature. And, I don't remember doing that, but I cosigned dig. And they showed me the Pyxis records then, they had the records and they showed me how, I guess, I'd canceled orders for the dig, ordering it under another patient. I'd ordered dig for another patient and then canceled the order."

"You *did* that?"

"Yeah, I did," Charlie says. He gives Amy his sheepish look. "I did that."

"Charlie, you're a dumbass," Amy says.

"I know, I know!" Charlie says.

———————

Hear that?" Danny said.

"Lund had the Pyxis for Gall."

"And the cancels."

"Yep."

"Fuckers."

———————

The Southwestern spring rolls are laid like daisy petals around dipping sauce.

"Wait," Amy says. "You actually have the papers *with you*?"

"Yeah," Charlie says. "Well, just the one." He flops the paper on the table like a winning poker hand and watches for Amy's reaction.

"The—the *New York Times*?" Her shock is genuine.

That is the reaction. "Yeah," Charlie says.

Amy shakes her head, not sure what the proper reaction should be.

"Um, wow," she says. "The freaking *New York Times*."

"Yeah." Charlie nods toward the paper. "It's the Metro section."

Amy reads. He takes in the raw amazement on her face, the way her lips form words as she scans the story, the wisps of blonde hair that fall as she bends to read the description of him.

"It just says 'a male nurse,'" he says.

"And, oh, gee," Amy says, her voice doofy. "I wonder who it is, '...was fired in late October.'"

"Yeah," Charlie says.

"Blah blah blah...five other hospitals." Amy looks up, squinting and serious. "Charlie, is that *true*?"

"Yeah, see, I mean—I jumped around five other hospitals—"

"Is it *true*?"

Charlie reaches for his beer. "I had—a problem, when I first started out, with uh—the first hospital I worked at was Saint Barnabas, and there was a patient there who crashed with low blood sugar, and there was some question." He takes a sip. "But nothing came of it. There had been other problems at Saint Barnabas. Somebody had been spiking IV bags in the store room with insulin, and—"

"*What?*" Amy says.

"Yeaaaah...," Charlie says.

"But—knowing your ICU, I mean, how would they—"

Charlie explains the process and how, after the crashes and confusion, somebody finally checked the IV bags and...

"*All* the IV bags, or—"

"Oh, no. No no," Charlie says, as if that was the craziest thing he'd ever heard. He reaches casually for a spring roll and holds it, waiting.

"So...why did they pinpoint...but they pinpointed *you*," Amy says, as if making the connection for the first time. "They *tried* to..."

"Yeah, but—"

"Were these older patients?"

"No," Charlie says, chewing. "One of these was younger.[3] But, the others...they questioned me."

"What did you think? What did you think, when they were questioning you?"

It was like a big deal at Saint Barnabas; Charlie wants to make that clear. A mystery. There were all sorts of nurses that hung the bags. Even a smart person couldn't figure out a pattern from something like this.

"But what did *you* think? When you were going through that, what did you think *could* have happened?"

Charlie chews his spring roll, thinking on it. "I wasn't sure. I wasn't," he says. "There was one patient, that was an HIV patient, she had terminal AIDS, and the mother wasn't involved, but the *father* wanted the patient…um, and he thought that, maybe, I would do it. But I really didn't know, about that." Charlie quickly adds, "You know. I never got accused. But I left there."[4]

"But, when did that happen? That happened *years* ago."

"Yeah."

"So, what is your opinion? Because *it looks bad.*"

"Oh, I know. I know."

"I mean, Charlie—it looks *bad.*"

"I mean, I was a target. I've been looked at, you know, in Warren County. Warren Hospital, they did interviews. They said, 'We want to talk to you.' They said, 'Now, it would be a long investigation, we don't have enough to charge you.' "

"Yes, but, are you *capable* of doing it?"

Charlie lowers his head. He remains still for a long time. When he speaks again, his voice is unnaturally slow.

"As far as abnormal lab results, I was…the other time, that was dig. That was at Warren Hospital. A patient that died, twenty-four hours after I'd been her nurse. Someone said, the son had said, that I injected her with something."

"The son?"

"The. Little. Little woman. The—mother…mother said, that, she said—yeah, I don't remember, uh…that, at all," Charlie says, struggling. "Other than, you know, that the doctor…thought it was a bug bite, and they investigated." He insisted on taking a lie detector test about the woman's death. And how, yeah—he passed.

"Nice!" Amy says.

Charlie brightens. "And then I sued them for discrimination," he says. It was actually an administrative leave with full pay from Warren, which kept Charlie out of their wards for nearly three months, but the cash settlement was basically the same thing, and it makes a much better story. "They settled out of court, and I got, like, $20,000,[5] so..."

"*Nice!*" Amy says.

"Yeahyeahyeahyeah," Charlie says. "And that's where I was admitted as a patient, to that hospital, after my suicide.... And so—there's another twist to that story, too." The newspaper story had mentioned his stay in the Muhlenberg psychiatric ward. It's a story he likes to tell. "I was going through my divorce at the time. I was at Warren. And then I started...talking with someone."

Bleep bleep bleep. Amy fumbles in her purse for her cell phone alarm clock. It's a signal for the detectives listening to flip the tape. Charlie waits until she's back in listening position again and he can continue the story.

"So, I started...seeing someone...romantically there. I was technically getting divorced and...whether or not she thought..."

Amy squeals. "You were having an affair?"

"Yeah—but I was actually going through a divorce."

"You *were* having an affair!"

"Well," Charlie says, "it *was* pre-divorce, technically."

"Technically," Amy teases.

"Technically," Charlie says. Just as now, he was still *technically* living with Cathy.[6]

But between the cops raiding the house and Amy's flirty messages on the machine, Cathy is already convinced that he and Amy are going to take off to Mexico like desperados. It isn't the worst idea; Charlie is dressed for the tropics.

Charlie tells Amy the Michelle Tomlinson stalking story again, making it sound like a slapstick romance. He liked her, but there was a misunderstanding, which led to this whole ridiculous thing where he sorta, um, *broke into her apartment one night,* and...

"Can I get you folks anything?" Amy turns. It's the pesky waiter again.

"I'll tell you what—what's your name? Jeff? Joel. Joel, we'll just call you over when we need you, okay?"

Amy watches him go. Between him and Charlie's free-associating, she is getting nowhere. Her bravery is wearing off faster than the beer can replace it. She has a brief image of her heart exploding, the microphone picking up the liquid sound.

"I just wanna poke his little eyes out," she says, and shoots Charlie a secret look. There is no way she can handle this much longer.

———

Over the headphones, a door squeaks, squeaks again. The restaurant noise is suddenly small and distant. Then another door, a woman's hard heel on tile, the hollow metal of a locking public stall.

"Okay, look, you better turn it down," Amy says.

———

She hasn't realized how public her life has become until she needs to use the ladies room. Who knows how many people are listening in. Amy squeezes her eyes tight, imagining away the high hiss sounding off porcelain. But she has a microphone strapped onto her heart. They can hear everything.

She let the sink run, the noise of it making her feel alone

at last, and studies the girl in the mirror, the one Charlie trusted, the one the detectives trusted, too. Who is she? A friend? A spy? Amy fingers the scar scalpeled across her breast plate, thinking of the damaged heart below it, the microphone strapped close by. This is her life now; you could listen to her pee over the radio. She is utterly transparent, like the clear plastic woman from biology class, the conflicting dimensions of her inner life encapsulated in parti-colored pieces: injuries and insecurities, the glandular excretions of fear and hope. She couldn't see inside of Charlie like this. Behind the computer screens and paperwork and cancellations and a uniform was a man she does not know. But maybe now, across a restaurant table, she can know him. "You can do this," she says, trying out the sound, liking it. Then she checks her gloss and pushes back out the door.

Amy figures Charlie might have bolted the restaurant. She has a sudden flash of him on the highway, headed north to her house, waiting in her driveway as her daughters returned from school, and—but there he is, slumping in the booth like an unplugged robot. Amy slides into her seat and watches his eyes flick up and register her. And suddenly, he is present, and the story picks up just where they left off.

Charlie speaks freely about the allegations and circumstances, providing details of patients who mysteriously died. He was comfortable with the details. *They* thought he did it, Charlie says. The hospitals. The investigators. He can talk about *Them*.

"Charlie?" Amy says. "I need to ask you something. Are *you* capable of doing those things?"

Charlie sags suddenly.

"Because that's what I want to know. Are you *capable*?"

Charlie sits, quiet. When his voice finally comes, it is in halting monotone bursts, directed at the appetizer.

"What they were saying...is that these people were die...were people that were going to die...were doing really poorly but..."

"Charlie?"

"I don't really want to talk to you about it," he says. He sits and stares for several more seconds. "Knowing that, you know...I mean...they even asked if I was attracted to patient death, you know...," he finally says. "They...they said I did."

"Charlie," Amy says.

He looks up again.

"Listen to me."

He's waiting.

"You are...*excellent.*"

Charlie is listening.

"You are—" Amy searches for the word "—a *phenomenal* nurse. And you are, my...my best...*partner.* That I've *ever* worked with. And I've...you know, and I *look* at this, and I, you know I'm *hearing* this, and I really wonder, Charlie, what...you know...I can't imagine being investigated *once*. But to be investigated *over* and *over* and *over* again..."

Charlie's eyes drop to his empty beer.

"Charlie?"

He looks up.

"What's your opinion of...*yourself*?"

Amy has just pushed Charlie into the deep end. "But I don't, I don't..."

"You know how much I care about you..."

"I know. I know, it doesn't, you know—" He shakes his head. "It's gotten to the point that, if I *do* get charged..."

"Charlie," Amy says. "Charlie. Look at me."

He looks.

"This is *over* and *over* again."

"Do I want it to be over?" he says.

"Do you want to be caught?" Amy says gently. "Do you want it to be really over?"

"I...really...as far as the charges...," Charlie begins.

"Charlie," Amy says. "Look at me." He's slipping away. She leans in close. "Look at me."

He looks.

"You are *not* stupid."

He watches her. "Yeah."

"And you know *I'm* not stupid."

"Yeah. I know, I know."

"And you know how much I care about you."

"I know, I know, I know, I know..."

"And I'm scared for you," Amy says. She can't help it—the wave of sadness has started rising in her chest. "Do you want to be caught?"

"It's to the point...if they bring the charges, and...I just feel a little...uh...overwhelmed," Charlie says. "And I feel, uh, you know, the hospital, the charges if they... when, um, I'm going into collection, and I have payments, and..."

She reaches for his hands, dead on the table. "*Please.*" She is crying now. "*Please* let me help you."

"I don't...I wouldn't...I can't."

"Let me help you."

"I can't. I can't..."

"*Let me help you.*"

Charlie has stopped moving.

"I see you, Charlie, and I'm *not* stupid. *Nobody* gets investigated over and over again, for *no reason*, Charlie. You *know* I know that."

He looks into a hole in the tabletop. "I—"

"What do you want?" Amy says. "How are you going to go on from here?"

"I don't know. I don't know. I—"

"Would it be easier if you were caught?"

"No," Charlie says. "It wouldn't. I—"

"How are you going to stop?" Amy asks. "Why? *Why?* You're *so good*. Do *you* know why?"

Charlie shakes his head at the floor.

"Charlie, what about Father Gall? What happened? *What happened?*"

"I just…can't…I can't…I…I can't…I…"

"I *know* you can. What happened? I know you're scared, but *what happened*?"

"I'll, I'll deal with the—"

"Charlie, I'm right here," Amy says. "*Right now.* Do you know?"

"It's…in the public," Charlie says. "I don't want…I can't…I don't want my life…it will…my life will…fall apart…"

"Your life *already* has fallen apart," Amy says. She lets that soak in. "It already did. *It already did.*"

"Hope not. Hope not. Hope not."

"Yes," she says. "*Your life fell apart.* And it's *falling apart.* And it's not going to come back together. I don't think so." She shakes the newspaper at Charlie. "And I read this…"

"People…believe…" His eyes search the table. "It… depends, what you think people are capable of."

"Please? Tell me how I can help," Amy says. "*Please* tell me. What I can do?"

"You. Do. Help. What I see happening is…unacceptable. You know…I…"

"*What* do you see happening? Charlie?"

"Being charged. Going to jail," Charlie says. He seems gone, the words leaking from his mouth like bubbles rising to the surface. "I lose. My children..."

"You're *already* losing them," Amy says. "You already are. And—I have *never* respected a nurse more than I respect you. And I am torn apart, watching you. I am *torn apart*. Because I see you. Out of everyone I know, I see *you*. And I *knew* you, and I *felt* you."

Charlie rocks gently in his seat like a child, mumbling, "I don't know, about, about, you know, what, your idea, of me... I just want it to be over..."

"How can we do that, then? How can we do that, then?"

"I...I...I...I, all I can do...," Charlie says. His voice is monotone, barely audible. "I've been giving them the truth. The truth. Truth."

"Not *enough* truth," Amy says. "What if you confessed?"

Charlie shoots a look at her. "I can't."

"Is there another option?"

"I...face the sources," Charlie says. "Face the accusations...they...I...they don't know, the...I can't handle the trial, the..."

"Charlie!" Amy cries. "This is me. Why? Just—why? Why did all this start? Charlie! Why? Are you ever going to stop? You can lie to the cops, but not to me. *Not* to me."

Charlie is muttering, talking circles, repeating words.

"I am *not* stupid," she says. "I'm not afraid of being your friend. I'm your friend."

Amy feels the vinyl of the booth rising around her, closing her off.

"I—like. Being with you. I love... when we worked the codes together. I *love it* when you were on with me. And you left me—abandoned."

She squares the newspaper to where Charlie's gaze is pinned to the table.

"Honey. I'm reading these, and you know what? I've been in nursing, for all these years. And *no one* has ever accused me of murder. And you've been accused now five times—more, maybe; you're telling me sometimes it's even more. And people think you actually killed people."

"No, I can't…it wouldn't…I can't…"

"I'm here, Charlie," Amy says. "I'm here, because—I love you. And I'm here because—I *know* you killed those people."

Charlie has stopped moving.

"I *know* it," she says.

The world has stopped. His lips move.

"Was it just—a rush?" Amy asks. She reaches across the table. His hand is cold. "Was it just for the kick of it, like when we're at a code?"

Charlie's eyes flick to the edges of the table, the space there.

"I don't know why," Amy says. "I—I don't know what your motivation was. But I know you're smarter than this. And I *know* you did it."

"I can't—"

"I know you did it. Let's go to the police station. We can tell them together."

"I can't I can't I can't…"

"Because I *know* you killed them, Charlie."

Charlie looks up.

This time, she feels a sudden wave of cold static. Then she sees the switch.

Sees his skin go slick and buttery. Watches his jaw reshape and his spine shift. Then Charlie's eyes began to drift apart.

The right eye unplugs and drifts lazy to the edge of the

table, reading the darkness there, pacing kinesthetic tracks back and forth and back. The left eye watches her. The wax head twists and speaks. The voice is low and toneless. Amy has never heard this voice before. It does not remind her of anything human.

There are undercover detectives here, men with guns watching, somewhere—but she isn't feeling that kind of fear. She doesn't sense evil in the man across from her. It's not rage or murderous lust. It's blankness, a horrible nothing. A wall has fallen. There is nothing behind it. In this moment, she knows. Charlie is not Charlie. If she did not know him, it was only because there was nothing really to know.

———

Tim had tried wiggling all the levels of the stupid wireless receiver, but they weren't getting squat out of there. The voices were distorted and drowned. They'd listen for a while, straining at the pips and pops and birdsong from the speakers. Then Danny would try the knobs. After a while they just stared ahead across the parking lot and watched the doors.

Charlie came out first, from the side door, alone. They watched him unlock his car and pull out onto 22.

"Where is she?" Tim said.

"I don't know."

"This isn't good," Tim said. "I'm going in."

Then Amy pushed through the front entrance. She hung to the door handle and stopped, dazed. The detectives hopped out of their car, waving and yelling. Amy looked to the sound, lost across a parking-lot sea.

———

She made the car before she fell apart and collapsed sobbing into Danny's arms. Tim opened the door and they slid her in to collect herself in the Crown Vic's heat. The recorder was there between the seats, a tape still spinning in the plastic window. The sight sobered her.

"So," she said. "Did you get it?"

Tim looked at Danny. "We'll get him," he said. "But—we were having a little trouble making out what he was saying."

"I told him," Amy said. "I told him that I knew. Something weird happened to him. His face. It was—awful. And he kept saying the same thing, over and over."

"What did he say?"

"He was talking weird," Amy said. "Low, almost a growl, one word at a time. But I think what he said was, 'Let. Me. Go. Down. Fighting.'"

60

Amy had statements to sign at the prosecutor's office before they let her go to her staff Christmas party. It didn't matter what kind of a day she had, Amy simply *had* to attend. It was the big-deal work event of the year, the sort of thing nurses pulled seniority on the schedule for. It was usually a good party as work parties go, docs and nurses, pharmacy and administration, secretaries and maintenance workers getting down beneath the disco ball of the Bridgewater Marriot ballroom. Amy's coworkers counted on an appearance by the outrageous party girl who wasn't afraid to hit on doctors or shake her ass on the dance floor or make them all drink shots with embarrassing names. A Christmas work party without Amy was like a year without Santa Claus. Amy wasn't the type to let anyone down except herself. Amy called Donna from Danny's desk, telling her she was running late, not able to say why.

Amy was a confusion of unprocessed emotions. One minute she felt sickened by Charlie's revelation, then guilty that she'd not felt his darkness sooner, then frightened by that darkness. She was nervous that her involvement might cost her job. Then, in the next stuttering breath, she felt a surge of pride. Wearing a wire, working undercover for homicide detectives, catching a serial killer. How cool was she? She felt extraordinary, and experienced a vain rush she hadn't felt since her days playing bass in a rock cover band. Then she realized that she was stoking her ego with her proximity to murder and infamy, the way Charlie had over lunch, showing her how famous he'd become in the newspaper, the Angel of Death. Amy's self-loathing set in, followed by guilt and anger. Each emotion pushed through in succession. Amy couldn't hold on to any one of them; it seemed so much simpler to just feel none. She craved numbness. Alcohol was the universal solvent. It might wash her mental whiteboard clean.

At the hotel she primped upstairs in a room rented with her girlfriends and had a few drinks, prepartying. She checked herself in the elevator mirror, looking hot—her hair in golden ringlets, makeup prom-perfect, and a dress she'd picked out weeks in advance. It was a tight, strapless thing that pushed her boobs up to her chin, done in satiny, bloodred material. Amy thought it gave her a fairy-tale look, like wicked Cinderella. When the elevator doors dinged open, she put a little extra wiggle in her stride and made her way toward the ballroom. She might not have known exactly who she was in that moment, or even how she felt, but she definitely was confident in her ability to make guys pay attention. With a dress like that, every man's face was a mirror. She knew it was shallow, but it was reassuring, too.

Somerset Medical CEO Dennis Miller was giving his speech to the troops as she walked into the crowded ballroom. Amy headed straight for the bar, ordering two Heinekens loudly enough that she got some looks. Miller was still talking. Amy took her beers, finished one, ordered another, then took them to where her nurses sat. She threw herself dramatically in a seat, giving an excited scrunch face to all the familiars, toasting, making too much of a fuss. The microphone man kept talking. Miller. Amy focused in on the CEO's red face and red tie. He was talking about Charlie. Miller never said the name, but that's what this was. He was congratulating Somerset Medical for standing up and reporting irregularities. "Blah blah blah," Amy said. That's what it was. A feel-good speech. He was taking credit. *I reported this, I reported that.* Amy was disgusted. *She* had reported things. *She* was risking her job. Didn't anyone else hear this crap? Amy searched the faces around the table for agreement but everyone was just listening to Miller, waiting for him to finish so they could get dessert. Amy wanted to puke. She flagged the waiter and ordered two glasses of white wine.

Miller saying how *Other hospitals had turned their heads, but we met this head on, as a team.*

"Bullshit," Amy said, maybe too loud.

Saying he was *proud of Somerset for keeping patients safe.*

"Lie lie lie," Amy said. "Blah blah blah."

Everyone at the table was watching her now. Some were smiling: *Classic Amy.*

Amy knew she was looking hot, but she had to wonder whether some of the looks she was getting owed something to Charlie as well. Of course, none of Amy's coworkers imagined she was a confidential informant working with the prosecutor's office, much less that she'd spent the afternoon at lunch with the killer, or the previous weeks secreting evidence out of the hospital. She could see them at the other tables, leaning in, whispering, staring. The rumors were out there, circulating, the looks said: *Is she one of us, or one of them?* At this point, she wasn't sure herself. She clapped a little too loud when Miller got offstage, and followed that with a round of shots. The party had turned a corner now, speeding along a course powered by the open bar. The lights dipped, the music came up, a few stray coworkers clapped their hands and bent their knees and shot finger pistols in the air.

Amy saw Miller working the tables, a drink in his hand. She stood up and sidled next to him, waited for him to notice. He noticed. Liked the dress. He leaned into it, yelling something in her ear, the music too loud but Amy couldn't miss the point. She said "What?" anyway.

Miller signaled for the girl with the drinks tray, flashed two fingers. He seemed cocky. One of those power guys with clean-shaven jowls and a full head of gray hair. She hated the man. He leaned in toward her bosom. "I need to know your name!" he said. "Who are you?"

Amy finished her wine, kept it wet on her lips, put them in his ear. "I'm Charlie Cullen's best friend!" she said.

Miller straightened up. He seemed to change color, but Amy couldn't be sure if that was just the disco lights. She thought he'd leave her, flee to the bar, but he didn't. "I know you," she said. She leaned back, looking him in his eyes.

"Oh you do, huh?"

Amy could tell the guy liked leaning in, the way the music forced them to breathe on each other. "Yeah," she said. "Do you know me?"

"I do now," Miller said. Amy saw his little smirk. He didn't know her. He probably didn't know anything at all. The guy was cocky. She wanted to smack that smirk off his fat face.

"Yeah, well, I know you're a liar," she shouted.

"Let's dance," Miller said. He took her hand. She let him lead toward the floor.

"I know things," Amy said into the music. "I know what

happened. You've got secrets, mister—behind the scenes."
Miller grinned at her. He seemed to think she was flirting
with him. She watched him, doing some sort of vague twist
like a chaperone at a high school dance, that cocksure smile.
She wanted to vomit everything she knew on this man. Just
empty her whole day on him, every unchecked emotion,
every fear, all the secrets and anger. She wanted him to be
scared, like she was. To be humble, at least. They weren't
dancing together so much as at each other, each in their own
rhythm. Amy was actually making a shame-shame-shame
dance out of shaking her finger at her CEO. "I know things,"
she yelled. "Big news. Big big big news."

Miller cupped his ear, not even trying, and took her hand
to spin her. By now her friends were taking pictures. *Classic
Amy!* The flashes were like a strobe light. Amy looked down
at the hand, up at the man in the tie, the photographers. What
was she? Enjoying the spotlight, angry at the man, dancing…
Drunk was what she was. Drunk and confused and at an
office party. "You're a liar," Amy said, and turned and walked
back to her friends at the table. "Dennis Miller is a liar," she
announced. "He lies."

Amy didn't know what to do next, so she went back to the
bar. She tried drinking some more, tried flirting with one of
the cuteish residents. Finally she wandered out into the parking lot. Distant highway sounds mixed with the music. Amy
looked up but saw no stars there, no sky.

61

Charlie steered his Ford Escort out of the Office restaurant parking lot and into the flow of traffic along 22 West at 4:40 p.m. Danny had radioed ahead to officers Timothy Musto and Michael Vanouver and Detective Douglas Brownlie, positioned just down the street in a marked Somerset County Sheriff's Department car. He and Tim wanted to do it themselves, but the officer who arrested Cullen and Mirandized him couldn't be part of the team that interrogated him later. Tim had found that you arrest a guy and tell him, "You have the right to be silent," and then later ask him to talk, he thinks you're joking. Better to have a uniform stop him, using something recognizable as a police car, make it seem like a routine traffic stop. Then hopefully, Cullen would be willing to talk later with the guys in suits.

Fifteen minutes later, the radio car came up behind Charlie and hit the gumballs. Charlie steered onto the paved shoulder just before the turnoff to Frontier Road. The officers ordered him out of the car and onto the ground, where Charlie was cuffed and searched before being placed in the rear seat of the marked unit. He was then driven to the prosecutor's office at 40 North Bridge Street and secured to the handcuff cable bolted to the floor in the upstairs Interview Room. Then Tim and Danny made their appearance.

Charlie looked up at the men in suits, big guys in a little room. Two guys standing over him while he's chained to the floor.

"Hi there," Tim said. He jerked his thumb between himself and Danny. "Remember us?"

Charlie looked at the ground.

"And where are you now, asshole?"

Charlie tried to turn away, but he was stuck on a short leash. The man kept talking.

"Yeah, that's right, you sick son of a bitch," Tim said. "I told you so. Didn't I tell you?"

Tim was a smartass, and he'd admit, he enjoyed it. But laying into Cullen served a purpose besides sport. Tim knew that Charlie Cullen had been investigated repeatedly and never suffered any consequences. He was a guy who had made decisions and paid for them with other human lives. No matter what he seemed like at the moment, that fact alone meant Cullen was a pretty cocky guy. There was no greater measure of control one man could exert over another than murder.

The detectives needed to make Cullen understand that he wasn't in control anymore. This wasn't some late-night hospital shift where Charlie called the shots; it was the interrogation room of the state. The man needed to comprehend the full ramifications of his new reality. He had to internalize them. He needed to be torn down and broken. Meanwhile, the rest of the SCPO team watched through the two-way mirror, wondering how long the guy would sit there before he smartened up and asked for a lawyer.

The truth was, they couldn't *make* Charlie talk, nobody

could. The best the detectives could hope to do was create an environment in which Charlie *wanted* to.

They were asking Cullen to tell them things that Cullen believed he could not tell them. The detectives' job was to help resolve this paradox for him. They needed to challenge his belief system so deeply that the architecture of his universe failed. Then they needed to rebuild the world into one in which confessing to murder seem like a good option. And the only way to do that was to create a situation where not talking was actually worse.

"I tell you what I see, Charlie," Tim said. "I see you jerking off on dead people. We've seen your Cerner. We've seen your drug orders and cancellations. We have you, asshole. We just want to hear you say it, is all. That what you did? You jerk off before or after you killed these people, Charlie?"

Charlie didn't look at him. He studied the corner.

"You know what the world is going to know about you?" Danny said. He walked around to get in Cullen's field of vision. "A sick fucking monster. Charlie Cullen, oh yeah— that nurse who got off on dead old guys. That was how you did Gall."

"I can't," Charlie said quietly. "I can't. I—"

"Why don't you tell us about it, asshole?" Tim said. "Because otherwise that's the way they'll know you. The twisted sex monster who killed to beat his meat. Nice for your kids. How could you do that to them? You ever think about your kids, Charlie?"

After a few hours of this, Charlie was curled up in the fetal position, crying into his palms. Tim had only seen a guy do that maybe two, three times in his career. It was the last stop on the trip over the edge. Every other guy he'd broken like that had gone. But Charlie just stayed out on that edge. It was as if he somehow couldn't. So Danny and Tim tried another tack.

They took turns telling Charlie, "Hey, your girlfriend there? She's been calling the jail. This girl Amy. The two of you were at a lot of the same deaths at the same time. How about we bring her in for this, too?"

"I can't. I can't. I can't..."

"Did you take turns, or did you push the needle together?" Seeing if maybe they could motivate him to protect Amy.

Then they'd give Charlie a little break, step outside the room to let Charlie steep in it for a while, then come back in. The breaks weren't regular. They'd come in when they wanted to, leave, then return, sometimes appearing with Captain Nicholas Magos, surprising him, showing Charlie that he was not in control. Showing him they could go all night.

"You're either a sick fuck or you're the Angel of Mercy, up to you. Meat beater or mercy killer—which one will your kids like for a dad?"

At that for an hour, leaving, getting a coffee, watching the guy roll around on the monitor, coming back in the room, grilling him: "What if I told you we had fingerprints on some IV bags?" Giving him the bluff, but leaving some wiggle room with the what-if in case the guy had worn gloves.

Six hours in and Charlie was still rolled up and rocking, making guttural animal sounds. The detectives stood over him, listening. Sounds of frustration. Communication without words. Still not a confession. Sometimes Charlie stopped and seemed to compose himself, only to bury his face in his hands again and cry. Sometimes he studied the floor as if it were a map and he was lost. Sometimes he just said, "I can't," repeating it for half-hour stretches like a mantra of abnegation. He was tired. Cullen was a night nurse, he was used to late shifts, but he had to be exhausted by now. That was a good thing. The detectives stepped out of the room again to let him say his *I can't*s to the walls. They grabbed fresh coffee, talking through whether they should go next with the Amy angle or the sick-creep angle, when Forrest said, "Send him back." Meaning, it got shut down, and Cullen would go back to the jail.

Tim and Danny weren't finished, and they didn't think Charlie Cullen was finished, either. Sometimes a guy gets to a point and that's it, he's done, but Charlie wasn't there. The guy was going. They were close enough that one more push might do it. Push him and he might go. Quit now, and he wasn't going anywhere but court.

But Prosecutor Forrest was worried that any more would look bad. It was 3 a.m., and the guy was grunting on the floor, practically frothing. They'd been pushing him for nine hours.[1] Forrest didn't think they could push him much further. They were done. Tim and Danny knew the guy would have a lawyer before morning.

———

Tim drove home and hit the bed by 4 a.m. He hoped his internal clock would allow him to sleep in the next morning but nope, there was the sun, and he was up. Tim hated coming off a big case, dumping it into the institution. He wasn't even the lead and he felt like that. Danny had to be worse. It was disorienting; it never felt right. His mind was still on emergency mode, trying to crack this guy. Instead, he was supposed to relax, recharge, let it go. He'd done his job. This was the weekend. Doo-dads to take care of around the house. Now there was time. Run down to the cabin, check the pipes. Errands. By early afternoon Tim found himself sitting in the mall parking lot, thrumming his finger on the steering wheel while his wife shopped at the craft store.

What burned Tim was, they weren't done with the guy. He would have gone, given another few hours. He had that look. Now, get a lawyer in there and the guy's not opening his mouth again. It would drag on for a couple years and go to jury trial for one murder and one attempted—and that was *if* Somerset Medical Center didn't have the juice to keep the whole thing under seal with a grand jury, which Tim figured they absolutely did.

Would the charge of killing Reverend Gall stick? Did they have enough to convict him, or would they have to cut a deal? Tim flashed back to his Duryea murderer, the guy convicted of one attempted, then walking after serving seven years. Tim could picture the guy. He was probably walking down the street, whistling a happy little tune at that very second. Maybe he was here at the mall right now, doing a little weekend Christmas shopping. Why not—everyone else in the world seemed to be here. After all, it was the friggin' weekend.

Tim thought about that, drumming the steering wheel. Thought about it some more. And then Tim thought, *Maybe.*

Tim punched numbers on his phone and caught Assistant Prosecutor Tim Van Hise at home, who told him, sure, it was still legal, and he'd be willing to vouch. Cullen had signed his Miranda forms. He'd initialed that he understood his rights. He'd agreed to let them question him without the presence of an attorney. That was yesterday, but it still applied, absolutely.

Cullen's arrest had been made after hours on a Friday. He'd gone straight to the interview, and he hadn't been processed at the county jail until early the next morning. It was the weekend. The judge was probably out Christmas shopping with his wife. Cullen hadn't been arraigned yet. He hadn't seen a judge. Tim called the clerk at the jailhouse. He had Charlie's file still sitting there. It hadn't been flagged by an attorney yet. Then Tim called Danny. It was the call Danny was waiting for.

They could still take one more run at the guy. They weren't finished. They just needed Amy back in Somerville one last time.

62

News of an arrest for patient murders at Somerset Medical Center was reported on Friday afternoon. The phone calls started less than a minute later, flooding the prosecutor's office switchboard with over 175 inquiries and potential victims from tipsters and concerned family members. It was late afternoon before Tim and Danny could break free, leaving Detectives Brownlie and Magos to deal with the public while they walked across to the county jail.

The sergeant led them past the screaming metal detector and the two-way mirrored wall, through the series of buzzing electronic doors to the lockup. Tim and Danny found Cullen curled on his bed, staring at the wall.

"Hey, *there* he is," Tim said.

Cullen turned. He gave them a flat look. Then he looked at the floor.

"Treating you all right in here, Charlie?" Danny said.

Charlie glanced down at his new prison sneakers. "Yeah, it's okay. These shoes don't quite fit, but...you know. It's cold..."

"Yeah, well. We'll see what we can do about that," Danny said. "Meanwhile, tell you what. I don't know if you—well, it's like this. Your friend called again."

"Amy?"

"Yeah," Danny said. "Amy. She keeps calling."

"Won't leave us alone," Tim said.

"She's real worried," Danny said. "Said she needed to talk to you. She's upset."

The story Tim and Danny had concocted had Amy as a hysterical but loyal friend with influential friends in local government. "It doesn't matter to us," Danny said. "But now our boss is on our back. So, tell you what. Tim and I, we want to bring you back over to the interview room, continue our conversation."

"And you can talk to your little friend."

"Amy."

"Yeah, talk to Amy. You guys can talk, get her off our back. Afterward we talk, you and us. Good?"

"Sure," Charlie said. He had no problem with that.

The sergeant opened Cullen's gated door and escorted him to a metal table, where Danny handed him a Miranda Warning Form to read aloud. This was the second since his arrest, but Assistant Prosecutor Tim Van Hise had suggested the caution. Danny watched Charlie print "YES" and his initials by each line then sign the bottom, then they handed it to the sergeant to be time-stamped. Danny took the pen away again, in case Cullen got any ideas, and led him to the car for the ride back to the prosecutor's office.

————

Amy waited in a room[1] in the prosecutor's office, her eyes fixed on the flickering closed-circuit television. The screen showed the interview room, a plain cinder-block space with a table and plastic chairs made greenish and blurry by the video feed and reminding Amy of news footage from the war in Iraq. It was not a happy room to look at, at least not on the monitor, and worse when Charlie appeared. He was stooped and affect-less. His arms and legs were bound in chains. He shuffled forward in beige prison scrubs and shoes without laces. Amy felt nauseated. She had done that to Charlie. The guilt over-whelmed her, and she burst into tears. What had she done?

There were other detectives in the room with her: Captain Nick Magos, the lawyer from the prosecutor's office, Tim and Danny, maybe others coming and going—by now she knew the guys by sight, at least. They certainly seemed to know her. She was Amy, the confidential informant. They told Amy she was great, a natural, pumping her up. Words. She heard other words, like *death penalty*, *life in prison*. On the screen, Amy watched her friend, the one they wanted to kill, the meek little man shivering on his plastic chair in the war bunker. The killer the men talked about wasn't here now. She saw only a little boy, frightened and alone. She had sent this boy to prison and yet there he was, waiting for her, honestly believing that she had come as his friend. And in that moment, he was right. She was his friend, somehow, still. Charlie's eyes darted around the room, then found the camera mounted on the wall, and held it. Amy felt herself blush with terrific shame. He couldn't see her, she knew that. But it didn't change the way she felt.

The detectives started in on Charlie from the top, tag-teaming like the night before.

"Look, you know, Charlie, this is going to come out that you were getting off, sexually, on killing these people. Or we can go with the mercy-killing thing. It's up to you."

Then Danny came in, with his own version.

Then it was Tim. Then Danny.

Then it was Amy's turn.

The detectives led Amy along a maze of corridors and office doors, the men talking, Amy not hearing anything but her own heart. The doors all looked the same. She felt like she was in hell, or on a game show. Finally they stopped at one, opened the door, and left Amy in a room with a couch. She sat down on one end, then the other, deciding eventually on a perch farthest from the door. And then finally she allowed herself to look around. It was an especially plain room with unadorned walls. The only other furnishings besides the hard couch and a few scratchy woolen pillows were a coffee table, a cabinet, and a wall-mounted camera. She assumed the camera was on. The coffee table had a tape recorder taped to its underside, the kind she remembered from fifth grade. The cabinet was full of dolls.

Amy looked closer. The dolls were all anatomically correct. It was the room used to investigate sex crimes against children. She sat on the couch, staring at the little Muppet-type penises and vaginas. She hadn't told anyone from the prosecutor's office that she'd been sexually abused; she hadn't shared that with anyone, but still she wondered if there was something about her that telegraphed this fact, if they'd put her here on purpose. Hell or a game show. Amy couldn't help but think how different it would have been if a lady cop had brought her to a room like this when she was seven, how her life could have gone and the nightmares she would never have had to know. But nobody had protected her then, and when she had tried to protect herself, her family didn't believe her. They had told her the man she accused wasn't like that. He was so nice. He was a good uncle. But Amy knew that inside the good uncle was a monster. He was there during birthdays and Thanksgivings and Christmases. He was always there whether anyone saw him or not. This was the truth of Amy's life. And it was also the truth of Charlie's.

Charlie entered the room, unshackled. Amy gave him a sympathetic smile. It didn't feel false. She wasn't nervous anymore. Charlie sat next to her on the couch. He was still small, still meek, like a frail stick figure in beige PJs and blue canvas shoes. He still looked like the scared little boy. The short-sleeved jail shirt showed his bare arms. It was the first time Amy had ever seen them. They were blue-pale and thin. Her eyes ran to a thick scar along his biceps.

He'd done that himself, he said. A botched suicide attempt. Charlie told her how, in basic training, they'd said, "If you're going to kill yourself, ladies, do it right!" and showed them. The standard method—slicing across the wrist, as if slitting the arm's throat—resulted only in pain. But cut down the arm, longways, you bleed right out. "This way for show, this way to go," they said. It was just tough-guy talk, the sort drill sergeants yell, but Charlie remembered, and one afternoon he put down his mop, walked to the bathroom, and drew a line down his arm with a razor blade. The drill sergeants were right. And when he saw the blood, how thick it came and saw, *My God,* his own muscle down there, the white cord of tendon, he started screaming.

"So, basically, I'm a screw-up in everything," Charlie said. Twenty suicide attempts, and here he was, still breathing. They laughed about that. But that suicide *had* taught him something. In crisis, whenever he felt cornered or impotent, Charlie's instinct had always been to subvert those feelings with the threat of death. But in truth, he wasn't particularly interested in being dead, not personally. His nursing career resolved the paradox. Access to the vulnerable allowed him to manifest death without dying. He'd learned to kill himself by proxy.

You couldn't tell Charlie what to do. He would never be forced, the child with his arms pinned, helpless to the older boy on top, no. The detectives couldn't make him do anything like that. But he could do something. Amy didn't demand the truth, but Charlie could give it.

Amy looked into his eyes and knew where he needed to go. Charlie didn't need to be a saint, lord knows he wasn't one. He knew right from wrong, knew what he'd done was bad, in that it was illegal. No, he wasn't a saint. But he needed to be a hero. He could be that, for her.

Once he started, it was easy. It wasn't a confession so much as a story about himself, and one that he liked to hear. He sat in the interrogation room chair with his feet tucked up and Amy's soft cardigan caped across his shoulders. Charlie had the floor. The detectives wanted him to talk about Reverend Gall. He told them about Gall. Then he kept telling. His was a long road backward, and he walked through it carefully.

Charlie hadn't kept a written list of what he'd done, he didn't keep mementos of his crimes, and he had never told anyone his full story aloud. But all along, he'd been telling himself, reliving the edited memories like a song stuck in his head. He started talking at 6:15 on Sunday night, stopping only for food and coffee and toilet breaks. He spoke for seven hours in a hushed, level tone, patiently pausing mid-sentence whenever Tim flipped a tape, then picking up again at exactly that point, expounding on the technical complexities of the profession, the vagaries of a lifetime of expertise, and vignettes of depressions and suicides, loves hilariously squandered, situations that did not suit. Each was a data point in service of the agreed-upon arc of a misunderstood wanderer wielding a benevolent, if criminal, compulsion.

The patients "passed" or "expired" or sometimes "died"; he "intervened" or was "compelled to intervene"—but Charles did not "kill," and there was no "murder." It was a gentle story, a narrative long rehearsed but never performed and only a small fraction of the whole truth. But it was a good story, and enough; for the sick, for their families, death was a grace that not only God could give.

They only needed one; Charlie had given them forty when the last tape ran out. It was late, and the detectives were done for the night. And at 1:31 a.m. Monday morning Charlie left it at that, leaving the detectives to their paperwork, and so much so unsaid.

Post Script

The media quickly dubbed Charlie "the Angel of Death." We will never know exactly how many patients Charlie truly murdered. The source for most of the evidence in the cases against Charles Cullen came, by necessity, from Cullen himself. Cullen initially confessed to perhaps forty murders, specifically. In his recounting, Cullen skipped entire years and hospitals, and wouldn't hazard guesses regarding those he wasn't absolutely certain he had killed. At Lehigh Valley Hospital, for example, Cullen recalled that he was responsible for four or five victims; so far, only two have been positively identified. And though Cullen initially said that he hadn't overdosed anyone at Hunterdon Medical Center, five victims would ultimately be discovered there. Experts with an intimate knowledge of the case say that the real number of his total victims is likely closer to four hundred. Charlie has heard this number, and while he does not like it, he does not deny it, either. Nor does he acknowledge that this number, if accurate, gives him the ignominious distinction as the most prolific serial killer in American history.

The problem in accounting for Cullen's exact death toll was evidence. By the time the SCPO was alerted, many of the medical records were missing or incomplete, and most of the dead were already dust, making autopsies impractical. Sorting Cullen's private death toll from the general cadence of hospital mortality would prove extremely difficult. At the first hospitals where Cullen worked, where the records have been destroyed, a proper accounting would prove nearly impossible.

His formal confession contained only one name from his five years at his first job in the Burn Service at Saint Barnabas Medical Center—that of Judge John Yengo, on November 6, 1988. But Cullen had earlier recounted that his first murder was that of a young Saint Barnabas AIDS patient, in 1987. This patient has never been identified. Nor have any others at Saint Barnabas. The only surviving records from that time were the incomplete file the detectives had retrieved, and some handwritten pages later discovered in a desk drawer in storage which detailed Barry and Arnold's investigation into the spiked bags of insulin and the rash of insulin overdoses on the CCU. Later, Cullen admitted to homicide detectives that he had been both targeting patients and spiking insulin bags at random, sometimes three or four times a week at Saint Barnabas. Without medical charts and autopsies, these numbers could not be verified. As of this writing, he has been convicted of only one murder or attempted murder from his five years at this hospital. He worked at eight others, for eleven more years. It is perhaps useful to contrast this number with the list of victims specifically identified when detectives had access to complete and computerized medical charts and drug data, as they did at Somerset Medical Center.

Led by the tireless efforts of Detective Danny Baldwin, Tim Braun and the Somerset County detectives cross-referenced some 175 tips with Cullen's work schedule, assignment sheets, Pyxis records, and Cerner transactions. The initial result was a list of twenty-six high-probability victims from Charlie Cullen's year at Somerset Medical Center alone. Charlie said a few names "jumped out at him." For the rest, he said, he'd need to review the charts.

In April 2004, Charles Cullen pleaded guilty in New Jersey court to thirteen murders and two attempted murders, crimes that legally qualified him for the death penalty. Charlie had initially claimed that he in fact wanted to be put to death. He told this to Amy, as well as to the Somerset County detectives during his taped confession. But he never told it to his court-appointed lawyer, senior public defender Johnnie Mask. But then, even Charles Cullen's suicide "attempts" had never truly been about dying. Charles Cullen wanted to live. He and Mask cut a deal with New Jersey prosecutors, who agreed to take the death penalty off the table in exchange for his cooperation. Danny Baldwin and the SCPO team would spend the next three years investigating.

———

Months turned to years at the Somerset County Jail in Somerville, and Charles Cullen's life assumed a regularity he had rarely known as a free man. He had his cell, his spy novels, time to exercise or shower or meet with the Catholic deacon or the head chaplain, with whom he was studying the lives of the saints. The guards would escort him across the lawn to the prosecutor's office, to sit with Danny or Tim and pull through the arrhythmic EKGs, the final flatlines, and the bloodwork of thousands of patients. The spotlight was always on him. Nothing could have suited him better.

There were new charts nearly every week, boxes of them, covering sixteen years of death at nine hospitals.

The detectives and lawyers ordered donuts, sandwiches, and chips—little perks for dealing with the paperwork of death—and as winter became spring and winter again, they packed pounds beneath their chinos. But Charlie just squirreled through the case files with a cup of black coffee, growing thinner and thinner, getting it done; eventually, when the investigations were closed and the shouting was over, he could take his life sentences into his cell and disappear completely.

Then, in August 2005, an envelope arrived at the Somerville jail. By now Cullen was inured to the interview requests and the hate mail, even the odd "fan letter," but this was something new: a thin clipping from a Long Island community newspaper with a few paragraphs about a man named Ernie Peckham and a margin note jotted in girlish cursive: "Can you help?"

Cullen knew Peckham—a guy about Charlie's age, with four kids and a wife at home and a job shaping metal for window casings and revolving doors in Farmingdale. He was the brother of Catherine Westerfer—Charlie's estranged ex-girlfriend and the mother of his youngest child, whom he had never seen and probably never would. Maybe he and Ernie had said *hey* at a wedding a few years ago, Charlie couldn't recall, but they weren't friends, they weren't even acquaintances, they certainly weren't close enough to swap organs. But according to the article, that was what Ernie needed.

Doctors don't know exactly how or when, but at some point in 2003, Ernie contracted strep. Probably it was just a little scratch that got infected, the sort of thing that either swells up and goes away or takes you out for a week with a sore throat and a dose of antibiotics. But Ernie didn't notice the infection, and it spread. His immune system attacked the burgeoning bacteria, creating complex protein knots that caught in the microscopic filters in both his kidneys. Normally, these filters would have been removing toxins from Ernie's blood and excreting them with his urine; now, they were like a sink clogged with hair. Ernie's body began to bloat with its own poisons, swelling his hands and face and turning his urine the color of cocoa. By the time he saw a doctor, his kidneys were dead. Untreated, he'd be next.

Charlie had never worked as a nephrological nurse, but he knew that once a kidney's filters are bunged up, you can't really fix them. Dialysis is the most common option, a method of removing fluid and filtering blood through a machine. Ernie regarded his three weekly two-hour dialyses at Stony Brook Hospital "another full time job," and the hassle hadn't stopped his deterioration. His access veins kept clotting off. The access port that surgeons had sewn into the major vein in his neck was like a wound that never closed, and it opened him to dangerous new infections. Ernie had been forced to give up his scoutmaster post and had scaled back his time at the local VFW. But if he really wanted to get his life back, dialysis wasn't going to do it. What he really needed was a new kidney.

At the time, there were around sixty thousand people waiting for a kidney in this country. Most would come from cadavers (donation rates are highest in early spring, when new motorcyclists take to roads still edged with winter sand). But a cadaver kidney has a lessened life expectancy of six years compared to that of a live donor; the waiting list for such a random cadaver donor was between five and seven years long—a wait that, as Ernie's health deteriorated, was beginning to look like a death sentence.

The best way to match kidney with recipient is through a

blood relative, but nobody in Ernie's family was medically eligible to donate one of theirs. Now his only chance was to find the perfect stranger. Unfortunately, the odds of one random individual being a perfect tissue-typed match for another random individual—of a donation being personal—are staggeringly small. Ernie Peckham had a better chance of being struck by lightning. Ernie's mother, Pat Peckham, had already mortgaged her house to help with her son's medical bills, and she contacted the local paper to run a public-interest item with Ernie's blood type and the hospital's donation hotline number. She was hoping for a miracle donor. But no miracle donor called. Pat was running out of options for saving her son; she was willing to try anything or anyone who might help. And what would it take except a stamp? So she clipped the article out of the paper, stuck it in an envelope addressed to the Somerville prison, and waited for her miracle. The thing about miracles: you couldn't really predict what form they might take, or what wings would bear them. It might be anyone, even the serial killer who had knocked up her daughter.

But Cullen's plea to become an organ donor from jail struck such a nerve, especially with the victims' families. The nurse who killed dozens of sick people suddenly wanted to save one? It seemed at the least ironic, at worst manipulative. In theory, the state had neutralized Charles Cullen in prison. Then, suddenly, there he was again—he wasn't neutralized, he was in the headlines, manipulating court proceedings, "playing God" with yet another life and using his own bodily organs as his last piece of collateral. Was Charles Cullen motivated by compassion or a sick compulsion? Was it all just an attempt to redeem himself in the eyes of his baby mama, or Jesus Christ, or himself? It was impossible to know. Most of those answers lay within Charles Cullen himself, and Charles Cullen wasn't talking.

"People look at Charles, they look at what he's done, and they see a monster," explained the Rev. Kathleen Roney, Cullen's chaplain in the Somerset County Jail. "You can understand why of course—Charles has killed people, more than you'll ever know. The families of the victims are owed something for that. But he isn't a monster," she added. "He isn't the Angel of Death. Charles is much more complicated than that."

Charles Cullen sat on the bed of his cell, reading and rereading Pat Peckham's note. *Can you help?* He wasn't sure. Cullen understood the medical implications of Ernie's disease—which might kill him soon—and the benefits of having a living donor, which might extend the kidney's life by six years over a cadaver donation. But he also knew the downside. He was the Angel of Death. He didn't think about himself in this way, but that's how he was known, the papers said so. And he knew: the Angel of Death donates an organ, that's going to bring some publicity. In giving a piece of himself to Ernie, he'd be giving Ernie a piece of the Angel of Death, and a piece of that publicity. Not just for him, but for his family as well. In jail, Cullen often agonized over "the scary stuff" happening to his family outside—the reporters who followed his ex-girlfriend and threatened to print her address unless she talked, the man who cornered his eleven-year-old daughter in the driveway.

"I know I'll be afraid of what is going to happen after I die, but I'm more afraid of seeing, feeling what I think my kids will have to go through for the rest of their lives," Cullen told me, during one of our visits. Cullen didn't like that his children would have to grow up as "the kids with the serial killer dad." And he didn't wish that for Ernie's kids, either. Which was why he wondered: could the Angel of Death really help Ernie Peckham?

Charles always liked to be helpful, especially medically. He was always an especially enthusiastic donor, having given some twelve gallons of blood and registering to become a bone marrow donor—not that he personally knew anyone who needed his marrow, but just in case someone ever did. Cullen was healthy and still relatively young; odds were he'd be at least physically eligible to donate one of his kidneys to someone. Being a specific match for a random request was a long shot; the best-case scenario, being a 6-for-6 antigen match, would take a miracle. But Charlie was in prison, and, he told me, somebody asked for something he could give. It was worth a try.

During his time in Somerville, he had a weekly service with the visiting Catholic deacon, and now Cullen asked him a question, casually, like an idle curiosity: was it possible for an inmate to donate a kidney? Deacon Tom Sicola wanted to sit down—they didn't teach him anything about this sort of thing in seminary. After lockdown he went back to his office, closed the door, and dialed the extension of his supervisor, Reverend Kathleen.

Kathleen Roney wears rock-collection-sized birthstone rings on her fingers and Celtic charms around her clerical collar, and her brown eyebrows flicker like pinball flippers as she talks. She'd dropped two hundred pounds from illness and surgery that year, but she still maintained the command of her old heft, and she has the bullhorn voice and direct manner that first earned her the Somerville jailhouse nickname of the "kick-ass Reverend." Roney and I met at a small wooden table behind the magazine rack of the Bridgewater, New Jersey, Barnes and Noble. Roney's into Templar stuff, Irish spirituality, Druid mysticism; Charles liked spy novels and whodunnits. "But nothing about murder," she said. "Do you know how hard it is to find a mystery that doesn't have murder in it?"

Kathleen started ministering to Charles when he came to the Somerset jail in 2003, and she had recently begun teaching him the meditation techniques of the Desert Fathers. She figured whatever worked for the first-century Christian mystics who kept their faith alive during years of hermetic desert asceticism might come in handy for a man spending his life in a nine-by-five box. The "Jesus Prayer," which Charles recited during his Somerset sentencing, had come from one of these tutorials. Jail only intensified the need for religion's comforts, and Charles had a lot of catching up to do; most of his knowledge of Christianity was either from grainy memories of Catholic grade school or the Technicolor drama of Cecil B. DeMille epics, which he preferred.

Over the course of nearly three years, Roney had gotten to know Charles, but that didn't mean she understood him. She didn't understand, for instance, why Charles had killed so many people. And she couldn't quite understand why, exactly, he suddenly wanted to donate. "So that night I went to the jail and I grilled him. I needed to know his heart on this, to make sure I wasn't being used.

"I asked him, is someone going to pay you? Are you doing it for fame? Are you thinking this is some sort of a deal with God, a bargain: 'I'm going to save this life, and this wipes out the lives I took'?"

The questions seemed to hurt his feelings. "But that was okay," she told me. "I needed to know his heart on this, if I was going to get involved especially." So Roney asked him another question: was this a sort of passive suicide attempt— did he think he might die on the table?

No, he told her. That's not it.

So a third time she asked him, Charles, why this? Why now? Would you have done this ten years ago, seventeen years ago, before everything changed, before all this started?

" 'Yes,' he said. 'And why? Because I can, it's possible. Somebody asked for something that is possible. Why now? Because this is when it was asked. And I think it's the right thing to do.'

"I believed him," she said. She pushed aside her grande iced tea and took my hands between her painted fingers. "Charles had an absolutely horrible childhood, and all sorts of problems, but he has never once blamed any of that on anyone else, or made any excuses to me for what he did. That person that killed all those people is the same person who would make this decision. Absolutely."

The kit from the hospital contained a series of color-coded tubes for Cullen to bleed into. Afterwards, Stony Brook Hospital would test the antigens in his blood against the antigens in Ernie's, the most basic matching criteria to see if Cullen could actually donate his kidney. "That's how I became the blood mule," Roney laughed.

The odds of Charles actually matching were incredibly long, but there was a life at stake, and she had made a promise, one she was still struggling to understand the full ramifications of. That night, when she asked her friends to help her with prayer, she didn't tell them what they were praying for, or for whom. "We needed to keep it secret," she said. "And besides, could you ask every person to pray for a serial killer?"

———

Every equinox, Reverend Roney and like-minded Celtic Christians spent a week at a Druid spiritual retreat near the Pocono Mountains. It was a spiritual time for her, a time of dancing around bonfires and meditating to icons and spirit-voyaging among life-size reproductions of Stonehenge and unbounded acres of blonde Pennsylvania Dutch farmland.

Every morning she'd walk the hard earth between the corn stubble, reciting her prayers under the recessive blue sky, feeling the ancient wisdom, looking for a sign. It was then that she felt the vibration.

This, of course, was her cell phone—they encourage silence at these things, so she had to keep it on vibrate—and right away, she knew what had happened. And her prayer group knew, too. In fact, the whole of the spiritual retreat knew what had happened, she can't say why, she'd never told them, they just felt it and started to cry, because they knew. And she thought, *This is it, it's meant to be.*

She was crying now, ruining her mascara as she remembered how Charles was a perfect 6-for-6 antigen match, like winning the Clearinghouse Sweepstakes. She wiped the tears away with a Starbucks napkin. "Honestly, we thought it was a miracle," she said. There would be more tests, X-rays, CAT scans, tests with machines you couldn't send to the jail by mail. But these were trivial compared to this spotlight in the darkness, a sign of God's larger plan.

"At the time, I didn't know this was just the beginning," she remembered. "But when I told Johnnie, all he could do [was] shake his head. He knew this was going to open up a whole can of worms."

The New Jersey Public Defender's office is four stories of chocolate brick with handicapped spaces and shrub landscaping and three-hundred-pound women in nightgown-sized Tweety Bird T-shirts smoking menthols by the glass double doors. In the offices upstairs, there are people waiting nervously under yellow mercury-vapor lights, and a hole in the Plexiglas where you can announce yourself by sticking your mouth in and yelling politely. Johnnie Mask's office was in the back, one of the few in the building with both windows and a door. With his gray Ishmael-like beard and broad leonine features, the Somerset County deputy public defender looked something like an Old Testament James Earl Jones, and he spoke with the same authoritative baritone. "Someone," he said, "is trying to shit-can this donation." After nearly three years representing the biggest serial killer in New Jersey history, Mask was tired, and playing point man for the legal side of Cullen's donation hadn't made his job any easier. "I made a promise to try and get this donation to go through," he sighed. "But it feels like we're getting played." Mask squinted and shook his head at what had become an old joke. "Basically, I don't think anyone's very motivated to make this happen for a serial killer."

The Lehigh County Courthouse
Allentown, Pennsylvania
March 20, 2006

Allentown is a poor steel town living in the ruins of a rich one, and the downtown is a grand, ceremonial public space of imported stone and soaring colonnades and busted crazies rooting for cans, joined now by a small parade of families in dark, formal clothes with little blue stickers from OfficeMax gummed to their lapels to show they're victims of the Angel of Death.

The old courthouse is largely gutted, part of a stalled renovation project, and the family members are guided through a spooky house tour of rooms stripped to the lathing and rooms of chrome-green file cabinets, up stairs, and through flicker-lit halls. At the end of this trip is a surprisingly bright, nineteenth-century Italianate courtroom. It is a high-box gilt with every splendor of Beaux Arts rococo and every pound of marble that steel money could buy. The ceiling is forty feet above and wreathed with concentric rings of filigree and a Medusa chandelier, under which sits the judge, cordoned off by a giant desk festooned with Federalist-style lamps and railings as intricate as the back of a two-dollar bill.

Cullen's hands are chained in front of his groin, and his legs are manacled into loops of institutional leather, giving him the air of being extremely physically dangerous. Of course, he isn't, at least not in this context, but the effect is that for perhaps the first time, Charles Cullen looks like what one expects from a serial killer. One senses that if Lehigh County could have put a grilled mask on him and bound him to a dolly, they surely would have. As it happens, Charlie will give them their chance.

After all of our conversations about Cullen's sensitivity to the suffering of other people, one might think that he would be on his best behavior here, especially if his one remaining action in public life—the donation of a kidney—still hung in the balance of public opinion. At the least, one wouldn't expect him to take his public opportunity to torture the families, short-circuit their grief, and build more bad will. But strangely, that's exactly what he does. Cullen begins the process by reciting, from memory, statements that Judge William Platt has made to the press.

"And for this reason, Your Honor," Cullen says, "you need to step down."

"Your motion to recuse is denied," says Judge Platt.

"No no, Your Honor," Cullen interrupts, "you need, you need to step down. Your Honor, you need to step down."

"If you continue this I will gag and manifold you," the judge warns. But Cullen shouts over him. "Your Honor, you need to step down! Your Honor, you need to step down! Your Honor..."

The court is a beautiful room, but a terrible courtroom,

formed entirely of hard marble surfaces that amplify and distort sound. Charles Cullen fills this room. The families wait, holding their carefully prepared statements to their chests, as Cullen gets to speed-shouting his statement ten times, thirty, forty. He is not going to stop, and now the court officers are on him. They pull a spit mask over his head—a mesh veil that keeps a prisoner from hawking lugies on his captors—but the noise continues.

They wrap the spit mask with a towel and push him into the chair, bunching the towel at the back of his head and screwing it tight, so that now all that's left of the tantrum is the bass cadence, like a man screaming into a pillow while the families of the victims try to read. "You are a total waste of a human body . . . You are the worst kind of monster, a son of the devil . . ." Only fragments can be heard beneath Cullen's gagged scream, and soon the sergeant's hands begin to cramp. His grip loosens, and chorus by chorus, Cullen's voice gets clearer, almost operatic. The judge scowls and the sergeant puts his back into it, wringing with both hands. Several women in the jury box raise their hands to their faces in horror.

"I will not allow him to leave this courtroom!" intones Judge Platt, but there's no order in this court. Cullen's getting off three *Your Honor*s per second now, and the sergeant motions to the judge, making a sign across his mouth. The judge nods and the sergeant ducks from the room and returns with a roll of duct tape the size of a dinner plate. They tape up his mouth like a cartoon, making a big X over his lips, which does essentially nothing. The victims read their personal statements, and Cullen screams his, like a nightmarish version of "Row Row Row Your Boat."

"If my grandmother was alive right now, she'd say to you, 'I hope you rot in hell, you sick son of a bitch . . .' "

"Your Honor you must step down Your Honor you must step down..."

"...three more life sentences, served concurrently with those already handed down..."

"...must step down Your Honor you must..."

And with a final "Such that you will remain in prison for the rest of your natural life," it's over. Once again, the court officers frog-march Charles Cullen—bound, gagged, duct-taped—out of the courtroom and into a waiting elevator. He still is chanting when the doors close. The silence that follows is terrible, too.

Afterward, the families huddle in the hallway, shaken and unsatisfied. "I think he intentionally meant disrespect to everyone in that courtroom," vents Julie Sanders, whose friend was OD'd by Cullen. "He says he is a compassionate man. He says he wants to donate a kidney to save someone's life, he wants to do it out of compassion. Where's the compassion now?" Sanders stabs her finger at the hole in the air where Cullen had been. "I needed to say something to him. Does he even know what he did? Does he know what he's done to our lives?"

———

All the precautions about me killing other patients," Cullen sighed, and subtly rolled his eyes at the idea. Over the course of our visits, Cullen was becoming increasingly depressed. This recent depression was specific to the delays in his donation. Cullen likes to be helpful, but here he was, sitting in jail, while someone out there needed a piece of what he was sitting on.

"The state's concerned that since my crimes were committed in a hospital, I might commit them again. Why did they think it was easier to kill yourself in a hospital than anywhere else?" he wondered. Especially when he'd be shackled to the bed and under guard. It made no sense. It was just another false stumbling block to his donation. And that was depressing him further. He had a signed order from the Somerset judge. His lawyer, Johnnie Mask, had been beavering away on the paperwork, Reverend Kathleen was working as a liaison between the recipient's family and the hospital. And yet nothing was happening.

Cullen studied my hands across the glass, then stared back down at his piece of steel counter. "When we got past the blood tests I felt like, okay, this is going to happen," he said. "But now I don't know.

"I mean, I'm not getting anything special for this, I'm not asking for special treatment for jail, I'm not getting paid or anything...what's the harm?" Cullen's eyes scanned the glass for an answer. "What would the families rather I did, just sit here and watch TV?

"I grant that I certainly have done some very bad things, I've taken lives," he said quickly. "But does that prevent me from doing something positive? The only thing I can do is sit in a cell and cost the taxpayer $40,000 a year. And I know that New Jersey doesn't make license plates anymore." He motioned into the air and shook his head. "So what positive contribution can a person make in jail?

"I know people say I'm playing God, but I can't really do that," he said. "The only thing I am doing is giving an organ up. As for what happens afterward, that is in God's hands. As a nurse they saw me directly taking life, but I can't give life, I can't extend life. We give love. To our children. But we don't own them or control them. We do a lot of things but we don't consider these things playing God. For some reason I matched, six out of six antigens. The recipient did put publicity out to get the good citizens of New York, to see if anyone matched. But nobody came forward. Not one person came forward. Not one single person."

Cullen fixed me with a look, then took his glance away, as if to study my response in private. "It really depends on how you think of people," he said. "And what you think people are capable of."

After his final sentencing at the Lehigh County Courthouse in Allentown, Charles was handcuffed and shackled and put in the back of a windowless van. No light entered his mobile cell, and as the van careened onto the New Jersey Turnpike, Cullen began to feel nauseated. He tried to use the techniques that Reverend Roney had taught him, visualizing Jesus in a halo of fire in the darkness, but then Jesus started to look nauseated, too, so he stopped and went back to the Jesus Prayer.

He was met at the New Jersey State Prison in Trenton by about ten guards, four of them in riot gear. He was led to a detaining cell, where two guards strip-searched him on camera. One guard told him that he had read about him in the newspaper. The other said that any move would be taken as a sign of aggression. He was given new clothes and taken to the prison psych ward, where they took the clothes away and strip-searched him again. He was given a sort of toga made from plastic sheets he thought looked like the stuff they wrap around new TV sets, and put into a cell for seventy-two hours. The toga ripped after the first day, so for Monday and Tuesday he was naked and embarrassed under constant camera surveillance. He tried not to listen to the guards, the *Time for your insulin* comments, focusing instead on Psalm 25: "My enemies are many, they hate me. Deliver me, let me not be ashamed." And gradually, he was given pieces of his new life. His cell was smaller than in Somerville, and the guards played games with him, telling him there was no library, giving him sneakers two sizes too small, little things. Things that taught him not to assume anything anymore. He was in the noncontact wing, locked down twenty-three hours a day and segregated from the other prisoners for his own safety. By the time he was eligible to see visitors for a phone visit, he was visibly thinner and had grown a gray beard, but his donation seemed no closer than it had five months earlier, and he was even more frustrated.

To Cullen, the delays just didn't make sense. If this match was God's will, if it was supposed to happen that he was a perfect match for a man who needed it, why then wasn't it happening? Was it a sort of punishment, a sort of medical tantalization? Had there been some sort of mistake?

"And meanwhile, the kidney recipient is getting sicker and sicker," Cullen said during one of our visits. This time, his speech was laconic, and he seemed both tired and depressed. "He's back in the hospital, and averaging one complication a month. At least, that's what I hear."

He knew the families of the victims saw his donation as an exercise of his personal will, just the sort of freedom that prison was supposed to confiscate. "But the fact that I was even able to take a blood test, it's not my will, it's the efforts of a great number of people—Mr. Mask, Reverend Roney, Judge Armstrong. I'd mention the DA but, ah, he's not on my good list," he said. "And Ernie's family has certainly gone through a lot of waiting." He thought about it a second, shook his head slightly. "A lot of waiting."

Cullen stopped for a moment, looking down, blinking away tears. Finally he breathes and tries again. "It's hard, knowing that if I wasn't in here they could go ahead and do this...It's hard to see this as just playing God. It's not like Ernie was given a choice between a good person and a bad person," he said. "If he was offered a matching kidney from a good person, I'm sure he'd take it." Cullen folded an arm tightly across his chest and studied the counter. "I still love people, I care about people. Maybe, maybe people don't think that I should be allowed to do something for people that I care about. But if I just picked someone out of the blue to donate to—people would think I'm just totally crazy." He looked up. "That's the funny thing. People think you're crazy for doing something for someone else if you don't know them personally."

"I can't take back the harm that I've done already, but a good thing, why can't I do that?" Cullen asked me. "I know that [people] think that I should go straight to hell and take my kidney with me. People think that they can figure out how God thinks. But God alone knows somebody's heart and soul and mind."

Johnnie Mask had long been convinced that the process was derailed, and Roney had bet a dinner on it. After all, it was God's plan, wasn't it?

Ever since Charles had first arrived in her jail, people had treated Reverend Roney as an accomplice. Maybe she'd gotten too close and enjoyed the excitement a little too much, she could see that, it was a temptation. Kathleen didn't agree with what Charles Cullen had done, of course, his crimes—nobody could—but she still didn't understand the comments, some from people she'd once called friends, others from fellow pastors, Christians who would ask, *How could you possibly think a serial killer is a child of God?*

One of the first letters she received was from an Evangelical Christian who warned her away from ministering to a monster. "He said, 'If you save him and he goes to heaven, that's not fair,'" Roney remembered. "That's the way

Evangelicals think. It was so stupid, but I was like hysterical for like two days after that."

The hate mail followed, some of it threatening. Nothing came of it, of course, and she tried to shrug it off—it was understandable, natural even, that the community felt threatened by a man who had used a position of trust to murder their most vulnerable family members. Then around the time of the arraignment, she was walking from the jail when someone yelled at her, calling her "Satan's pastor," and threw something in her face. She didn't know what kind of blood it was, probably pig's blood like they use when protesting abortion clinics. She tried not to think about it and just went home and washed off the sticky brown mess. "Yes," Kathleen laughed, "if there's a heaven and I end up there, I should definitely get a crown."

Of course, when the donation became public, it just made everything worse. "I have one friend, who is no longer a friend," she said to me. "She told me that by helping Ernie get a transplant from Charles Cullen, I was ruining his life, because I was helping him receive Satan's kidney."

Kathleen remembered when she first started in her job, she thought that if you were a decent human being and you were Christian, you would be nice to everybody. "Doesn't that make sense?" Roney asked. "I mean, as much as my parents hated Hitler, they still said, 'Well, he is a child of God.' I thought that was the Christian way. But this trial changed it. Man, did I learn that Christianity can be vicious."

Just the day before, Kathleen had gotten a call from Ernie Peckham's mother, Pat. "She informed me that I was never to talk to them again," she said. "Ever. Before she hung up on me, Pat basically said that it was me, and that damned lawyer, we were ruining her life! Well, I don't mean to be cute about it, but if it wasn't for me and Johnnie, they wouldn't be thinking about getting a darned kidney!"

All she could hope was that the donation had been scheduled by the hospital, and since Charles was such a security threat, Pat had been told to be careful, to keep it as secret as possible. "I mean, I don't expect flowers and chocolate cake, but we're not trying to ruin Ernie's life, we're trying to save it."

Roney stopped talking and let herself breathe. Slowly, the anger faded. And as it did, she began to cry.

———

They came for Charlie Cullen in the night, guards with keys and handcuffs. He was going to St. Francis Medical Center. If they knew why, they wouldn't say. They gave him the paper gown again, drew his blood, cuffed him to the bed. The television in the corner was always on, local news, *Oprah*. A day passed, and he thought, *Here we go again.* It wasn't the donation. It was something else.

The guards came again in the morning. They were taking him downstairs, they didn't say why. He was instructed to only address direct questions. He was told that Charles Cullen was not his name. His name was now Johnny Quest. The doctor called him Mr. Quest. The nurses called him John. Cullen thought it was ridiculous. He didn't know what was happening.

They gave him something to relax him—Valium, he thinks, they wouldn't say. It made him woozy. They gave him forms to sign. He held the pen, unsure of which name to use. "Use the one you're supposed to," the doctor said. He'd watched the cartoons as a kid, he remembered the handsome blond boy and his adventures, a useful boy with skills, full of potential. Charlie signed the paper "Johnny Quest." It wasn't legally binding, of course, so they gave him another form that he was to sign "Charles Cullen, A.K.A. Johnny Quest." The nurse looked away while he did this. It was supposed to be a secret. Then they gave him another shot and now he was feeling kinda gone.

An hour later, Johnny Quest's kidney was tucked into a red Coleman cooler and loaded onto a Lifestar helicopter. They flew north from Trenton, kept Manhattan on their left, banked up Long Island. August 18 was a perfect summer night, and the traffic far below was heavy with Hamptons weekenders filing past the massive Stony Brook medical complex, lit on the dark hillside like Bilbao under construction.

I parked in the C lot. On weekend nights, hospitals are usually busy only after the bars close, and usually only in the emergency room. At 8:00, the main lobby was quiet as a dead department store. A guard read yesterday's newspaper again, the gift shop was just Mylar balloons in darkness. Surgery is on the fourth floor with the burn unit and radiation. The kidney took the back elevator; I took the front.

In the surgical waiting room the TV is always on, approximating normalcy for the families camped there, the women and their mothers with running mascara, the men clutching Dunkin' Donuts cups. This TV had the movie *Freaky Friday*, two people switching bodies and identities and, it being Hollywood—and Disney, at that—coming closer together as a result. But that was just a movie. For transplants, parts are parts. You take what you can get and survive.

And so, while Jamie Lee Curtis and Lindsay Lohan had their first mother-daughter argument about whose life was more difficult, Ernie Peckham lay faceup on a table, anesthetized and encircled by masked strangers in disposable blue clothes. Some traced a curved incision through the fat of his left abdomen; others parted the draped muscles of his belly wall with cool steel clamps. Johnny Quest's kidney was about the size of a surgeon's hand, a quivering bean-shape mottled in pinkish fat that nested neatly into the half shell of Ernie's pelvis. A stump of renal artery, pruned only hours before from its owner's aortal stalk, was patched into Ernie's blood supply with 5-0 suture wire, and vein was stitched to vein. And, hours later, as Jamie Lee and Lindsay, back in their bodies again, smiled knowingly at each other across a climactic concert scene, a surgical clamp was removed from an external iliac artery, and Johnny Quest's kidney swelled pink with oxygenated blood, alive again, and Ernie's.

Underneath the xenon lamps, this medical miracle didn't look like much more than cauterized gristle in a blue paper hole. It showed nothing of the millions of tiny tubules stacked inside its medulla, or the branches, as infinite as crystals in frost, which would filter and titrate his blood as a brain filters choices, sorting bad from good as well as humanly possible.

The civil trials followed on the heels of the criminal. The families of his victims, or potential victims, sued the various hospitals at which Charles Cullen had worked. All of the suits were settled out of court.[1] The files are sealed, as are the settlements and non-disclosure agreements. There have never been any criminal proceedings against any administrator at any of the hospitals that employed Charles Cullen, nor any Grand Jury convened to consider such proceedings.

The New Jersey State Legislature passed two new measures in reaction to the Charles Cullen case. The Patient Safety Act, passed in 2004, increased the responsibility of hospitals to report all "serious preventable adverse events"[2] that occur at their health-care facilities to the Department of Health and Senior Services. The following year this was supplemented by the Enhancement Act, which requires hospitals to report to the Division of Consumer Affairs (including the Board of Nursing) certain limited facts about the health-care professionals at their facilities, and to keep records of all complaints and disciplinary actions related to care of their patients for a period of seven years. These measures were adopted by thirty-five other states. A hospital in compliance with the provisions would not be liable for civil actions that might arise from their reportage. There is no penalty or civil liability for hospitals that fail to comply.

All of the hospitals at which Cullen worked were contacted in the course of researching this book. Several did not respond to repeated requests for interview or comment. Several were prevented from doing so due to the civil litigation by the families of victims, would not comment on Charles Cullen's employment due to Human Resources policy, or stated that they did not want to "comment or be involved." Somerset Medical Center continues to be one of the top health-care centers in the state of New Jersey. A spokesman stated that "Somerset Medical Center fully cooperated with all interested parties and agencies throughout the course of the Cullen investigation. At this time, we are devoting the full extent of our resources and efforts on delivering the highest quality of care to the members of our community."

———

Tim Braun retired after Charles Cullen's conviction. He now has a private investigation practice specializing in medical murder, and he volunteers as part of a national task force that mobilizes to help local law enforcement catch child murderers.

The murder of Ethel Duryea which had so plagued Tim

Braun had partial resolution—in 2010 it was finally leaked that the murder weapon had been traced, years before, to another murder, as Tim Braun had known. But Duryea's killer has never been named, and her case remains officially unsolved.

Danny Baldwin transferred from the Somerset County Prosecutor's office soon after the Cullen case; in 2017 he retired from active duty to head DLB Investigative Services. He is also an adjunct professor of criminal justice.

Both Danny and Tim received numerous commendations and awards for their investigative work on the "Angel of Death" case, as the prosecution of Charles Cullen came to be known. Their distinctions include several official congressional citations and the National Association of Police Organizations' "Top Cops Award."

In their acceptance speech, the detectives gave special thanks to the confidential informant identified only as "Agent Amy."

Amy Loughren quit nursing soon after Charlie's arrest. She is now married, and works as a hypnotist and past-life regression therapist, a calling directly inspired by her experiences with Charlie.

Her involvement in Cullen's arrest and conviction was never made public; this book marks the first acknowledgment of her existence as a CI in this case. Even Charlie wasn't told what Amy had done.

In October 2012, Amy traveled to the New Jersey State Prison in Trenton, to see Charlie for the first time since his confession. Amy asked for his forgiveness; Charlie told her it wasn't her fault.

Amy still has not told Charlie that she was the confidential informant.

ACKNOWLEDGMENTS

I want to acknowledge the anonymous sources, the families of the victims for allowing me to wade into their grief, and the shocked family of Charles Cullen, particularly Adrianne "Baum" and her daughters. I also need to acknowledge the contribution of Charles Cullen himself for talking to me. He said he didn't want this book—that he wanted to disappear. Perhaps now he can. My hope for all parties is that the truth will be some consolation.

Special thanks to all those who were assigned the role as lead detectives within each of their respective jurisdictions, and those whose untold stories and diligent investigative work greatly contributed to the overall success of the case, including: Somerset County CID Commander Det./Capt. Nick Magos; Det./Sgt. Russell Colucci; homicide detectives Doug Brownlie, Lou Demeo, and Matt Colucci; Somerset County assistant prosecutors Robert Lang and Tim Van Hise; and of course Somerset County prosecutor Wayne Forrest; as well as Somerville PD Det. Ed Purcell; Essex Co. homicide detective Tom Kelly and Agent Jack McGarry; Essex Co. assistant prosecutor Howard Zuckerman; Morris County Prosecutor's Office detective Barry Bittenmaster; Raritan Twp. (Hunterdon County) detective Scott Lessig; Warren County Major

Crimes Det./Lt. Richard "Dick" Dalrymple and Det. Stephen Matuszak; Pennsylvania State Police detectives Ron Garza, Robert Egan, Tpr. Bruchak; Lehigh County district attorney Jim Martin; NJ Regional Medical Examiner's Office doctors Nobby C. Mambo (lead ME) & state toxicologist George Jackson; and Northampton Co. coroner Zachary Lysak. Detective Sergeant and Unit Commander Tim Braun and Lead Detective Daniel Baldwin gave especially generously of their time and honored this book with their honesty and patience, and a vetting and corrections of the manuscript. Amy Park Loughren shed her anonymity and broke her silence for this book; her time, energy, and bravery made every difference. Sustaining support came from Jim and Joan Reichardt, Julian Porta, Saskia Lane, Mike Didovic, Nicole Davis, Scott Jardine, Jeff and Mina Kauffman, Lisa Santandrea, Richard Ketchum, Nick Gault and Caroline Cole, Señor Pip Wood, Liz Gilliland, Kathryn Fitzgerald, Katie Trainor, Kari E. P. Niles, the Jeffreys-Osbornes, and West-Staceys, and of course my brother, Matthew Waterbury Graeber. Steve Byers at National Geographic Adventure schooled this young writer on priorities. Adam Fisher at *New York Magazine* saw a story in the ragged news clipping in my wallet; Diana Mason, PhD, RN, Rudin Professor at the Hunter-Bellevue School of Nursing and Co-director, Hunter College Center for Health, Media and Policy, offered fierce vigilance for the profession and reached whistleblowers too frightened to speak to anyone else. Mary Jennings, Muse of Madaket, knew that writers need to read too. Maura Egan gave advice, work, and her apartment so I could begin this book; her sister, Kathy Egan, gave me hers so I could continue it; Reverend Kathleen Roney shared her spiritual insight on the humanity of Charlie Cullen behind the headlines; and I owe a debt to Barbara Morgan, and the island of Nantucket, where there's always work to support a writing habit. The patient judicial clerks of NJ and PA lent many hours, especially particularly Steve and Sal at the Middlesex County Court archive. The work was buoyed by the early encouragement of legendary mystery man Otto Penzler and his anthologizing the original article from which this book grew; the Virginia Center for the Creative Arts provided crucial monastic months for its writing, as did the staff of the New York Writer's Room, which generously keeps desks cheap and clear twenty-four hours a day and where Donna Brodie traffics in luck and magic. The brilliant editorial insights of the unflappable Ann Patty helped tame madness into structured narrative—she gave more than she had to, and just what I needed. I'm grateful to Devereux Chatillon, Esq., who was somehow tireless yet never humorless in her legal vetting. Fine writers and editors including David Evanier, Bliss Broyard, Jill Frayne, Michael Fitzgerald, Owen Matthews, Brad Wieners, Tom Downey, Thomas Coleman, George Hodgeman, Jane Ciabattari, Thomas Pettit, and the talented Douglas Rogers provided advice, comfort, and the taunting example of their own work and also sometimes bought drinks, as did the late and legendary sportswriter Trent Frayne, who first warmly welcomed me to "the toy department" and who with his wife, June Callwood, graciously treated this kid as a peer. Bill Abbott and the Allens of Harpswell, Maine, lent desks with an E.B. White view. The painter Karl Franke helped re-engineer inaudible audio overhears into dialogue, the designer Ahmer Kalam generously lent his valuable design talents, and celebrated surgeon and author Dr. Jamie Koufman generously kept me walking and talking. And it was Robert L. Powley, Esq., of Powley & Gibson P.C., whose assurances of having my back made moving forward possible. The esteemed

John T. Schulz III, MD, PhD, associate chair, Department of Surgery and Medical Director of the Connecticut Burn Unit, facilitated my weeks shadowing burn nurses under Jacqueline Laird, RN, on the long and often heartbreaking overnight shifts at the Bridgeport Hospital Yale–New Haven Health System. They face the unbearable with uncommon grit, compassion, and soul-saving humor and exemplify the greatest of the good nurses everywhere. Personal thanks too to the nurses of Des Moines General, the University of Iowa Medical Center, Manhattan's Beth Israel Hospital, New York Presbyterian and Weill Cornell Hospitals, the Nantucket Cottage Hospital, the dialysis units of Newington and New Britain General Hospital, and especially the nurses of C5 at the Hospital of Central Connecticut, with whom I spent my sixteenth birthday in traction.

I'd still be grunting or grammarless if not for my loving mom, Diann Waterbury Graeber, a former English teacher who knows doctors as only a daughter and wife can and loves writers as only a mother should. A book about murder by chemistry only seemed palatable because of my father, Dr. Charles W. Graeber, the kindest and hardest-working man I know; following him on rounds as a kid has left me with a sense memory of the hospital night shift inextricable from childhood itself. Both he and my grandfather Dr. Carl Waterbury D.O. (whose first date with my grandmother Patsy ended up as an emergency house call and home birth in Des Moines's southeast "bottoms") inspired a reverence for the art of medicine which, I hope, informs the grim details with higher purpose.

Somehow I was lucky enough to have the tireless advocacy of the Golomb Agency's Susan Golomb, who, from the moment I first sweated through her office chair one hot August afternoon, was a champion for my work as I could not be. And particular respect and gratitude are owed to the Twelve/Hachette Book Group team: the indefatigable efforts of Libby Burton and Tony Forde, the tolerance of Grand Central Publishing senior managing editor Bob Castillo, the patient wisdom and handholding of veteran Twelve/Grand Central associate publisher Brian McLendon, the support of interim publisher Susan Lehman, the sustaining vision and professionalism of publisher Deb Futter, and the faith of former Twelve publisher Cary Goldstein. Cary fought for this book and I owe him a debt, as well as a fresh red pencil. He's a true mensch.

Most personally, I cannot begin to count the saving insights and raw kindnesses of my beloved Gabrielle Allen, who somehow tolerated this Charlie writing about that Charlie, which wasn't always fun, and whose partnership makes everything seem possible.

NOTES

CHAPTER 1

1 Born February 22, 1960.

2 After his father died seven months later, the eight Cullen children survived on church charity, the sewing his ailing mother took in, and the disability checks his paternal aunt received for her deformed leg.

3 On Kling Street.

4 He was twenty-four years old.

5 In an eighty-seven-person class.

6 Charlie didn't like the risk of humiliation that running for election, or anything else, seemed to promise, but his friend insisted.

7 Information about the relationship between Adrianne Baum and Cullen was gathered through interviews with both parties; Ms. Baum has never before allowed herself to be interviewed. Names have been changed at Ms. Baum's request.

8 Adrianne felt that she really knew her beau, but she knew him alone; other than his sister Maureen, who had worked at Roy Rogers for a time, Adrianne had met none of Cullen's family or friends. When she asked to see where Charlie had grown up or to meet the brothers, her boyfriend went mumbly and defensive. She remembers that Charlie's brother James died soon afterward, right in Charlie's old bedroom—an apparent drug overdose, possibly a suicide. The eldest Cullen brother, Edward—the one called Butchy—called from a pay phone drunk and overwhelmed with the news; Charlie drove him back to Adrianne's apartment to let him sleep it off on the couch. That was their first meeting. The only other time Adrianne saw Butchy was at her wedding.

9 He was twenty-six years old.

CHAPTER 2

1 As Charlie started his career, he was aware of the shocking head-lines regarding another killer just finishing his. On April 6, 1987, a depressed, suicidal, Air Force dropout turned nurse named Don-ald Harvey was arrested for murders committed while he worked as a nurse in Ohio and Kentucky. Harvey had been given the nick-name "Angel of Death" by his coworkers, for his constant proxim-ity to coding patients. Harvey would be convicted of thirty-four murders.

2 These are often referred to as "granny burns" because they are most commonly seen in the elderly, when loose clothing catches fire over an open flame such as a stovetop.

3 They are called *escharotomies*, from the Latin for "scar."

4 The practices described in this chapter date to the early '90s. Modern burn wards are far quieter, and pain and anxiety are carefully titrated with new classes of drugs.

5 While other dates have been offered, this is the most likely; Saint Barnabas Medical Center records from 1987 were lost or destroyed sometime prior to the Somerset County Prosecutor's Office investiga-tion. As it happens, this is also the date, in 1992, when Charles Cullen murdered Judge John Yengo. While Cullen acknowledged at least one other victim prior to Yengo, his was the first murder victim to whom he confessed by name to the police.

6 A Levite from Cyprus who facilitated the church's destiny, it was Barnabas, sent to the booming Christian population in Antioch, who recognized the importance of having a Christian beachhead in Greece and pulled the apostle Paul out of retirement.

7 As a newly minted apostle himself, Barnabas preached to the pagans in Lycadonia. The Lycadonians assumed that he was not a preacher, but God himself. Barnabas was talking Jesus; they called him Jupiter. Was the Son of Encouragement discouraged?

   Sources: *Little Pictorial Lives of the Saints*, a compilation based on *Butler's Lives of the Saints*, and other sources by John Gilmary Shea (Benziger Brothers: New York, 1894); *Les Petits Bollandistes: Vies des Saints* by Msgr. Paul Guérin (Bloud et Barral: Paris, 1882), Vol. 6.

8 He was stoned to death by recalcitrant Jews in Salamis on the island of Cyprus.

CHAPTER 3

1 The children's names have been changed at the request of Adrianne Baum.

CHAPTER 4

1 The details of these incidents and the investigation that followed come from police investigation reports, witness statements, and court documents, in addition to interviews with Charles Cullen and Thomas Arnold.

2 Heparin is an anticoagulant, useful for thinning the blood to prevent the clots that can precipitate heart attacks and strokes, but antithetical to stopping bleeding after surgery.

3 By Endocrine and Radioisotope Laboratories of Livingston, New Jersey, and Abbott Hospital Products Division of Abbott Park, Illinois.

4 Arnold told investigators that the units on which their Charles Cullen investigation focused was the old Cardiac Care unit on the sixth floor and the 5700 unit, both cardiac units. Arnold and Barry were so focused on Cullen as the suspect that they concentrated their analysis of death rates only upon the units in which he worked; Arnold stated that he had not looked into the Burn Intensive Care Unit (BICU) due to Cullen not having worked in that unit at the time when their investigation was being conducted.

5 Initially, Cullen and two other female nurses were under suspicion. One of the nurses was cleared, and the other was found to have been stealing morphine for her own personal use.

6 This was the first of two interviews Arnold and Barry would hold with Cullen regarding their investigation.

7 The investigation included patient chart reviews, work schedules, Pyxis medication dispensing cabinets, video surveillance of medical rooms, interviews, evidence (IV bags), and pathological analyses.

8 Police investigation records. This was Charles Cullen's recollection, as well as that of his ex-wife, Adrianne, in a witness statement to police, and expanded upon during a 2010 interview with the author. Cullen being the primary focus of the investigation was the direct statement to the Somerset County Prosecutor's Office by Betty Gillian (the woman who, as administrative director of critical care, had fired Cullen); Gillian's testimony was given November 14, 2003, when she was serving as supervisor and vice president at the Saint Barnabas Hospital corporate offices. Thomas Arnold independently confirmed that Charles Cullen was the primary focus of their investigation.

In a response to uniform interrogatories arising from civil litigation in the wake of Cullen's sentencing, Saint Barnabas Medical Center counsel Sills Cummis Epstein & Gross P.C. rejected the claim. "Saint Barnabas did not perform or cause to be performed any internal investigation as a result of unexplained laboratory results regarding medications in patients or unexplained patient deaths while Charles Cullen was an employee of Saint Barnabas, Livingston Health Care Services, or Medical Center Health Care, Inc. In February and October of 1991, internal investigations were conducted at Saint Barnabas regarding unexplained low blood sugar levels in several patients...In this regard, Saint Barnabas notes that it has only been able to retrieve a portion of the documents related to these investigations; the rest are believed to have been destroyed years ago during the course of an office move." The brief goes on to state, "The 1991 internal investigations regarding unexplained low blood sugar levels in several patients did not focus on Charles Cullen." This document was signed by Nancy Holecek, senior vice president of patient care services at the Saint Barnabas Health Care System, speaking on Saint Barnabas's behalf. Ms. Holecek was a former Telemetry unit director, and also involved with Barry, Arnold, and Gillian in the investigation.

9 Then Telemetry supervisor Nancy Holecek would later compare the process to finding a needle in a haystack.

CHAPTER 5

1 Charles Cullen, interviews by the author.

2 Cullen was technically employed by Medical Center Health Care Services, formerly Livingston Health Services, a wholly owned for-profit subsidiary of the Saint Barnabas Health Care Corporation, which supplied staffing to the units. Depositions of Medical Center Health Care Services staffers explain that between January 6 and January 10, 1992, Cullen became a "do not book," as the terms *terminated* and *fired* were as policy not used. The cause given for termination was poor documentation and a "decreasingly poor attitude." For example, Cullen was found on June 20, 1990, to have canceled a physician's continuous ventilation order for one burn patient and, on the morning of June 21, canceled another vent order for another patient. Among his documented issues are several medication errors, including a March 14, 1991, occurrence in which an incoming nurse found Cullen had failed to give his patient the medicine the doctor had prescribed, and

instead hung an IV marked only with a red label without writing on it. His coworkers expressed a "deep concern re: Charles's attitude toward making this dual medication error" and felt he was "not at all concerned about the error or the welfare of the patient." Among several other incidents potentially affecting patient safety was a July 26 occurrence in which Cullen had written on a patient's chart a doctor's order for four units of insulin; in fact, no insulin was to be given that patient. In court records of the deposition of Nancy Holecek, senior VP of patient care services for the Saint Barnabas Health Care System, she explained that Cullen was fired for "nursing care issues."

CHAPTER 6

1 Details of Cullen's application process and the events at Warren Hospital come from Warren Hospital's file on Charles Cullen, police investigation documents, police witness statements, and court records.

2 The exact dates of Cullen's termination at Saint Barnabas are unclear, but his interview at Warren Hospital occurred January 21, 1992.

3 The available records from this time contain Cullen's inclusion of these references and numbers, but leave it unclear as to whether anyone from the Warren Hospital HR department did call to confirm references at Saint Barnabas Medical Center or Medical Center Health Care Services.

CHAPTER 8

1 Details from court documents, interviews with Adrianne Baum, and police reports.

2 He'd learn later that his mother's body was still there.

3 Charlie turned eighteen three months after his mother's death, and at the Navy recruiter's suggestion he got his GED. He enlisted in April 1978 for eight weeks of basic training at the Great Lakes training facility in Illinois, then seven months at the Naval Guided Missile School in Virginia Beach, Virginia, followed by three months of submarine school in Groton, Connecticut. He would ultimately be stationed in Charleston, South Carolina.

4 Several captain's masts, or disciplinary hearings, stemmed from his refusal to urinate in front of another sailor for the mandatory drug tests; Charlie maintained that while marijuana use was common in the Navy, he never personally tried it or any other illicit substance,

and he bristled at the humiliation of exposing himself during public urination. His inability to void publicly would cause him conflict for his whole life.

5 This included an incident in which one of Cullen's shipmates reported finding him at the launch panel for the nuclear missiles while wearing a green surgical gown, mask, and gloves from the medical supply closet. This anecdote was relayed to reporters by one of Cullen's former superior officers following news of Cullen's arrest. Cullen says that he finds this story about him to be very funny, but that it is not true.

6 Finally, Cullen was transferred off the sub to a supply ship, the USS *Canopus*.

7 Cullen was anxious about his upcoming discharge from service, which was expected to be dishonorable; he told Navy psychiatrists that he wanted to kill himself because he "didn't want to return home a failure." In previous alcoholic suicide attempts, the Navy doctors had found him to be sane and fit for service, and they prescribed alcohol counseling and Antabuse. Charlie had used the drug to attempt suicide again.

8 He was treated for methyl salicylate poisoning.

9 "Eye contact poor and voice soft," the physician noted. "Verbalizations concise and evasive." The physician also noted that Cullen showed poor insight as to his alcoholism, and was passive-aggressive and resistant of ward routine and rules. But soon he became more verbal, particularly about his sense of loss of his mother (with whom Cullen was "unusually close") and an unnamed fiancée. "He has always been shy with few friends," the report noted. "He has shown dependency, particularly in relationships with females, becoming intensely involved in a short time."

10 Cullen's older brother, James, who died of a drug overdose in 1986 at the age of thirty-six, had been an apparent suicide. While some police investigators have speculated that Charles Cullen may have been involved in his brother's death, there is no direct evidence to support those speculations.

11 January 31, 1993.

12 Civil Action docket no. FM-21-229-93, Superior Court of New Jersey, Warren County, October 19, 1994.

13 It was located at 263 Shafer Avenue.

CHAPTER 9

1 Phillipsburg, Pennsylvania, police records.

CHAPTER 10

1 All quotes come either from my interviews with Charles Cullen, from his confession to police, or from Pennsylvania State Police transcripts.

CHAPTER 11

1 Greystone was the "State Asylum for the Insane," an updated version of the "New Jersey State Lunatic Asylum at Morristown." The name changes provided a coded history of the public perception and private care of "diseases of the mind" (the term itself a more modern take); it was, by the time of Cullen's incarceration there, a "psychiatric hospital."

2 Sources conflict as to the exact dates of his treatment. On March 24, Cullen was first checked into the Carrier Clinic, in Belle Mead, New Jersey; he was then transferred to Greystone Psychiatric Hospital in mid-April.

CHAPTER 12

1 There are other vital signs telemetry can monitor—blood pressure, blood oxygen level, temperature—but the electrocardiogram is the most common.

2 In Cullen's accounting, the judge who had ordered him to pay for this was responsible for forcing him back into nursing. Given a free hand, Cullen maintains, he would have quit. But nursing was the core of Cullen's self-definition, and one that clearly offered him enticements beyond a good wage. While it is possibly true that he would have had difficulty earning as much money at another job, what is certain is that he would have been far less likely to get away with murder in another work setting.

3 Cullen would later characterize the relationship as romantic but not sexual.

CHAPTER 13

1 Statements by Larry Dean and police investigative records.

2 Larry Dean would die in 2001, still attempting to prove his contention that his mother had been murdered. After his death, his late mother's blood and tissue samples would be found in his home freezer.

3 Cullen had given Helen Dean an intramuscular injection that should have taken maximum effect in three to four hours. But Mrs. Dean

died the next day, nearly twenty-four hours later and shortly after her release from the hospital.

4 Det. Richard Clayton and Lt. G. Dundon.

5 The results of the autopsy of Helen Dean, as written by Dr. M. L. Cowen, Warren County medical examiner: "The injection site was examined for chemicals and toxic substances…the chemistry evaluation was negative…The male nurse suspected of injecting an unknown substance into Mrs. Dean's anterior left thigh successfully passed a polygraph test indicating that he was truthfully stating that he did not inject Mrs. Dean with a needle."

CHAPTER 14

1 Fair Oaks Hospital (formerly Summit Hospital), Summit, New Jersey.

2 Police investigative report.

3 It appears that the Saint Barnabas Human Resources department was never reached by anyone at Hunterdon, but several Warren Hospital employees vouched for him, including Charlie's nurse supervisor, and the ICU nursing manager. Both gave Cullen positive remarks, his ICU manager adding only that Cullen had left their hospital for "personal reasons."

4 Charles Cullen has changed his accounting many times. After his initial confession, he would go back and decide that in terms of actual deaths, he probably was responsible for at least one patient in January. Also, definitely one in April, and yes, another about a week later, then two weeks after that, then two weeks after that—not able to really keep the details, knowing only that all of them would have been injections while he was working in the ICU.

5 Police investigative records and witness statements, in addition to Cullen's personnel file.

6 One patient, discovered in a room strewn with bloody cloths and empty bottles, was naked and oxygen-starved, staring at the ceiling. Physicians contended that these factors contributed to, if they were not responsible for, the patient later suffering a stroke.

7 The spellings and spacings herein are from the original letter.

CHAPTER 15

1 Carco Research.

2 Police investigation records. The Hunterdon and Warren HR departments both confirmed that Cullen had been employed by them;

Medical Center Health Care Services, the staffing agency owned by Saint Barnabas Health Care Corporation, indicated that they could vouch for Cullen being employed there from 1990, but Saint Barnabas itself did not locate a file for Charles Cullen.

3 From Cullen's Morristown personnel file and documents from court records.

4 A short-acting sedative, usually used to initiate anesthesia.

5 This was Cullen's recollection, as stated to detectives on December 14, 2003. Cullen believed "there could have been one or two at Morristown," and that while he "didn't remember specifics," he "could have been involved in something there." Cullen did not provide any further details at that time, and during the subsequent investigation he failed to identify victims among the Morristown Memorial Hospital patient records.

6 April 7, 1997: "Tammy, I really don't want to write this, but for the patient's sake and safety, as well as for the unit's reputation. This is just one of many patients who verbalized the same thing. Call me." This was but one of the handwritten notes, presumably from Cullen's supervisor or colleagues, found jotted on paperwork relating to Cullen's employment at Morristown.

7 This and all subsequent details taken from police investigation reports.

8 $500, according to Cullen's testimony and police investigation.

9 This was to be a serious review, and lawyers for Morristown Memorial and the American Arbitration Association exchanged letters in preparation.

CHAPTER 16

1 A company called Medical Staffing Network took over for the Health Force staffing agency in 2000, at which point all old employee records were purged from their system.

2 It is impossible to say exactly when the problems started at Liberty, but Mr. Henry was the earliest Liberty patient with whom Charles Cullen would admit to having "intervened."

3 Police investigative records and Pennsylvania State Nursing Board investigative reports.

4 According to the brief filed by Kimberly Pepe in her lawsuit against Liberty, Henry was taken to nearby Lehigh Valley Hospital after he began having respiratory problems that morning. Hospital officials discovered the insulin overdose. Henry was later returned to Liberty,

placed on a morphine drip, and subsequently died. Liberty's records don't say if his death was a result of the insulin overdose. Charles Cullen would ultimately confess to being responsible for Henry's overdose.

5 Pepe's suit alleged that administrators at Liberty "intentionally chose to ignore and overlook any evidence pointing to the fact that Cullen may have been the nurse who administered insulin" despite the fact that Charles Cullen's repeated medication issues had put him under "a cloud of suspicion." Charles Cullen was not Henry's nurse that night, but he was in and out of the room frequently for another patient. Pepe also filed a complaint with the Equal Employment Opportunity Commission.

6 According to a February 29, 2004, *New York Times* article ("Death on the Night Shift: 16 Years, Dozens of Bodies; Through Gaps in System, Nurse Left Trail of Grief," by Richard Pérez-Peña, David Kocieniewski, and Jason George), Julie Beckert, spokeswoman for HCR Manor Care (which owns Liberty), would not discuss Mr. Henry's case, but she denied that Mr. Cullen had been under investigation for stealing drugs. Liberty settled Ms. Pepe's lawsuit on terms that both sides have kept secret.

7 Four years later, in January 2002, the Pennsylvania State Nursing Board would initiate a background investigation into Charles Cullen in response to complaints from another incident. At that time, Liberty Nursing and Rehabilitation Center nursing director Dawn Costello was interviewed and asked whether "any drugs or unexplained deaths had occurred during his [Cullen's] employment." Ms. Costello replied "No."

8 Liberty admitted their investigation into the patient's death was inconclusive, according to Pepe's 1998 lawsuit.

9 A Liberty spokesman stated that Charles Cullen's infractions were reported to the Pennsylvania Department of Health, which oversees hospitals but not nursing personnel.

10 Internally, Liberty listed the reason for dismissal as "failure to follow drug protocol." In 2003, the *Express-Times* of Easton, Pennsylvania, quoted Liberty spokeswoman Julie Beckert as saying that Cullen was fired in 1998 after he was accused of giving patients drugs at unscheduled times. Beckert said there was no evidence that Cullen, who worked at the center for eight months, had given patients medications they had not been prescribed.

While giving patients drugs in violation of a prescribed delivery schedule can cause serious harm, Beckert said Liberty was not aware of any cases in which a patient became ill. Liberty said it reported Cullen's actions to the Pennsylvania Department of Health, which regulates nursing homes but does not have the power to discipline individual nurses. According to a story in the December 18, 2003, *New York Times*,

> The year after Ms. Pepe was fired, she sued the nursing home and filed a complaint with the federal Equal Employment Opportunity Commission. She and the hospital settled her claims in 2001, and the terms of the deal were sealed. Yesterday, through her lawyer, Donald Russo, Ms. Pepe declined to be interviewed, and Mr. Russo said he could not say much about the case.
>
> But Ms. Pepe's account is laid out in detail in her original suit and in a statement she gave the employment commission.
>
> On May 8, 1998, she said, after Mr. Henry was taken to Lehigh Valley Hospital, staff members there called her three times to ask if she had given him insulin, and said his blood-sugar level had dropped to 25—so low that a patient is likely to lose consciousness and may suffer brain damage. Except in rare circumstances, a person's blood sugar does not drop below 70 on its own. But insulin, a hormone used by diabetics to combat high blood sugar, could force such a drop, with the effect peaking one to two hours after injection. Ms. Pepe said Mr. Henry was not diabetic.
>
> Ms. Pepe said that when she was asked about the incident days later, a nursing supervisor told her "they were not suspecting me at that time; they were, in not so many words, looking at my co-worker, Charles Cullen."
>
> In a statement yesterday, Liberty's parent company, HCR Manor Care, said, "To the best of our knowledge and according to our employee records, Charles Cullen was not under investigation by the center or outside pharmacy in May of 1998."

11 Charles Cullen was employed through Health Force, an agency Easton Hospital used for its staffing.
12 Details of this incident are corroborated with police witness statements and police investigative records.
13 Ottomar Schramm had been taken from his nursing home by ambulance with aspirated food in his lungs.

14 These conversations are reconstructed as recorded from Easton Police interviews with Kristina Toth.

CHAPTER 17

1 Northampton County coroner Zachary Lysek didn't see how Schramm could have been accidentally given a dose of the deadly drugs in his system, and undertook a rigorous eight-month investigation of the death, interviewing dozens of staffers who had been involved with Schramm's care, both in the nursing home from which he was transferred and at the hospital where he overdosed and died. He was aware from Toth of the mention of a man who seemed to be a nurse, but was unaware of that nurse's identity. The forensic pathologist found that Mr. Schramm had died of pneumonia with digoxin overdose as a contributing factor, and, as a result, reported that Schramm's "manner of death will be listed as accidental." Lysek was still suspicious, but despite his personal opinion, had no evidence to take it further.

According to court documents and police investigation reports, Lysek was contacted three years later by an unnamed source, who told him that the mystery male nurse Toth had mentioned was named Charles Cullen, and that Cullen might have had some involvement in Mr. Schramm's death. At this point, Lysek contacted the state police.

According to Mr. Lysek, he also called Easton to inquire about Charles Cullen's records there. The Easton administrator looked up employee records and reported that they had no record of having employed a Charles Cullen. While of little help to Lysek, this was in fact technically true; while Mr. Cullen had worked at Easton Hospital, his employment had come through a personnel agency called Health Med One of Harrisburg, Pennsylvania. This was a familiar problem in the tracking of Charles Cullen throughout his career, and it taught Lysek the importance of ensuring that forensic investigators asked the right questions when compiling complete and accurate lists of medical staff who might have had contact with a potential victim.

2 OxyContin entered the market in 1996.

3 This perception of the situation has been drawn from interviews, both by myself and by police detectives, with Charles Cullen; the facts surrounding his subsequent actions and the hospital's reaction come directly from police investigative documents and witness statements to police.

4 Although Cullen told police investigators that he recalled having killed four or five patients at Lehigh Valley, investigators were only able to definitively identify two of the victims: twenty-two-year old Matthew Mattern (August 31, 1999) and seventy-three-year old Stella Danielczyk (February 26, 2000); she had granny burns over 60 percent of her body, a death sentence by the rule of 9s.

5 The surgeons flapped out muscle to lay down a vascular grid over the bone to which they might eventually graft skin. The drugs in his system kept his body from fighting the transplant tissue, even as it prevented him from effectively fighting off infection. Each infection sent Mattern back to the OR.

6 This account comes from interviews and copies of Duddy's police incident report. The dialogue has been taken from these sources and framed into quotes by the author.

7 Charlie was examined and sent home. There was nothing wrong with him physically, and he appeared quite sane.

CHAPTER 18

1 In April 2000, Cullen used the unit's computer to send an e-mail to two nurses who had recently been fired by the hospital, expressing sympathy and solidarity. Cullen was leaving the Burn Unit too, he explained—he'd already put in for a transfer to the Cardiac Floor. He was one of them, he said, aligned against the "Senior Service"—the fifteen-year veterans of the ward. Charlie called them "the SS," for short, and continued on with the Nazi references—at the time, he didn't realize that his e-mail would be sent not only to the two fired nurses, but to everyone on the Burn Unit staff, including the "Senior Service" members themselves. After that, life on the Burn Unit was utterly unbearable, and the Cardiac Unit no longer had any room for his transfer.

2 Cullen's confessed recollection of his time at Lehigh includes having been responsible for the deaths of four or five patients there. Only two murders have been successfully identified from the Lehigh records: Matthew Mattern on August 31, 1999, and Stella Danielczyk on February 26, 2000.

3 According to police investigation reports, St. Luke's Hospital HR called for references from coworkers at "Liberty Nursing Home," and Lehigh Valley Hospital Burn Intensive Care Unit; the quotes in this paragraph come from those references.

4 According to a March 9, 2008, article in the *Morning Call*, St. Luke's share of the medical care pie grew at an astounding 25 percent between 1990 and 2007, outstripping neighbor Lehigh Valley Hospital's 2 percent gain, and taking between 29 and 39 percent of the patients and patient dollars from smaller Easton and Sacred Heart hospitals.

5 St. Luke's offered him full-time on the overnight shift starting at $21.45 an hour.

6 The nine patient rooms were arranged around the nurse's station in a semicircle, usually just one patient per room.

7 The perceptions of the nurses come from witness statements and police investigation records.

8 Taken from police investigation witness statements and police investigation documents, including subpoenaed records of reports and incidents from the hospital itself.

CHAPTER 19

1 Julie (family name withheld) was a unit clerk at St. Luke's.

2 From Nurse Brad Hahn's statement to Pennsylvania State Police.

3 The president of the hospital had a PhD in biostatistics. St. Luke's Hospital has been repeatedly honored by inclusion in both the annual *U.S. News & World Report* list of best American hospitals and Truven's "Top 100 Hospitals" rankings.

4 Statements of Cullen's recollection of events are all taken directly from Charles Cullen interviews and corroborated by police investigation records, including witness statements and Cullen's statements to police.

CHAPTER 20

1 Police investigation documents and court records.

2 Nurse Thelma Moyer's comment, as recollected in the confidential memo between attorney Paul Laughlin of the law firm Stevens and Johnson and St. Luke's Hospital attorney Sy Traub.

3 From personal and police interviews with Charles Cullen. This was only Charlie's perception of course, just as it was his perception that St. Luke's was a Catholic institution. Cullen's assumption stemmed from the medical center's use of a saint's name and with a cruciform apostrophe shaped like the Star of Bethlehem. In fact, St. Luke's had no religious affiliation.

4 Joe Chandler was a day-shift nurse who ordered the restock for the med room. He had noticed that the drugs had started going missing as early as December 2001.

5 From police investigation documents and witness statements, personal interviews with Cullen, and Cullen's own recollection and documentation to police. Three patients coded that night. Whether Charles Cullen was responsible for all three is a point of contention. Cullen was ultimately charged only with the death of Edward O'Toole, seventy-six, on that night.

CHAPTER 21

1 Extensive interviews detailing these incidents are contained in police investigative documents, Pennsylvania Board of Nursing investigative reports, and subsequent court proceedings.

2 Biohazardous materials, used gloves, bloody material, amputated limbs, and excised organs, the abortions and tumors and liposucked fat, etc.; hospitals use and remove a great deal of mass.

3 It is used to help becalm patients who couldn't keep their ventilators in—for patients whose diaphragm musculature had seized up as a side effect of other drugs.

4 For this reason, vec is always prescribed in as small a dose as possible for efficacy—enough to relax the diaphragm for breathing but not enough to impair oxygen delivery to the brain and other vital organs.

5 Cullen admitted to having used vec to kill at St. Luke's.

6 Reports of the exact numbers vary between sources, but most fall in the middle of Kimble's recollection of seeing between six and twelve used bottles of vec.

7 Because O'Toole's death was not specifically investigated until many years later, his cause of death cannot be officially determined. Charles Cullen would later confess to having killed O'Toole with vec in his voluntary statement to Somerset detectives.

8 Janice Rader's interview with Pennsylvania State Police was used to create this specific language regarding the reasons for contacting outside council, i.e., that it would be best for the hospital. Sy Traub is the individual cited in Paul Laughlin's confidential memo regarding his response to the call from St. Luke's regarding this issue.

9 The same firm which had been retained by Easton Hospital, in light of the suspicious death of Ottomar Schramm. Some partners, including Laughlin, have since moved on.

10 In a deposition before the civil trials, however, Laughlin made clear that his job here was simply to determine who had put the drugs into the sharps box, not to extrapolate as to what had happened to the drugs nor what the proper course of action for the hospital should be regarding that information.

11 Charles Cullen also said these words when security brought him out.

CHAPTER 22

1 Laughlin's brief to St. Luke's in-house counsel provides an account of his meeting with Cullen, and subsequent interviews with Charles Cullen have confirmed and colored in that account without contradiction; this passage reflects both. I have taken the liberty of inserting quotation marks into this account for clarity.

2 These are the questions and phrasings from Laughlin's report; the use of quotes is only perhaps appropriate.

3 Charles Cullen maintained that he didn't wear gloves for this, and the vials had his fingerprints on them. It's impossible to know what is true. This is Charlie's recollection; the vials are gone, and Laughlin has never commented.

4 Laughlin was part of an administrative meeting in which it was decided that Charles Cullen would be offered the opportunity to resign; it was not his decision.

5 Documentation detailed in court proceedings and police investigation documents.

CHAPTER 23

1 His references included St. Luke's nurse Pat Medellin, who would later alert Laughlin to a series of suspicious deaths on the unit that she believed were attributable to Cullen and ultimately take her concern to the police.

2 The St. Luke's HR department gave Charlie "neutral" references, according to documents which were part of the police investigation. However, it took them three weeks to respond to the request from the Sacred Heart HR department.

3 From court documents. New Jersey Superior Court Judge Bryan D. Garruto, in his Memorandum of Decision on two motions—(1) St. Luke's Hospital's Motion to Dismiss the Plaintiff's Complaint, and (2) Somerset Medical Center's Motion to Amend Its Complaint to Add St. Luke's as a Third-Party Defendant—rejected St. Luke's claim that

they were both unaware of and not responsible for informing Somerset Medical Center about the danger posed by Charles Cullen, and could thus be sued by the families of Cullen's victims at Somerset Medical Center. Garruto did not rule on the merits of those families' cases.

In an opinion filed August 21, Garruto wrote, "The record reflects that St. Luke's did not affirmatively misrepresent Mr. Cullen as a 'model employee.' However, because St. Luke's chose to omit information about Mr. Cullen's rehiring status to an inquiry by Somerset when at the same time St. Luke's officials were calling other local-area hospitals to inform them of Cullen's 'do not rehire' status, it is not immune from liability."

Specifically, Garruto cited the March 21, 2005, memo between Dr. Saunders and St. Luke's executive vice president and CEO, Elaine Thompson, in which Saunders acknowledges the sub rosa phone calls warning area hospitals off of Charles Cullen; this citation is the only reason this document is known to exist.

Judge Garruto's decision notes: "Specifically, Dr. Saunders writes that on or around August 2002, he phoned his counterpart at Lehigh Valley Hospital, Dr. Robert Laskowski, 'to inform him about the medication diversion found at St. Luke's Hospital; to see if there were any similar incidents in his employment file at Lehigh Valley; and to alert Dr. Laskowski not to hire this nurse because of his bizarre behavior.' Saunders also indicated that he informed Dr. Laskowski that Mr. Cullen was listed as a 'do not rehire' at St. Luke's. Dr. Saunders's March 21, 2005, memo also notes that the then chief operating officer at St. Luke's, Vince Joseph, was making 'similar calls to other area hospitals.' "

The "Memorandum of Decision on Motion Pursuant to R.1:6-2(f)" was filed August 21, 2007, and addressed "all cases and docket numbers arising out of the Cullen Litigation Case Type 270."

4 On December 23, 2003, Pennsylvania state troopers interviewed Easton Hospital assistant CEO Deborah Borse and Easton's risk manager, Georgianne Gerlach. Borse related that in August 2002, Gerlach, who was then the nursing recruiter for Easton, had been contacted by Paul Laughlin: "Laughlin advised that he could not tell them why, but they should not hire Charles Cullen."

5 No notes acknowledging these calls would ever be found in Charles Cullen's personnel file from Lehigh Valley Hospital, Sacred Heart Hospital, Easton Hospital, or St. Luke's Hospital.

6 In this same memorandum, Judge Garruto ultimately rejected St. Luke's motion, and granted that of Somerset Medical Center. "Here, the problem is that St. Luke's assumed a duty to patients who would be under Mr. Cullen's care," Judge Garruto concluded. "But then took it upon itself to choose who will live and who will die."

7 In ruling against St. Luke's Hospital's request for summary judgment in five civil suits brought against it by patients' families, the Trial Court of Pennsylvania offered the following opinion:

> It would be shocking to contemplate a state of affairs where society would condone a hospital keeping silent while knowing, or being aware that it is highly probable, that a member of its staff killed a patient. Accordingly, the duty to disclose such information surely flows not merely as a concomitant of the express duties set forth in Thompson, supra, but is also understood more profoundly as one of the collection of duties that civilized people have come to expect of each other and their institutions. Therefore, while the court in this situation may be perceived as "imposing" a duty, it is in truth only recognizing an obligation that, it may fairly be said, persons would widely expect ought to apply, even in the absence of a more formal judicial pronouncement. It is, after all, the extent to which our principles of jurisprudence resonate with our collective convictions and shared notions of right and wrong that ultimately lend vitality to, and command respect for, our system of laws. To fail to recognize such an obvious duty on the part of a hospital in these circumstances would, by contrast, render the common law not only effete but a legitimate object of derision. (Superior Court of Pennsylvania Trial Court Opinion, *Krapf v. St. Luke's Hospital*, July 9, 2009, at 25–26, upheld by the Superior Court July 27, 2010, http://caselaw.findlaw.com/pa -superior-court/1533011.html)

CHAPTER 24

1 Four hospitals and Liberty Nursing and Rehabilitation Center.

2 Also, his Pennsylvania nursing license would expire in October 2002. Applying for a new one seemed like pressing his luck, especially in light of his inglorious removal from St. Luke's. Cullen had prepared for this eventuality and had applied to renew his New Jersey license while still working at St. Luke's Hospital.

3 His New Jersey state nursing license was in good standing; it would not expire until March 2003.

4 Named for England's Somerset.

5 "It was once the country home of some of the 19th century's wealthiest families, and modern-day residents now include pharmaceuticals and chemicals barons." Sara Clemence, "Home of the Week: Peapack Palace," *Forbes*, March 14, 2005, http://www.forbes.com/2005/03/14/cx_sc_0314how.html.

6 Details from Somerset Medical Center personnel files and police investigative documents.

7 Charlie had, for a time, taken great pains to make weekend plans when he had custody of his children, arranging trips to museums, movies, or even the beach. But since he'd moved in with Cathy he'd stopped making such plans and often found excuses not to take the kids.

8 Cullen was a do-not-rehire at St. Luke's. On September 6, 2002, Connie Osinski, nurse recruiter at Somerset Medical Center, called St. Luke's Hospital to follow up on references listed on Cullen's application to work at Somerset. St. Luke's Human Resources confirmed Cullen's employment, the dates and position, but did not respond to the inquiry as to whether Cullen was eligible for rehire at St. Luke's. St. Luke's assistant vice president in Human Resources, Mr. Andrew Seidel, would later testify in deposition that "neutral references"—which is to say no references at all, neither good nor bad—were the standard, unwritten policy for all former employees.

Following St. Luke's internal investigation, Seidel said he had been present at an August meeting with other top-level St. Luke's administrators and legal counsel, including Amedeo, Saunders, Anderson, and Traub, at which the decision to formalize Cullen's do-not-rehire status had been made. Seidel further testified that, although Cullen had already offered to resign the night he was removed from St. Luke's, Seidel later spoke with Cullen by phone, informing him that "he had a choice"—to either resign or be fired. "The difference is by resigning he can save face, leave an organization, reapply for other jobs by indicating he resigned from his position," Seidel testified. "Firing someone becomes common knowledge, and if he's ever asked by future employers if he's been fired from a job, if he's truthful, he'd have to say yes." Seidel explained that, as the evidence at that time was circumstantial, and Cullen had not admitted to any wrongdoing, he did not, "based on the information I had...want to destroy his ability to get another job." Asked whether he "anticipated that by allowing Mr. Cullen to resign rather than be fired, it would make it easier for him (Cullen) to get his next nursing job," Seidel replied yes. Asked about Cullen's claims that he had "discussions about a neutral reference" with someone from St. Luke's around the time of his termination, and whether Seidel had discussed such neutral references with Cullen, Seidel replied "I do not recall that." He went on to explain that, in fact, neutral references were what they were giving at the time, "for anybody," regardless of whether, or why, that employee had been fired by the hospital. "So whether he resigned or not," Seidel said, "he was still going to get a neutral reference."

In the civil actions that followed Cullen's arrest, St. Luke's attorneys took the following position with the court: "There is no evidence to suggest that St. Luke's permitted Cullen to resign 'in exchange for a neutral reference' that would help him to obtain future employment," as Somerset contends. On the contrary, the evidence suggests that St. Luke's accepted Cullen's resignation and, consistent with the hospital policy, did not provide any reference—positive, negative, or otherwise—on behalf of Cullen."

9 For purposes of narrative expediency, another of Charlie's friends on the unit is not mentioned—Donna Hardgrieve, now Donna Scotty. Donna was also a good friend of Amy's; together they formed a group the other nurses referred to as "the Three Musketeers." Some of the stories that Amy initially heard about Cullen in fact came to her indirectly, relayed through Donna. Donna had no part in the investigation and never learned of Amy's involvement.

10 Amy was thirty-eight at this time; she'd received her nursing degree from St. Elizabeth College in 1988.

11 January 14.

12 This was Cullen's language; if he ever knew Mrs. Han's name, he did not remember it by December, when he would be questioned about it.

13 Each unit is 2 cc, or 0.5 mg; according to Dr. Shaleen, Ms. Han had been given only 0.125 mg on June 12 and 0.125 mg on June 13.

14 Gall's blood work showed low blood proteins, symptomatic of his immune system's impaired ability to fight infection (hypogamma-globulinemia).

15 Gall died on Saturday, June 28. According to police investigation reports, nurse Marty Kelly asked to meet with Risk Manager Mary Lund regarding the situation on Monday morning. Lund called a

meeting for the following day. Participants included William Cors, MD, chief medical officer; Sharon Holswade, chief operating officer; Anthony D'Aguillo, MD, chairperson of Pathology; Kathy Puder, Laboratory Services; Stuart Vigdor, director of Pharmacy; Nancy Doherty, Pharmacy; MaryJo Goodman, RN, director of Critical Care–Cardiology; Valerie Smith, RN, manager of Critical Care; Darilyn Paul, RN, Critical Care; and Linda Vescia, RN-C, manager, Quality and Risk Improvement. One of the several measures taken as a result of that meeting pharmacy was to check Pyxis access to the digoxin in the Critical Care unit and around the times of the abnormal lab values. Pharmacy was also requested to contact Poison Control to, among other things, obtain information on the dose of digoxin necessary to cause a serum digoxin level of 9, as found in Gall's blood work. The focus was on patients 4 and 3: Reverend Gall and Mrs. Han. The Pyxis reports were studied, with special concern over the canceled drug orders.

CHAPTER 25

1 From transcript of recorded call. These passages have been abridged for length and clarity. All calls between Somerset Medical Center and New Jersey Poison Control were recorded by NJPC, though Somerset Medical Center staff were unaware of this until much later.

2 Ruck was the director of drug information and professional education, and holds a doctorate in clinical pharmacy.

3 According to a time line later submitted to the Department of Health by Dr. William Cors, Kelly and Doherty contacted Mary Lund regarding these patients on June 19.

4 From police investigation records.

5 From police investigation reports and author interviews with Dr. Marcus.

6 It did—Vigdor was in fact named on all the civil suits against Somerset Medical Center, along with Somerset CEO Dennis Miller, William Cors, and Mary Lund.

CHAPTER 26

1 Police investigation records. For this conference, Somerset Medical Center had assembled Risk Manager Mary Lund, Senior Vice President for Medical Affairs Dr. William Cors, Quality Manager Linda Vashed, Pharmacist Director Stuart Vigdor, and Pharmacist Nancy Doherty.

The New Jersey Poison Control side was represented by Pharmacist Bruce Ruck and now his boss, running in late, Dr. Steven Marcus.

2   State regulations required hospitals to report to the Department of Health any events occurring within hospitals that jeopardized the health and safety of patients. The reportage was to be immediate; the cause of these events did not need to be known by the hospitals in order to be reported.

3   Witness statements from police investigation records and DOH records.

4   Police investigation records and DOH records.

5   Police investigation records and interviews with Dr. Marcus.

6   The e-mail, dated Thursday, July 10, 2003, and contained in the police records, reads in part:

> I spoke to the risk manager of the hospital, the director of pharmacy, the chief operating officer, and the chief medical officer, and they told me that they were not planning on reporting these incidents to anyone, not the NJDHSS or the police, until after they mount a thorough investigation.

7   According to DOH records and court documents, Assistant Commissioner Amie Thornton e-mailed Dr. Marcus again in December 2003:

> I've been meaning to contact you all, but things have been a zoo here (as you can imagine). Your call to Eddy and me in June seems to be the grain of sand in the oyster that brought this situation to light. [Your] ability to spot the trend and get the hospital focused on pursuing this issue proved quite valuable. Clearly your instincts were right on target! Thanks.

According to state records and court documents, Dr. Bresnitz e-mailed Dr. Marcus two years later regarding the calls:

> Ironic that Somerset portrays themselves as doing the right thing by notifying us when clearly it was in response to your informing them that if they wouldn't do it, you would.
>
> By the way, did you also tape our conversation and your conversation with Amie Thornton just so I know in case we get a call from the media? I imagine that the press will continue to inquire to find out exactly what the department did to investigate the deaths during that summer.

8 At 4:23 p.m. on July 10, 2003, several hours after Dr. Marcus had called and e-mailed the DOH.

9 Those patients were Joseph P. Lehman, who suffered unexplained hypoglycemia on May 28, 2003, and Francis Kane, who had a similar incident on June 4, 2003.

10 They'd hired an RN from an inspection agency, who spent two days interviewing leadership and checking the machines before submitting a report.

11 An internal memo on the interview (written July 25, 2003, and included in police investigative reports), written by Fleming, indicates that he had not interviewed any nurses other than Cullen, that he had some suspicion that the unexplained overdose incidents at Somerset could be connected, and that they needed to prepare for the possibility that such incidents might not yet be finished. Fleming's notes also indicate conflicting impulses and information.

"Ms. Lund and I discussed a variety of issues and planned some further investigation," Fleming wrote. "Some of the blood taken from patients in the CCE/ICU in recent days is going to be tested and the ICU/CCU blood taken from patients now and in the immediate future is being saved. In addition, we are going to speak to the nurses caring for Reverend Gall on the 27th and 28th of June. The billing records are going to be checked to see if Digoxin was billed to any of these three patients, even though the record doesn't show that it was given. Lastly, Ms. Lund is going to send me the Han medical chart and the Maurer medical chart." (Maurer was another, unknown patient who was also apparently within the scope of Fleming's investigation.)

The penultimate paragraph of Fleming's memo suggests that Lund and Fleming already suspected Cullen as a subject to be watched: "We agreed that there was nothing so overtly suspicious at this point in time (either from the records or Mr. Cullen's demeanor itself) that would necessitate a call to the authorities. However all the patients in ICU/CCU are being carefully monitored and red flags are going up for any Digoxin orders of medication administration.... Incidentally, the records also show a number of viles [sic] of Digoxin not being accounted for last month."

CHAPTER 27

1 Pasquale Napolitano, killed on July 13.

2 Dr. Max Fink, the head of the insulin coma unit at the Hillside Hospital in Glen Oaks, Queens, New York, from 1952 to 1958, described some of the effects of insulin for PBS's *The American Experience*:

Stages of Coma

0630–0715: Pre-comatose.
    Patient went gradually to sleep and then to coma. Two forms of coma were recognized, a "wet" and a "dry." In the "wet" form, sweating was profuse and was accompanied by "goosebumps" in the skin. Salivation increased, so much so that nurses sopped it up with gauze sponges. In the "dry" form, the skin was hot and dry, muscles twitched, in a sequence that began in the face, arms, and then in the legs. These were often small twitches, but from time to time, patients would move and jerk an arm or a leg. Occasionally, a grand mal seizure supervened.

3 Götz Aly et al., *Cleansing the Fatherland* (Baltimore: Johns Hopkins University Press, 1994). The Eichberg Station was designed to accommodate experiments with intentional IV overdoses; see Henry Friedland, *The Origins of Nazi Genocide* (Chapel Hill: University of North Carolina Press, 1995), 131.

CHAPTER 28
1 Details of this horrifying incident, and all patient deaths, are drawn from police investigation documents.
2 September 23, 2003.

CHAPTER 29
1 Tim got the call that he'd made the grade in Essex the same day that he got the call that his father had passed away. He didn't know if that was what changed it for him, but something shifted in the way he saw his role in life.
2 Fifteen years later, in January 2010, Essex County investigators finally made their knowledge of Duryea's killer's gun public. The Newark *Star-Ledger* would report "Robert Reeves, 44, used the same .32-caliber revolver involved in the Duryea slaying to fire five bullets into a Newark minister. When asked about Reeves, Anthony Ambrose, the prosecutor's chief of investigators, [confirmed] in an

interview that Reeves is 'a person of interest' in the Duryea case."
Philip Read, "More Details Emerge in the Killing of Glen Ridge
Grandmothers," *Star-Ledger*, January 10, 2010, http://www.nj.com/
news/index.ssf/2010/01/new_details_emerge_in_1995_kil.html.

CHAPTER 30

1 Dennis Miller at Somerset Medical Center contacted the office of
  Prosecutor Wayne Forrest on this date.
2 Details of the detectives' actions and interactions with the individuals
  at the hospitals are drawn from the police investigative reports and
  detailed by personal interviews.
3 In fact, the Department of Health and Senior Services had reached out
  to the New Jersey Attorney General's office before Somerset Medical
  Center administrators contacted the Somerset Prosecutor's Office.

   The full story of how these incidents were reported is a bit more
  complicated, and suggests that the process of reporting, investigating,
  and ultimately acting upon the incidents at Somerset Medical Center
  in a timely manner had been stalled or sidetracked at several junc-
  tures, both within Somerset Medical Center and at the highest level
  of the DOH itself.

   The DOH sent an investigator named Edward Harbet, an RN and
  a complaints Investigator from Health Care Systems Analysis. He
  visited SMC on July 11 and 14, reviewing the medical records of the
  patients involved and the summary of the SMC internal investigation,
  and interviewing several administrators. Harbet was unable to identify any specific findings that would explain the relevant lab values
  in the patient incidents. He told SMC administrators that the charts
  would be reviewed by others in his department.

   The sitting commissioner of Health and Senior Services at the time
  was Cliff Lacey. According to e-mails from the senior assistant commissioner, Marilyn Dahl, the incidents at Somerset Medical Center had been
  discussed with Commissioner Lacey following the reporting of both Steven Marcus and then Somerset Medical Center administrators. "Based
  on his experience with the drugs in question, and as the senior medical
  officer of a large hospital, *the commissioner thought it was extremely premature to start suspecting foul play. I had, at that time, raised the issue
  of a referral to the AG, and the commissioner declined*," Dahl wrote. "He
  was able to hypothesize several likely scenarios not involving foul play
  that could have resulted in the outcomes reported." (Emphasis mine.)

Then, on September 26, 2003, some members of the DOH became increasingly concerned about what was unfolding at Somerset.

A senior DOH staffer named Maureen F. Miller sent an e-mail to Marilyn Dahl. "While the Dept was aware that three unexplained incidents had occurred and was working with Somerset's administration who was investigating the incidents," Miller wrote, "Somerset reported to us today that a fourth incident occurred one month ago," despite being explicitly warned of the necessity of reporting any additional patients.

Dahl was deeply concerned. She reported that she had met with Alison Gibson, director of Inspections, Compliance and Complaints at the DOH, and Amie Thornton, assistant commissioner of Health Care Facility Quality:

> We all agreed that there may be sufficient reason to suspect foul play. *The disturbing part of this picture is that Somerset had made us aware of the 3 previous occurrences, yet chose to wait an entire month before reporting the 4th. We believe that this was irresponsible at best,* and would like permission to seek counsel's opinion from OLRA [the DOH office for Legal and Regulatory Affairs] for referral to the AG's [Attorney General's] office. [Emphasis mine.]

That day, the Department of Health reached out to the Attorney General's office regarding the issue at Somerset. Amie Thornton wrote Ms. Miller and others at the DOH later on September 26 to report that "I believe at this point the hospital actually suspects foul play as they have retained private investigators/attorneys to investigate this situation." Seven days later, Somerset Medical Center contacted the Somerset County Prosecutor's Office (SCPO).

CHAPTER 31

1 Sachs, Maitlin, Fleming, Greene, Marotte and Mullen.
2 This conversation is reconstructed from SCPO investigation documents detailing the meeting and the information Lund provided, aided by extensive interviews with Detective Baldwin.
3 Somerset hadn't called the police for a half-dozen patients who *had* been poisoned—then, months later, called to report the death of a man who hadn't.

CHAPTER 32

1 This call was part of an investigation at Easton Hospital, just underway at this time but already stalled.

CHAPTER 33

1 The info on this date (October 8, 2003) comes from various databases and contacted agencies, including the South Carolina State Police, the Summerville (South Carolina) Police Department, the Palmer Township (Pennsylvania) Police Department, the Phillipsburg (New Jersey) Police Department, and the New Jersey Board of Nursing.

CHAPTER 34

1 Those investigations were closed in late December 1991, with no conclusion. Charles Cullen was fired the first week of January 1992, and the insulin spikes stopped. Saint Barnabas has since maintained that these facts are unrelated, and that the administration did not have reason at that time to believe Charles Cullen was a risk to patients.

2 Fragments of this investigation would be recovered after Cullen's arrest.

3 Several incident reports described the MO of the crimes almost exactly. For example, Charlie had been written up for checking the insulin levels of a patient repeatedly and at inexplicable and inappropriate intervals, and for leaving an unprescribed and unlabeled IV hanging for a patient after his shift, rather than the prescribed KCL solution. Afterward, when his supervisor contacted him at home by phone, Cullen seemed apathetic, and he claimed that if it was hanging there, it must have been the prescribed KCL. It wasn't, but exactly what was in the bag, and whether this was one of the saline IVs which Cullen would later admit to having randomly spiked with insulin, would never be known. According to disciplinary records in court documents, this was not an isolated incident; a supervisor's write-up dated 3/14/91 stated that "Charles has a reputation for not showing reaction when making an error."

4 Cullen had signed up with MCHCS halfway through his years at Saint Barnabas in order to have more flexibility in the hours and units in which he worked. This was the reason that Cullen's Saint Barnabas file covered only the final two years of his five-year tenure; technically, a different corporate entity had hired him.

5 In fact, what was meant by "dual medication error" is somewhat more damning of the nurse. What was referred to here is a situation in which Cullen had (1) withheld medication the patient was prescribed; (2) in

its place hung an unlabeled bag that, strangely, he had (3) pinched off so that the next nurse would be the one to start the drip. It is, in fact, a triple error; exponentially less likely, and rather more troubling than a single dosage error, as it cannot so easily be written off as a simple mistake. The supervisor's reaction reflects this.

Ostensibly the IV bag in question contained only saline, though we cannot know for sure, as Cullen's practice at the time was to use such bags, spiked with insulin, to sicken patients; and he often covered his tracks by ensuring that the spiked bags were infused by other nurses when he was not present.

6 According to the DOH investigation and police investigation documents, SMC's legal counsel prepared a time line in "anticipation of potential litigation," in which "DBR, Paul G Nittoly, (PGN), [was] asked to participate in investigation of abnormal lab values with help of private Investigator, Rocco E. Fushetto (REF)."

7 This conversation is drawn from the notes and recollections of Detectives Braun and Baldwin and detailed in police investigation documents. The only liberty taken with the statements reported by the police investigation documents is the use of quotation marks to create the scene.

CHAPTER 35

1 Bruchak, Egan, and their commander, Cpl. Gerald Walsh, all participated in the briefing, but Egan was Detective Baldwin's main point of contact.

2 The details of this case could constitute a book in themselves. Several of these facts are referenced elsewhere; at the risk of some redundancy, and with the aim of greater journalistic transparency, they are presented again here, in fuller context and greater detail. The following information was provided in the course of the civil suits brought by five families of former patients against St. Luke's Hospital. St. Luke's argued that the cases should be thrown out because they were older than the two-year statute of limitations; Lehigh County Judge Edward D. Reibman ruled that they were still relevant. Ultimately, St. Luke's settled with the families out of court. While the specifics of the settlements are sealed, some details may be gleaned from court records (Case law: Superior Court of Pennsylvania, *Krapf v. St. Luke Hospital*, Lehigh County Judge Edward D. Reibman, Nos. 2958 EDA 2009, 2959 EDA 2009, 2960 EDA 2009, 2961 EDA 2009, 2962 EDA

2009. Before: Gantman, Shogan, and Mundy, J. J.): much of the issue facing the court was whether St. Luke's had reason to believe that Cullen had been involved in patient deaths.

Attorney Paul Laughlin recalled that he suggested patient charts be reviewed to ascertain whether the diverted vecuronium bromide had been improperly administered, thereby resulting in patient harm (Pl.Ex. VVV at 40–44); however, the question of what precisely Attorney Laughlin learned during and concluded from his investigation is not clear. And in that respect, the deposition testimony of the various witnesses diverges considerably. Laughlin indicated that particularized suspicion of Cullen harming patients was never brought to his attention. (See ibid. at 127–135.) However, notes from his interviews in combination with testimony of Nurse Patricia Medellin leave it within the purview of the finder of fact to draw a different inference.

Specifically, Nurse Medellin stated she met with Attorney Laughlin on the night he confronted Cullen and that he had instructed her to call him if she "had any additional thoughts." (Pl.Ex. III, at 72.) After learning that opened containers of vecuronium bromide had been found in the receptacles and that other nurses had concerns that patients may have been harmed, she telephoned Laughlin on or about June 7, 2002. (Pl.Ex., at 76–78.) She informed him that the unauthorized administration of vecuronium would be consistent with an unexplained slowing of patient heart rates, leading to codes when their hearts stopped. (Ibid. at 79.) She also told Laughlin that no one in the CCU at that time should have been receiving vecuronium. (Ibid.)

In response Attorney Laughlin informed Nurse Medellin that "the investigation was closed" and that he was "confident that Cullen was not in any way harming patients." (Ibid. at 80.) Medellin pressed Laughlin about how he could be so sure, especially when Laughlin had admitted to her that he had not compared the medications sent from the pharmacy versus those actually used on patients and had not compared the number of patient codes on day versus night shifts when Cullen was on duty. (Ibid. at 81–82.) Laughlin allegedly responded that based on his experience as a prosecutor in Philadelphia for eight years, he was confident in his investigation and was "certain" that Cullen "was not hurting anyone." (Ibid.) He then informed her once again that the investigation was "closed and not open [[001]] for further review." (Ibid. at 82.)

Nurse Medellin also testified at deposition that she voiced her concerns to her supervisors, but that she was met with an equally inhospitable response. (Ibid. at 96.) In particular, she stated that after Attorney Laughlin dismissed her concerns, she spoke to Thelma Moyer, the clinical coordinator at St. Luke's, and Ellen Amedeo, the CCU nurse manager at the hospital, both of whom dismissed her concerns and informed her that the investigation was closed. (Ibid.) She also testified that after speaking with Attorney Laughlin, she compiled a list of the patients who died in the CCU, compared it to Cullen's shifts, and determined that a disproportionate number of patients died while he was on duty. (Ibid. at 91–93.) However, because of the lack of receptivity and "almost anger" expressed by Clinical Coordinator Moyer and CCU Nurse Manager Amedeo to her previous entreaties, Nurse Medellin did not present the list she compiled for fear of "repercussions." (Ibid. at 97.) After he returned from leave in July 2002, the hospital's general counsel, Seymour Traub, directed Attorney Laughlin to prepare a report and ordered additional chart reviews to be performed by St. Luke's staff. (See Pl.Ex. BBBB at 30.) Risk Manager Rader and Nursing Manager Supervisor Koller were charged with reviewing charts of all of the patients who had died over the course of the weekend in which the diverted medications were found. (See Pl.Ex. UUU at 21.) However, Nursing Supervisor Koller testified at deposition that she had never before performed any similar such chart review and, in fact, was not even aware of the purpose of her review when Risk Manager Rader asked her to review the patient charts. (Pl.Ex. AAAA at 46–50.) For her part, Rader testified at deposition that Attorney Laughlin indicated to her at that point that he could not find "a scintilla of evidence that there was any foul play involved." (Pl.Ex. UUU at 114.) Risk Manager Rader and Nursing Supervisor Koller identified neither any suspicious administration of vecuronium nor any suspicious deaths. (Pl.Ex. UUU at 138.) Accordingly, the additional inquiries ordered by General Counsel Traub reported that they failed to find any evidence of Cullen's involvement in patient deaths; afterward, the hospital's chief executive officer concluded this part of the investigation by referring Cullen to the State Board of Nursing for follow-up as it saw fit. (Pl.Ex. III.)

After notification by the district attorney that the matter had been referred to law enforcement, the hospital undertook further investigations, including patient-chart review by an outside physician; however, this, too, failed to lead St. Luke's to conclude Cullen had harmed any patients. (See Pl.Ex. NNN at 51–55, 125–127.) Cullen ultimately confessed to killing, among others, the five decedents at St. Luke's at issue in these cases. (See Pl.Ex. B; Ex. C.) In total, seven patients have been specifically identified as having been killed by Cullen at St. Luke's.

3 From police investigation documents and Lehigh County district attorney James B. Martin's memo of September 9, 2002.

4 Also present were coroners Zachary Lysek and Scott Grim, and Easton County Police captain John Mazzeo, the acquaintance to whom Medellin had first taken her suspicions about Cullen.

5 While the St. Luke's administration had contended that Cullen had not harmed patients and their investigation had closed, they indicated less certainty several weeks later. On September 6, two months after Cullen's removal from St. Luke's, St. Luke's Hospital president and chief executive officer Richard A. Anderson finally wrote to the State Nursing Board, notifying them of the incident with the sharps box, the discovery of numerous empty vials of dangerous drugs, as well as unused drugs, and that Cullen's employment had been terminated following the discovery. The letter from Anderson reads, in part: "Based on the internal investigation conducted by St. Luke's the management believes that the drugs were wrongly diverted by Charles Cullen. St. Luke's does not know if or how Mr. Cullen used these drugs, or why he would discard unexpired, unused boxes of drugs. St. Luke's has reviewed the medical records of the persons who died in the CCU during the weekend in which the drugs were discovered. The medical records do not show that the deaths are attributable to anything but natural causes. However, the possibility of improper use of the drugs found in the sharps disposal container cannot be entirely ruled out."

St. Luke's was the only medical facility at which Charles Cullen had worked to ever contact a state nursing board about his actions. St. Luke's has since stated that its decision to notify the state nursing board at that time was in no way motivated or related to Nurse Medellin having notified the district attorney of these same events four days earlier, and that St. Luke's administrators had no knowledge of that notification.

6 In all, eighteen St. Luke's staffers were interviewed.

7 According to police investigation records, Tester had noticed the death trend early, going so far as to quantify the statistical increase in the death rate in the CCU.

8 Tester told the Pennsylvania State Police that she had brought her observation of this troubling trend to 'people on the CCU Unit' and her supervisors, but nobody had any answers.

9 According to documents supplied to the police investigation at St. Luke's. The hospital had supplied extensive investigations of its own in support of its assertions that administrators had no reason to believe Cullen had harmed anyone at their hospital, and that the death rate was within the statistical norm.

10 From witness statements in police investigation documents. Other nurses, including Judy Glessner and Darla Beers, also testified to their concerns that Cullen had harmed patients. (See Pl.Ex. RR at 72–77; Ex. PPP at 72–73; see also Ex. U at 2 [police report summarizing statement given by Nurse Gerry Kimble about his belief Cullen had harmed patients with diverted medications].) Assistant Pharmacy Director Susan Reed testified that she recalled expressing to Laughlin that the nature of the empty medications found, including vecuronium, raised a concern about potential patient harm. (See Pl.Ex. VV at 128–130.) Notes that Attorney Laughlin apparently took during his conversation with Nurse Medellin contain several abbreviated descriptions that could be understood as references to patients being harmed by Cullen including "cross ref deaths w/ Charlie" and "cod[ing] fast." (See Pl.Ex. CCCC.) Testimony from the hospital's vice president of risk management, Gary Guidetti, stated that Laughlin never apprised him of concerns about patient harm or otherwise passed those concerns on to upper management. (See Pl.Ex. FFFF at 36–39.)

11 Retired St. Luke's CCU nurse Susan Bartos, quoted in the *Morning Call*, February 15, 2004 ("Nurses' Warnings Unable to Stop Trail of Death," by Ann Wlazelek and Matt Assad; http://www.mcall.com/news/all-5nursesfeb15,0,4417146.story).

12 On May 18, 2003.

13 Working with the Pennsylvania State Police, the district attorney retained a forensic pathologist, Dr. Isidore Mihalakis, who reviewed seventeen patient charts selected by St. Luke's. (Pl.Ex. MMMM at 18–35.) However, Dr. Mihalakis was not provided with a written list of the diverted medications and reportedly had no contact with any

of the nurses or their statements regarding suspicions about Cullen. (Ibid.) Dr. Mihalakis was unable to conclude that Cullen had harmed anyone. (Ibid. at 50–55.)

14 Cullen killed Pasquale Napolitano on July 13—though at the time he didn't know the patient's name.

CHAPTER 36

1 According to the Somerset Medical Center executive report given to the board of directors on July 17, 2003, the DOH review at SMC took place on July 11 and 14. Edward Harbet, RN, Health Care Systems Analysis complaints investigator, visited SMC and extensively reviewed the medical records of the four patients reported, as well as the summary of the SMC internal investigation to date, and pertinent policy and staffing assignment documents. Harbet also met with administrators. He was unable to identify any specific finding that would explain the relevant lab values, but he was comfortable with the level of attention being paid to these events by SMC, and he did not advise any additional external agency report. He said copies of the charts and his report would be reviewed by his department.

On July 14, two clinical laboratory evaluators from the DOH reviewed SMC lab services, focusing on the testing procedures and facilities in validating the abnormal results reported. No deficiencies in the lab process were identified. The SMC executive report says that investigators were "satisfied that all appropriate steps had been and were being taken to identify the cause of the unexplained events."

2 Hundreds of pages of DOH files and internal documents, including e-mails, would eventually be made available by a police subpoena, but would shed little light on the incidents at Somerset Medical Center. They were of minimal use to the SCPO during their investigation.

CHAPTER 37

1 The pieces of this recording are abridged from the original transcript, but context has been carefully maintained.

2 A standard homicide term referring to a body newly murdered and thus potentially still bearing the greatest cache of evidence and trace, as distinct from a body discovered much later and disturbed by time and environment.

CHAPTER 38

1 He was still in his thirties at this time.
2 Details of Detective Baldwin's meeting and conversation with Lucille Gall were taken from police investigation documents.

CHAPTER 40

1 Dr. Smith found that two cases could possibly be medically explained without exogenous influence, and were thus not as suspicious as the other four.
2 Joseph P. Lehman and McKinley Crews were the two Somerset patients whose lab values were not as suspicious.
3 The manner and cause of death would be determined later by toxicologist George F. Jackson, PhD.

CHAPTER 42

1 According to documented court proceedings and police investigation documents, Laughlin hadn't provided specifics in his call to Easton, but had told them, in regards to reconsidering hiring Charles Cullen, "Don't"—this word was handwritten in quotes on the back of a page in Charlie's Easton personnel file, which was obtained during the police investigation.

CHAPTER 43

1 Coincidentally, from the standpoint of minimizing Somerset Medical Center's liability, this was the best possible situation.

SMC couldn't fire Cullen without a reason. If the reason was a suspicion of murder, Somerset might then be liable for those murders. But following directions from the prosecutor's office was not an admission of their own suspicions. It was reasonable compliance with the legal authorities based on the prosecutor's suspicions.

Instead, Cullen was gone—the detectives had investigated a crime, discovered Cullen's history, and advised SMC to fire Cullen. But if it couldn't be definitively proven that Cullen was actually the one responsible for the specific patient deaths, then SMC was not liable to civil suits.

2 From Detective Baldwin's interviews and SCPO records.

CHAPTER 44

1 From Tim Braun's notes.

2 This had been the pattern at many of the hospitals they'd looked into, a confusing thing to the detectives. During Detective Baldwin's November 14, 2003, interview with Betty Gillian, the vice president of the Saint Barnabas Hospital corporate office (and Cullen's former supervisor, the woman who had fired Cullen for "nurse practice issues" and remembered Cullen being the focal point of an internal investigation concerning IV bags that were contaminated with insulin), she recalled the Saint Barnabas staff had been upset when Cullen was accused of tainting the IVs, because "they liked him because he was very helpful."

3 Police investigation documents and interviews with detectives.

CHAPTER 45

1 On November 21, 2003.

2 Police investigation documents and interviews with Amy Loughren and Detective Baldwin.

3 This incredible detail is from a direct recounting in one of the author's interviews with Amy.

CHAPTER 46

1 Police investigation documents and interviews with Loughren, Baldwin, and Braun.

2 Amy had suspected something was off before, when she'd been asked to sign her name to the insulin levels without having any means to actually check them.

CHAPTER 47

1 The information in this passage is taken from author interviews with Amy and from her journals.

CHAPTER 49

1 Following Cullen's arrest, Pyxis bolstered the security of their dispensing system.

CHAPTER 52

1 After the exposure of what Charles Cullen had done, this loophole in Pyxis was fixed by the manufacturer.

2 Code status indicates whether or not a patient is to be resuscitated if they code, and what measures are and are not permitted for them—a decision made by the patient or the patient's family.

CHAPTER 53

1 Cullen was using his acetaminophen orders as a means to access the drugs he used to kill patients. At the same time, he was also establishing a public record of legitimate acetaminophen orders. According to police records, Lucille Gall, the Reverend Gall's sister, recalled for investigators a conspicuous argument about Tylenol she'd had with the male nurse; it was clearly a drug he favored, even when it was not clinically prudent. Charles Cullen could easily claim the rest of the Tylenol orders were valid as well; certainly nothing the SCPO investigation had turned up could prove otherwise.

CHAPTER 54

1 This was SCPO captain Andy Hissim.

CHAPTER 55

1 Benadryl and ibuprofen—though Benadryl is a sedative that Cullen's ex-wife Adrianne had accused him of using on his children, a charge Cullen adamantly denies.

CHAPTER 56

1 This material and all quoted matter here are taken and abridged from Detective Braun's notes, made during these calls.

2 Tim had faxed the completed questionnaire to them, but there hadn't been enough time to actually get the consultation before they kidnapped him.

3 After Cullen's arrest, the detectives would have the opportunity to speak with famed forensic scientist Dr. Henry Lee about the difficulties in bringing a case against Cullen. Dr. Lee's opinion regarding medical serial killers was captured in an April 29, 2002, interview regarding a different case in the *Los Angeles Times*:

"You have to figure out who the victims were long after they were buried," he said. "You have to dig up [bodies]. You are going to have a difficult time finding true trace drug or elements in there. The next issue is how to link to the suspect. Why him? What's the proof? Prepare to fail."

4 This was despite Charlie's having been investigated for suspicious deaths by all three hospitals. It's not clear whether Montgomery ever had the opportunity to call any of his references.

5 From a police investigation report.

CHAPTER 59

1 Cullen couldn't read without his glasses, either. Whether or not Charlie Cullen was wearing his glasses on a given night might have determined what he could read, and which patient got the deadly cocktail.

2 Cullen misstates the name of the paper; it was the Newark *Star-Ledger*, Rick Hepp reporting.

3 Amy remembers Charlie Cullen telling her that the first person he killed at Saint Barnabas was a young woman.

4 Cullen has never been tried for this patient's death.

5 It's more likely that Cullen was simply bought out of his contract and paid for the months of sick-leave time he accrued while in various mental institutions during his tenure there, and that added up to less than $18,000. Charles Cullen filed for bankruptcy the following year, claiming over $68,000 in debt; it is possible, but unlikely, that the settlement from Warren Hospital was an addition to his base salary.

6 In fact, with all the stories flying around and the police visit, Cathy believed that Charlie was going to run away with Amy to Mexico.

CHAPTER 61

1 Baldwin's report lists this as six hours; however, Cullen had been processed by 6 p.m., and the interview didn't wrap up until 3 a.m.

CHAPTER 62

1 Captain Nick Magos's office.

POST SCRIPT

1 The hospital civil suits each alleged that the fault lay with whatever hospital had previously hired Charles Cullen and then allowed him to move on. One of the larger battles occurred between St. Luke's Hospital and Somerset Medical Center. Somerset Medical Center's lawyers argued that St. Luke's should be responsible for any lawsuits brought by the families of victims at Somerset. As noted earlier, Judge Garruto of the New Jersey Superior Court sided with Somerset without weighing in on the specific merits of the actual cases. The fact that St. Luke's administrators had called other hospitals was one of the main contributors to his decision as to their responsibility for those suits. By making those calls, advising some hospitals against hiring Cullen but not alerting others, they had, in Judge Garruto's opinion, effectively "decided who would live and who would die."

2 An adverse event is one that results in death, loss of a body part, disability, or loss of bodily function lasting more than seven days or still
   present at the time of discharge, where the event could have been
   anticipated or prepared against, but occurs because of an error or
   other system failure [NJSA 26:2H-12.25(a)].

INDEX

ABOUT THE AUTHOR

CHARLES GRAEBER spent many childhood hours in hospitals, waiting in nursing stations and visiting patients with his physician father. He deferred Tulane Medical School to pursue a story in Cambodia and never returned. His writing has been recognized by awards from the Overseas Press Club of America, the New York Press Club, and the American Academy of Poets, and anthologies including *The Best American Crime Reporting*, *The Best American Science Writing*, *The Best Business Stories of the Year*, and *The Best of National Geographic Adventure*. He is a contributor to *Wired*, *GQ*, *The New Yorker*, *New York*, *Outside*, *Bloomberg Businessweek*, the *New York Times*, and others. A native Iowan, he now lives in Nantucket and Williamsburg, Brooklyn.

MISSION STATEMENT

Twelve strives to publish singular books, by authors who have unique perspectives and compelling authority. Books that explain our culture; that illuminate, inspire, provoke, and entertain. Our mission is to provide a consummate publishing experience for our authors, one truly devoted to thoughtful partnership and cutting-edge promotional sophistication that reaches as many readers as possible. For readers, we aim to spark that rare reading experience—one that opens doors, transports, and possibly changes their outlook on our ever-changing world.